HOW TO DESIGN YOUR OWN CLOTHES
AND MAKE YOUR OWN PATTERNS

CLAUDIA EIN

HOW TO

ILLUSTRATIONS AND DIAGRAMS BY THE AUTHOR

DESIGN YOUR OWN CLOTHES

AND MAKE YOUR OWN PATTERNS

DOUBLEDAY & COMPANY, INC., GARDEN CITY, NEW YORK
1975

Library of Congress Cataloging in Publication Data
Ein, Claudia, 1943–
    How to design your own clothes and make your own
patterns.
    1. Dressmaking—Pattern design.   2. Costume design.
I. Title.
TT520.E42   646.4'3'06
ISBN 0-385-07434-4
Library of Congress Catalog Card Number 74–12682

To Richard

CONTENTS

PART I: MAKING YOUR CUSTOM-FITTED MASTER PATTERNS

PART II: DESIGNING YOUR OWN CLOTHES

INTRODUCTION

How often have you had fantastic fabric ruined because the pattern was wrong?

Or fallen in love with a dress costing $75 and known you could make it for $20 if you just had the pattern?

Or started sewing for the joy of it and ended up in tears because the pattern didn't work?

You may have picked up this book to see if it's just another sewing book. It's not. This book will show you how to design your own clothes and make your own patterns that really *fit*. (Most sewing books are put out by pattern companies that naturally want to keep how to make patterns a CIA secret.) If you're thinking this sounds like a textbook for a structural engineer and you didn't even take plane geometry, don't worry. If you can sew, you can make a pattern. The sewing-direction sheets included with ready-made patterns are more complicated than the directions for making most of the patterns in this book.

I am a professional designer. I've designed sportswear and dresses as well as needlework, soft toys, and home-decorating items. In this book I've adapted the methods used by designers and patternmakers so you can use them at home.

You will learn how to make your own set of five master patterns called slopers (pronounced slow'-pers) that are custom fitted to *your* figure. The slopers are used as patterns, as the basis to make new patterns, and to check the fit of and alter ready-made patterns.

This system will save you a great deal of time and money. With the cost of fabric these days, few of us can afford the cut-the-pattern-and-pray-it-fits routine. And sewing is certainly quicker and more enjoyable without spending a lot of time on boring fittings. Using a sloper, you can cut a style and whip it up that same day, knowing it will fit properly.

This book will also show you how to restyle ready-made patterns so that you can make a collar round instead of pointed, add a pleat to a skirt, put cuffs on pants, and so on.

I hope that by sharing my professional experience with you, your sewing will be more fun and more creative.

PART I

MAKING YOUR CUSTOM-FITTED MASTER PATTERNS

Basic Blouse
Basic Pants

Basic Dress

Basic A Line Dress

Figure 1

CHAPTER 1

INTRODUCTION TO PATTERNMAKING

THE BASIC-SLOPER SYSTEM

The sloper system is used by professional designers and patternmakers. The basis of the system is the master pattern called a sloper. Each sloper is made from a muslin that has been made to fit your figure perfectly. Once you have the perfectly fitted sloper, you can use it to make a tremendous number of different styles. For example, from the basic-pants sloper, you can make any pants style from flared-leg evening pants to shorts.

The basic slopers are shown in *Figure 1*. For the most versatility, you can make all the slopers, but this is by no means a necessity. You can make only those slopers you need for the kind of clothes you wear most. There are so many design possibilities with the set of slopers because the pieces are interchangeable. The A-line dress, bodice, and blouse all have the same armhole and neckline. Therefore, the collar sloper, all of the sleeve slopers, and any sleeve pattern you make from the slopers will fit any of the other slopers. The skirt of the basic-dress sloper is also used alone to make many skirt styles. The bodice of the dress can be combined with the pants sloper to make jumpsuits, the blouse sloper used to make jackets, and so on.

If you are making only one or two of the slopers, you might want to make all of the sleeves so that you can interchange the sleeve styles. Before you decide which slopers you want to make, look through the design chapters in Part II and see the styles that can be made with each sloper. You'll probably be amazed at how many different designs can be made from one master pattern.

In the sample room (designer's workroom), slopers are made by a complex system of drafting or by fitting muslin on a dress form. As a home sewer, you can begin with a commercial pattern cut in muslin. You can use a regular tissue-paper pattern or one of the computer patterns made to your measurements which can be ordered in some sewing stores and notions departments.

If you have invested in a computer pattern, this book can be especially helpful, since it will enable you to make much more use of your pattern. I would still recommend checking the fit of a computer pattern in muslin because the body has so many variations. The specific requirements of each pattern needed to make a sloper are given in each chapter.

After the muslin garment has been fitted, it is taken apart and traced onto heavy paper to make your permanent sloper.

The slopers can be made extra sturdy by attaching them to adhesive-backed clear plastic such as Contact. This product is available in housewares and hardware departments. Stick the Contact onto the wrong side of your sloper and trim away the excess. To store your slopers, don't fold or roll them but hang them in a closet using a skirt hanger with clips.

In the sample room, patterns and slopers are used differently from the tissue patterns that you are used to. They are not pinned to the fabric but are placed on top of the fabric and held down with paperweights. Because they are made of sturdy paper, the outline can be traced like a giant stencil. After it has been traced, the paperweights and slopers, or patterns, are removed, and the fabric is cut just inside of the line so that no line remains on the fabric. This method is faster, easier, and more accurate than cutting with a tissue pattern. It will also keep your shears sharp because you are not using your fabric shears to cut through paper.

HOW TO USE THIS BOOK

Each chapter in this section tells you how to make one of five master patterns you need to design your own clothes.

Before making a sloper, read through this chapter and the chapter on the sloper. Work carefully. Accuracy is important.

When you make a new pattern, read through the directions and have an understanding of the procedures before you begin. I have included here a set of miniature slopers (*Figures 2* and *3*), which you can use to experiment with your own new ideas and to try out some patterns shown in this book in Part II. Trace the miniature slopers, glue them to thin cardboard, and cut them out.

When you first began sewing, you probably made something like an A-line shift. It's not likely you started out making a shirtwaist dress with a placket, collar, and cuffs. Do the same with learning to make patterns. Start simply and work up to the

more complicated ones. In the sections on making patterns I've tried to begin each chapter with the easiest patterns and gradually proceed to the more difficult ones toward the end of the chapter, although in some cases keeping a logical order made this impossible.

Once you learn the general procedures used in making patterns and understand how patterns are made, you will be able to make other styles besides the ones shown in this book. You might want to try working with a friend; you can help each other fit muslins and work on making patterns together.

Even though you probably won't want to spend the time to make all of your own patterns, you can also learn a lot from this book on how to restyle commercial patterns. The information on designing new necklines, collars, sleeves, adding fullness to skirts, shifting darts, and much more can

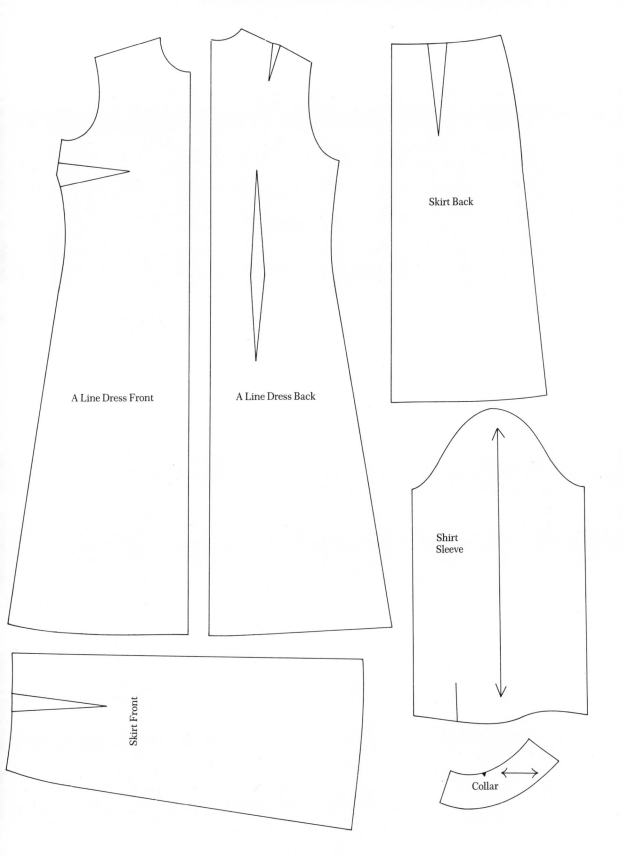

Figure 2

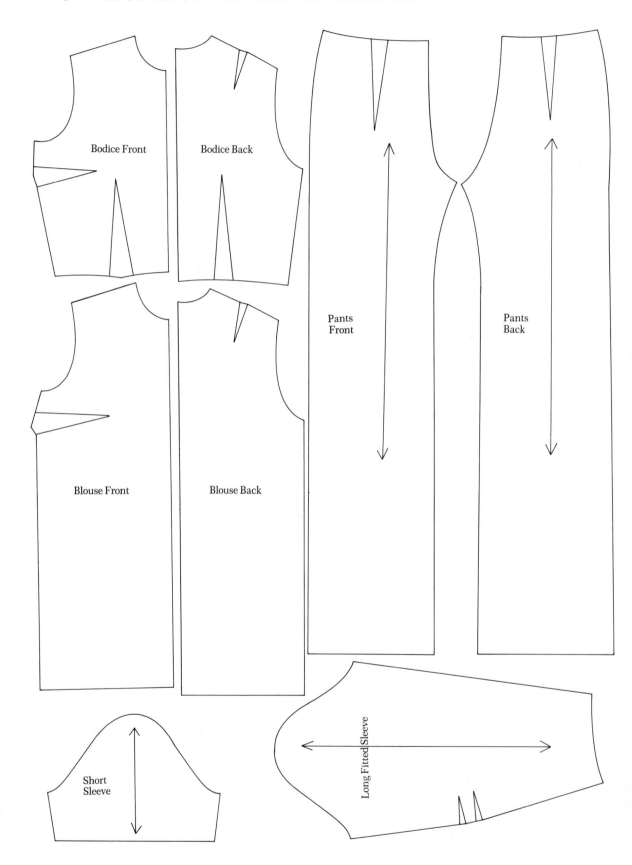

Bodice Front

Bodice Back

Pants Front

Pants Back

Blouse Front

Blouse Back

Short Sleeve

Long Fitted Sleeve

Figure 3

be used in restyling commercial patterns, as well as in making new patterns from scratch.

When making your pattern, it would be helpful to use this book with a cookbook stand that will hold the book upright and keep the page open to the pattern you are working on.

PATTERNMAKING SUPPLIES

You already have on hand a number of the supplies needed to make patterns. The items you should have are pictured in *Plate 1*. Most of the items which are not available at a notions department can be found at art or drafting supply stores. If you would like to order your supplies by mail, my company has a mail-order division which can provide you with patternmaking needs. To receive a leaflet, send your name and address and twenty cents to Claudia Designs, Inc., P. O. Box 88, Pound Ridge, New York 10576.

1. *Shears:* You should have two pairs of shears. One for fabric and one for paper. Don't use your fabric shears on paper, or on anything else but fabric, or you will ruin the blades. A good size for paper shears is 7″–8″ and for fabric shears 8″– 10″. Your shears should be fairly loose at the pivot (screw) and of course have sharp blades. Clean away the dust and lint that accumulate around the pivot occasionally and lubricate with a drop of sewing-machine oil. When you buy fabric shears, take along scraps of a number of different kinds of fabrics and try out the shears in the store.

2. *Paper:* Pattern paper should be about the weight of typewriter paper. Brown wrapping paper called kraft paper is available at stationery stores and works well. The paper with the rows of dots is called true-mark. It is used by professional patternmakers and is available only by mail.

When making your slopers, you need a heavier paper or you can use a clear Contact covering for sturdiness. (See page 4.) For making small patterns, a roll of plain white shelf paper is convenient. Tissue paper does not work well.

3. *Muslin:* You need muslin to fit your pattern before you make your permanent sloper. This should be unbleached muslin about the weight of broadcloth. You can also use a light-color broadcloth or something similar.

4. *Triangle:* A drafting triangle is used to check the grain of the fabric. Also in patternmaking, a line is often marked at a right angle to another line and a triangle accomplishes this. Ask for a 90°/45° triangle with the short leg at least eight inches long.

5. *Ruler:* For patternmaking, you need a clear plastic ruler. One of the best is called C-Thru and has lines in both directions like graph paper. Twelve or eighteen inches long by two inches wide is a good size. Another good ruler, made by Dritz, has slots in it for drawing parallel lines. This ruler is good if you have trouble figuring fractions of an inch because the fractions are clearly marked. A six-inch C-Thru ruler is also convenient.

6. *Yardstick:* Paint stores often give wooden yardsticks away free. The best kind are made of metal and are practically indestructible.

7. *Tape Measure:* You should have a

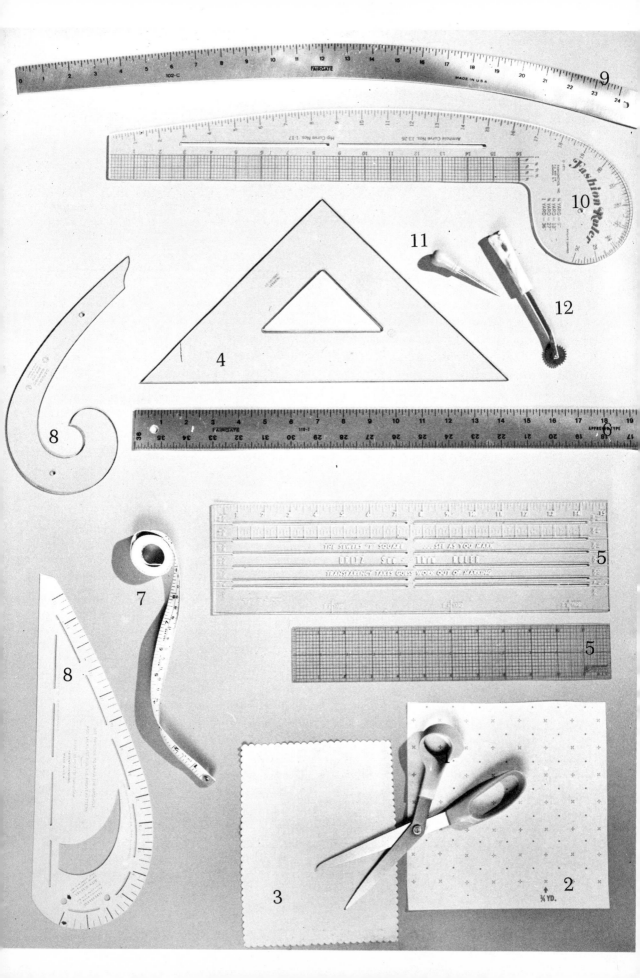

good-quality tape that is sturdy enough to stand on its edge to measure around curves.

8. *French Curve:* The French curve is an important patternmaking tool. It is used for marking necklines, armholes, and many other curved lines. A clear plastic French curve is best because it lets you see the lines underneath it. Deitzgen number 17 SP French curve has the shape of an armhole and neckline and is used by professional patternmakers. Another French curve, made by Dritz, is available in notions departments.

9. *Curved Rule:* This is also called a curve stick or hip curve. It is used for marking long curved lines such as hems, sleeves, skirts, etc. It has a more gradual curve than the French curve. There is another curved tool available called the Fashion Ruler (number 10) which combines the French curve and the hip curve into one clear plastic tool.

11. *Awl:* An awl is used for punching holes to mark dart points and to make other marks. You can also use a tapestry needle or a thin knitting needle to do this job.

12. *Tracing Wheel:* One with a bent handle is easiest to use. In making patterns, the tracing wheel is often used without dressmaker's carbon paper.

(*Not Pictured:*)

13. *Tailor's Chalk:* This is used for marking the fitting muslin before you make your permanent sloper. Before marking your muslin, check to see that the tailor's chalk marks won't disappear from the heat of the iron when the muslin is pressed.

14. *Colored Pencils:* You need colored pencils for two purposes. First, in making patterns, often lines are drawn in different colors to avoid confusion. You also need colored pencils to trace around your patterns or slopers when you mark them on the fabric. For accuracy, keep the points of your pencils sharp. Venus Paradise or Eagle Prismacolor (available at art and stationery stores) are good pencils for both purposes. White, yellow, red, and blue make a good color selection. Marking on fabric can also be done with dressmaker's pencils, which are like tailor's chalk in pencil form. You will also need an ordinary lead pencil (black) for making patterns.

15. *Dressmaker's Carbon:* Never use regular carbon paper on fabric; use only dressmaker's carbon paper.

16. *Tape:* Scotch Magic Tape is best for making patterns because it folds easily and can be written on.

17. *Eraser:* The Pink Pearl type is a good all-purpose eraser for pattern paper. When you make long incorrect lines on your patterns, it is often quicker just to cross out the line rather than erase it if this won't be confusing.

18. *Paperweights:* You will need two or three paperweights. You can make your own by filling small jars with gravel or dried beans.

Plate 1

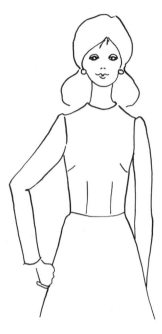

Figure 4

PATTERN PRINCIPLES

Patternmaking is not hard to learn because so much of it is based on a few principles used over and over in various ways. When you first look through this book, it might seem as if there are an incredible number of different instructions. However, once you begin making patterns, you will realize that most instructions are variations and combinations of only a few basic steps. Once you understand the principles, you can apply them to making many different designs, including ones not shown in this book.

CHANGING THE DART

One basic method used in designing and making patterns is changing the dart. Most often it is the bust dart, but any dart can be changed (*Figure 4*). The bust dart can easily be moved from the usual underarm position to the shoulder, neckline, center front, french dart, or any place in between (*Figure 4A*). Moving the dart to any of these positions follows the same steps.

Moving the dart also follows the same steps whether you are working with the A-line, blouse or bodice sloper, or a ready-made pattern, so once you learn to move a dart to one new position, you can move a dart to any position. Another way to change the dart is by converting it into ease or tucks (*Figure 4B*). A dart can also be changed into a seam. This is done in making a pattern for a princess line and for some yokes (*Figure 4C*). Detailed instructions for making all these patterns are found in Part II.

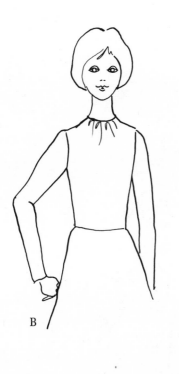

Figure 4

Figure 5

SLASHING AND SPREADING

Slashing and spreading is another basic technique of patternmaking. It is used to add fullness whether flared or gathered. Slashing and spreading is used to make patterns for such different styles as flared skirts, puffed sleeves, bell-bottom pants, and tent dresses. Slashing and spreading is essentially what the term says. You cut the pattern into strips (slashing), then spread the pattern to add the amount of fullness you want, where you want it.

A slashed pattern may be spread at the top only, at the bottom only, or at the top and bottom. The sleeves shown in *Figure 5* illustrate this concept. The first sleeve (A) is tight at the bottom and has gathers at the cap because only the top of the sleeve pattern has been spread. The second sleeve (B) has a smooth cap and gathers at the bottom because only the bottom of the sleeve pattern has been spread. The third sleeve (C) has gathers at the cap and at the cuff because the pattern has been spread at the top and the bottom. The flared sleeve (D) is made from the same pattern as (B), and the gathered flared sleeve in (E) is made from the same pattern as (C). (C) and (E) look different because (C) is gathered at the arm and (E) is left free at the arm.

The drawings here are only meant to show the concept of slashing and spreading. Detailed instructions are given in Part II wherever slashing and spreading is necessary to make a pattern.

USING A SLOPER TO ALTER A COMMERCIAL PATTERN

When you use a ready-made pattern, you can save time on alterations because the slopers can be used to check the fit of commercial patterns. To do this, first iron your tissue pieces, then place your tissue-pattern piece on top of the corresponding sloper. For example, to check the fit of a pants pattern, place the front pants tissue pattern on top of your front pants sloper. See if the commercial-pattern leg length and crotch length are the same as the sloper. Check the hip and waistline measurements of the tissue pattern against the sloper. Remember to measure the waistline along the finish line, not including the dart. Make necessary adjustments on the tissue pattern before you cut the fabric. Use the same method to check the back pants leg.

Use this same procedure with the bodice, A-line dress, and so on to check the position of the bust dart, back-waist length, dress length, sleeve length, etc.

COMBINING PARTS OF A COMMERCIAL PATTERN WITH A SLOPER

Sometimes you may also want to combine part of a tissue pattern with a sloper. For example, you may want to use a tissue-pattern sleeve with your A-line sloper. Before you can do this, you must find out whether the two pieces will work together by comparing the armhole of the sloper with the armhole of the tissue pattern.

Place the front tissue pattern that goes with the sleeve on top of the front A-line sloper and compare the armholes. If the armholes are the same size, the new sleeve pattern will fit the A-line sloper. If the tissue armhole is slightly larger, or smaller, you can add or subtract at the seam of the sleeve. However, if there is more than $\frac{1}{2}''$ difference, you will have trouble with the sleeve and should not use it. You should also check the back armhole the same way. Use this same method to check the neckline if you want to use a collar pattern, the waistline if you want to join a skirt tissue pattern to the bodice sloper, and so on.

TERMS USED IN PATTERNMAKING

ABBREVIATIONS

See *Figure 6A*. Sample pattern.

1. C.F. is the abbreviation for center front.

2. C.B. is the abbreviation for center back.

TERMS REFERRING TO LINES

1. *Cutting Line:* This is also called the cut line or the seam-allowance line. It is, of course, the line that you cut on and includes, in most cases, the $\frac{5}{8}''$ seam allowance. In some of the diagrams the cutting line is indicated by a scissors symbol.

2. *Stitching Line:* Also called seam line or finish line—this is the line that you will sew on when you sew your garment. In making some patterns, the stitching line will not be indicated.

3. *Grain Line:* This is the line that indicates the way you place the pattern on the fabric. In many cases the grain line is the same as center-front or center-back line; in that case, it is quicker and more accurate to use the center front or center back as the grain line instead of drawing a separate grain line. If you are using one-way fabric, draw an arrow to remind you to place all the pattern pieces in the same directions.

4. *Design Line:* This is also called the Style Line. It is the line drawn on the pattern to create a new style. For example: In making a scoop-neck pattern, using a sloper with a regular neckline, the line indicating the new scoop neckline is the design line.

5. *Slash Lines:* These are lines drawn to indicate where to slash a pattern when you're making a pattern that requires slashing and spreading (page 13).

6. *Blend a Line: Figure 6B.* This means to draw a smooth line connecting several points. It often refers to a curved line and, in that case, is drawn with a French curve or curved rule. Blend a line also means smooth out a jagged line. Sometimes a step in making a pattern results in jogs which must be smoothed out to finish the pattern, as shown in the drawing here.

7. *Draw a Line Parallel: Figure 6C.* In making patterns, it is often necessary to draw a line parallel to another line. This is very easy using the C-Thru transparent ruler shown on page 8. For example, suppose you want to draw a line parallel to another line $\frac{5}{8}''$ away and parallel to another line. To do this, place your transparent ruler on top of the line so that you can see the line through the ruler. Position the ruler so that the red line on the ruler is

⅝″ from the edge of the ruler and is directly over the pencil line. With your pencil, draw along the edge of the ruler, as shown here. The second line will be parallel and ⅝″ from the first line.

8. *Square a Line: Figure 6D.* In making patterns, it is sometimes necessary to draw a line at a right angle to another line.

This is done using your triangle. To square a line, place the short side of your triangle against the line you have drawn as shown. The second short side of the triangle will be square to the first line. Instructions to square a line will have a triangle symbol where the line is to be squared (*Figure 6A*).

SAMPLE PATTERN

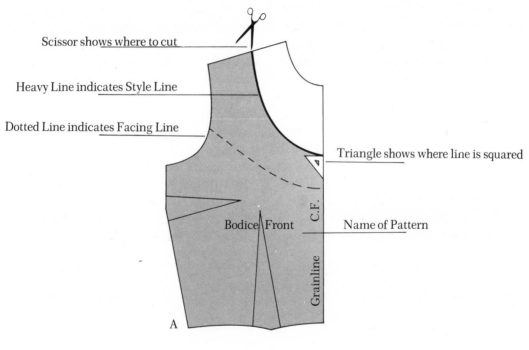

Scissor shows where to cut

Heavy Line indicates Style Line

Dotted Line indicates Facing Line

Triangle shows where line is squared

Bodice Front

C.F.

Name of Pattern

Grainline

A

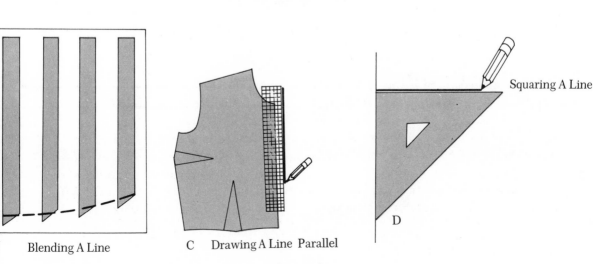

B   Blending A Line

C   Drawing A Line Parallel

Squaring A Line

D

Figure 6

TERMS REFERRING TO PATTERNS

1. *Commercial Pattern:* This is the ready-made tissue pattern that you are used to.

2. *Pattern:* In this book the word pattern refers to a new pattern which you make.

3. *Sloper:* This is also called master pattern. It is the basic pattern from which new patterns are made. The sloper itself is used as a pattern when styling changes are not needed.

4. *Trace Your Sloper:* This is the first step in making most patterns. Put one or two paperweights on the sloper and trace around the outline of the sloper, like a giant stencil, onto a new sheet of paper. Mark the notches and indicate any dots and the grain line unless otherwise noted. Remove the sloper and mark the darts and grain line in pencil on the new pattern. Write center front (C.F.), center back (C.B.), or whatever other information from the sloper you need on the new pattern.

If you are using a ready-made pattern,

place the pattern on a new sheet of paper and hold it in place with Scotch tape. Trace around it with your tracing wheel, without carbon, marking the darts, grain line, and so on. Remove the tissue pattern and mark the darts and grain line in pencil on the new pattern.

5. *Bust Point:* Also called apex. This refers to the tip of the bosom. In pattern-making, this is used as a reference point.

6. *Crossmarks:* When making patterns, crossmarks are lines drawn across two pieces of the pattern to indicate how the pieces fit together—like notches.

7. *Trueing:* This word has two meanings. A) The first refers to making a muslin garment. Trueing a muslin means correcting a muslin garment to make it into an accurate pattern. B) In making paper patterns, if you change one pattern piece, in some cases you will need to make a corresponding change on another pattern piece so that the two will fit together.

PATTERN REMINDERS: MISTAKES TO AVOID

Don't be discouraged if you make a few mistakes at first. Remember when you first learned to sew, you didn't do everything right. Here are a few common mistakes which beginners make that you should watch for.

1. Confusing the cutting line with the finished line. To avoid this confusion, it

helps to use two different colored pencils—one color for your cut line and one color for your finish line.

2. Not remembering to add seam allowance. In some styles, especially those with curved lines, the pattern must be worked without seam allowance, then the seam allowance added as the last step.

3. Forgetting to true your pattern.

4. A paper pattern must be cut the same way it will be sewn in order to have the right shape. For example, if the pattern has a dart, you must cut out the paper pattern with the dart folded closed, the same way as the dart will be stitched closed in the finished garment. If it has a pleat, the pleat must be folded when you cut the pattern, just as it would be pressed in the garment.

The directions for making these patterns will instruct you to do these things, but sometimes they may still be overlooked.

CHAPTER 2

BASIC A-LINE-DRESS SLOPER

Please read Chapter 1 before following instructions in this chapter.

The A-line sloper is used to make dress patterns with no waistline. If you make only this sloper, there are so many different designs you can create from it, you're sure to be pleased with your efforts. When buying your tissue pattern, look at the size chart and select the size in which the bust measurement is closest to your own. The hips are easier to fit, so don't worry if that measurement is different from yours. As you see in *Figure 7,* the pattern should have a jewel neckline and a long fitted sleeve with one or two elbow darts. The back should have a center-back seam, shoulder and waistline darts; the front should have underarm bust darts. The best patterns are either Butterick Personal A-line Fitting Pattern (⚹3001 in misses sizes) or Vogue Basic Fitting Pattern (⚹1001 in misses sizes). They are listed in the catalogue index as fitting shells. The Butterick comes in all size ranges and both patterns include detailed instructions on altering and fitting. When fitting your muslin you can refer to these instructions, as well as the directions

given in this chapter. In both these patterns, the long sleeve is shown with a zipper at the wrist. I have omitted the sleeve zipper, but you may include it if you prefer.

For the muslin dress, use only the front, back, sleeve, and neckline-facing patterns. No other facings, zipper, or other finishing touches are needed. Press the tissue-pattern pieces, using a warm iron and no steam. Check the muslin to make sure the grain is straight and press it. Lay out and pin the pattern pieces, being sure the grain line on the pattern follows the grain of the muslin. This is important because if the grain is off, the dress won't hang properly and will be difficult to fit. When cutting the dress, leave 1″ seam allowance instead of ⅝″ at the side seam for extra leeway in fitting. You can use your ruler and colored pencil to add an additional ⅜″ to the pattern seam allowance. After you cut the muslin, use your tracing wheel and carbon to mark the bust, waist, shoulder and elbow darts, grain-line arrows, and the ease line on the sleeve cap.

Once the pieces are cut and marked, they

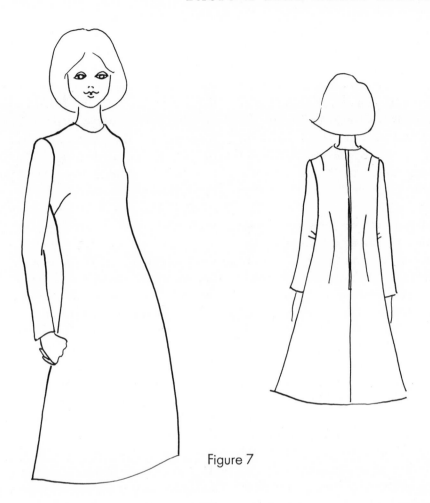

Figure 7

are ready to be sewn together. Use a bright-color cotton thread, a long stitch, about eight to the inch, and loose tension. This will make seam ripping easier when you take the dress apart later. First stitch around the neckline so that it won't stretch out of shape while you're working. Then stitch the bust darts and press them down. Sew the back-shoulder darts and waist darts and press them. Join the shoulder seams and facing seams and press them open. Attach the facing to the neckline. Stitch the center-back seam and side seams, leaving an 8″ or 10″ opening at the center back so that you can try on the dress. Now you're ready for your first fitting, which is without sleeves.

Put the dress on, right side out, and stand in front of a full-length mirror. Let your arms hang at your sides. Turn sideways and check the bust darts. They should be in the middle of your bust at the fullest part. If the bust darts are too high or too low, use your red pencil to mark where the point of the dart should be. Then check the hips as described below. After you have made any adjustments in the hips, take off the dress and open up the side seams. Using your paper pattern, re-mark the bust darts so that they are positioned on the points you marked with your red pencil. If you are flat-chested and the dress pokes out in front, make the darts smaller. If you have a full bosom, you may need to make the darts larger.

Now stand sideways and check the hips.

The dress should not cup under your fanny. If your dress is too tight at the hips, it will get lap wrinkles, ride up, and look terrible. You should be able to pinch at least an inch of fabric at the side seams at the fullest part of your hips. Take in or let out the side seams and/or center-back seam to achieve proper fit. If the waistline looks too wide, you can shape the side seams a bit and also take in the back-waistline darts.

The next place to check is the neckline. It should not cut in at the front of the neck or stand away from the neck in back. If the neckline cuts into your neck, mark the uncomfortable place with a pencil, take off the dress and reshape the neckline with your French curve. Stitch the facing following the new neckline. The neckline should not be any lower than what is needed for comfort. If it is too wide or too low, you will have trouble when you want to add a collar. If the neckline stands away from the back of the neck, it should be lowered ¼″. If you do this and it still pokes out, you need to adjust the shoulder darts. Open the shoulder seams and take in the shoulder darts ⅛″ to ¼″. Press the darts and stitch the shoulder seams again.

The last places to fit are the armhole and shoulders. The armhole should not come up too high under the arm. If the armhole needs lowering, use your red pencil to mark on the muslin where the armhole should be, take off your dress and reshape the armhole, using your French curve.

Now you have fitted the dress except for the sleeve. If this part seems tedious, remember that after you have done this once, you'll hardly have to fit any dress again when it is made from this sloper. Now for the sleeve. Sew the elbow darts and press them toward the wrist. Run an easing stitch following the ease line on the cap. Stitch the seam closed and press. Carefully pull the thread of your stitch to put ease in the cap. If you have trouble with the thread breaking, use a heavy thread like button twist in the bobbin and pull on that. Pin the sleeve in place, matching the side seam of the dress with the seam of the sleeve, and center the center of the cap with the shoulder seam. Stitch around the armhole just outside of the easing stitch of the cap. Very lightly steam the seam allowance of the cap toward the dress. A sleeve board or sleeve roll is helpful if you have one. If you don't, you can improvise by rolling up a heavy towel tightly into a cylinder and pinning it.

Put the dress back on. Look at the sleeve. If it is too full at the cap or has bunchy gathers, it needs to be adjusted (*Figure 8A*). Take out the sleeve and open up the seam. Press the seam flat. Bunchiness is usually caused by the cap of the sleeve being too high. To correct this, fold the sleeve in half to find the center of the cap and mark with a notch. Open the sleeve flat and measure down ⅜″ from the notch and mark. Starting at the new mark, lower the cap as shown in *Figure 8B*. Cut on the new line. Finish the sleeve as before.

Now try on the complete dress with two sleeves. Bend your elbows. The dart should come at the point of your elbow. If there are two elbow darts, your elbow should be in the middle of the two darts. The sleeve should not be so tight that it binds across the bend of your elbow. If the dart is not in the right place, put a mark on your elbow with a red pencil. Open up the sleeve seams and the darts. Press the sleeve flat. Using the tissue-paper sleeve pattern, line up the elbow-dart points on the tissue-paper pattern with the new elbow-dart point on the muslin, and redraw the darts with tracing wheel and carbon. Stitch the new darts and stitch the seam closed. Put your dress on

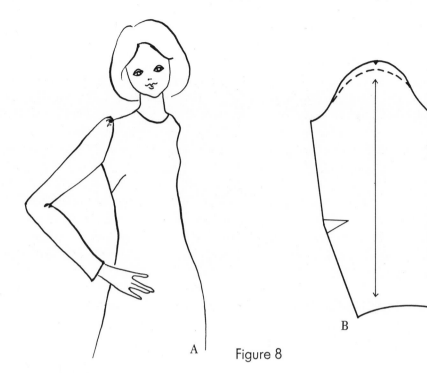

A   Figure 8   B

again. If the sleeve is too tight, let the seam out. If it looks too loose, take it in, but don't make it so tight that you can't move comfortably. Mark the correct finished length of the sleeve all around with the red pencil or chalk. The sleeve should end just at the wristbone.

When you're satisfied that your muslin fits comfortably and looks right, you can mark the hem. Wear the kind of shoes you usually wear with a dress. Don't try to judge the length with your bedroom slippers on. A hem marker is best if you have one. If you don't have one, use a yardstick and have someone mark it while you stand up straight. The important thing is to measure up from the floor exactly the same amount all around. Be sure to place hem crossmarks at the side and center-back seams.

With tailor's chalk, make a mark at the center front, side seam, and center back at your waistline. Do the same to indicate

your hipline at the fullest part. These marks will be guidelines on your sloper that you'll refer to when designing new patterns.

Now you're ready to make your heavy-paper pattern. After you take off your dress, but before you take it apart, the seams and darts should be marked so you'll be able to tell the stitching lines. Since you will only use the right (not left, as you wear it) side of the dress to make your sloper, you need to mark only the right side. Use tailor's chalk, of the soft chalky type rather than the waxy type, in a color which contrasts with your tracing-wheel markings (*Figure 9*). With the dress right side out, beginning at the side seam, carefully draw the chalk along the seam so you have a narrow line marking each side of the seam. At the hemline and armhole, draw a crossmark across the seam to indicate exactly where the seam ends. Follow the same procedure to mark the armhole seam, sleeve seam, shoulder seam, and center-back seam. Be sure to mark the beginning and end of each seam with a cross-mark. If the hem is marked with pins, use the chalk to make a line where the pins are placed and remove the pins. Mark all the darts the same way as the seams and draw an X at the point of each dart. Rub the chalk along the edge of the neckline. Your marked muslin should look like *Figure 9.*

If you are going to make the short-sleeve or shirt-sleeve slopers to go with the A-line (instead of making the entire basic-bodice or blouse sloper), remove the long sleeve, then follow the directions in chapters 4 (short) and 5 (shirt).

Once your muslin is marked, use a seam ripper or small scissors and carefully open each seam and dart except the shoulder in the following order: 1) center-back seam; 2) remove sleeves at armhole; 3) side seams; 4) sleeve seam; 5) bust and waist darts on the right side; 6) neckline

facing. You will need only the right sleeve, the right back, and the front. Open the shoulder seam of the left (unmarked) side and discard the left back. The other pieces won't be used, since you need only one pattern for each sleeve and back. Carefully press each of the pieces you will use.

The next step is what designers call "trueing." It means marking and trimming each muslin piece so it becomes an accurate pattern. Before you separate the right shoulder seam, the neckline and armhole must be trued (*Figure 10A*). Using your French curve and soft black pencil, blend the chalk line at the armhole to form a smooth line. You will have to reposition your French curve several times to mark the entire line. Follow the same steps to mark the neckline. Once you have marked the neckline and armhole, open the shoulder seam and dart, then press each piece.

Fold your dress front in half carefully and pin together. Be sure the shoulders,

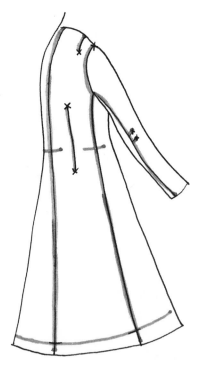
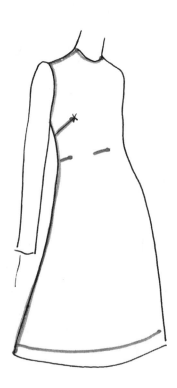

Figure 9

armholes, and side seams are together exactly. Press the center-front fold to form a crease. Open up the front and press it flat lightly, but don't press out the crease. Cut on the center-front crease line and discard the unmarked half.

Using your ruler, yardstick, curve stick, and soft black pencil, smooth and blend any uneven parts of the chalk outline on the muslin. Blend the dart line and hem-line. When you finish this part, your front muslin should look like *Figure 10B*. Now pin the dart closed with the fold down. Carefully cut on the outline around the neck, shoulder, armhole, side seam, and hem. You now have a muslin pattern with no seam allowance. The seam allowance will be added when you transfer the muslin to the permanent paper pattern.

Now you can work on the back muslin. Using your yardstick, ruler, and curve rule, use a black pencil to smooth and blend the chalk lines at the center-back, side, and shoulder seams, hem, and darts as you did on the front muslin. With the shoulder dart pinned, cut out the back muslin.

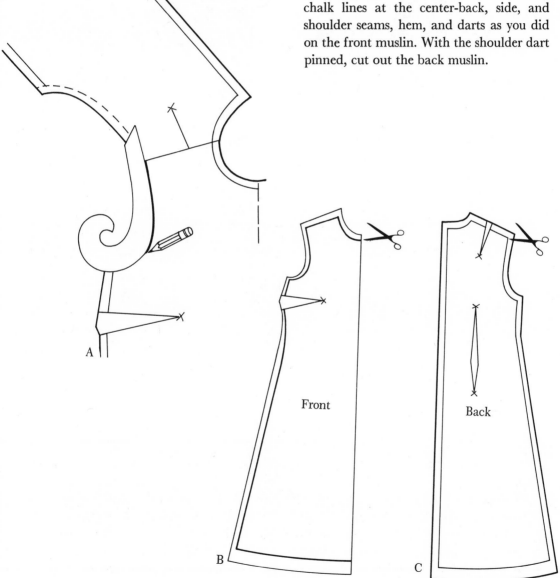

A

B   Front   C   Back

Figure 10

Use the same method for marking the sleeve muslin. Mark the cap, darts, wrist, and seam as shown in *Figure 11A*. Mark notches at each end of the ease line on the cap, two in back and one in front. Cut out the sleeve. Now you have your three pattern pieces ready to transfer to heavy paper.

all sides. Using cellophane tape, tape each side to the paper, using the tape at right angles to the sleeve. Keep the sleeve smooth and flat and don't pull on it. You can use your paperweights to help hold the muslin. Once the sleeve is taped in place, carefully draw around the edge of it like a stencil,

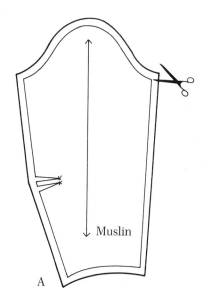

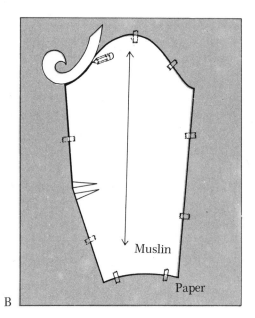

Figure 11

Press each piece carefully, moving the iron with the grain so as not to change the shape.

To make your sleeve sloper, cut a piece of heavy paper several inches larger, on all sides, than the sleeve itself. Lay the paper on the table and place the sleeve muslin on the paper, leaving some excess paper on

using your ruler and French curve to keep the lines smooth as in *Figure 11B*. Make V-notch marks to indicate the end of the two dart lines and to indicate the position for the ease on the cap. Use your tracing wheel and ruler to mark the darts and grain line. The lines will transfer without carbon. When you have finished tracing the muslin onto the paper, carefully clip the tape where it meets the muslin and remove the muslin which you can discard. Your sloper now has what is called the finish line, or stitching line. To finish the sloper, you must add seam allowance. Use

darts closed before you cut along the seam with the darts. Cut little V notches in the end of the dart lines and use your awl or heavy needle to make a hole in the dart point, and at each end of the grain line, big enough to stick a pencil point through.

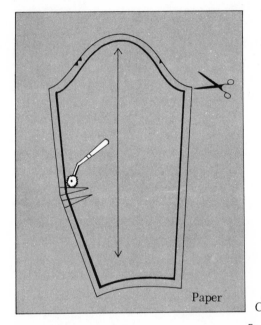

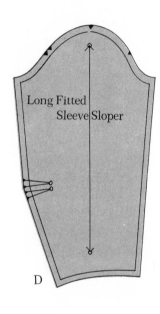

Long Fitted Sleeve Sloper

D

Paper

C

Figure 11

your ruler and red pencil to add ⅝″ seam allowance all around. Draw in the dart on the traced marks. Use your ruler and pencil to mark the grain line. Your sleeve sloper should look like *Figure 11C*. When this is done, you can cut out your sleeve sloper on the red line. Be sure you do not cut on the stitching line. Fold and tape the

Cut little V notches at the ease marks on the cap. Lightly fold the sleeve in half longways to indicate the center of the cap and mark a notch at the center. This notch must be matched with the shoulder seam when stitching the sleeve into the armhole. Label the sleeve. Your finished sleeve sloper should look like *Figure 11D*.

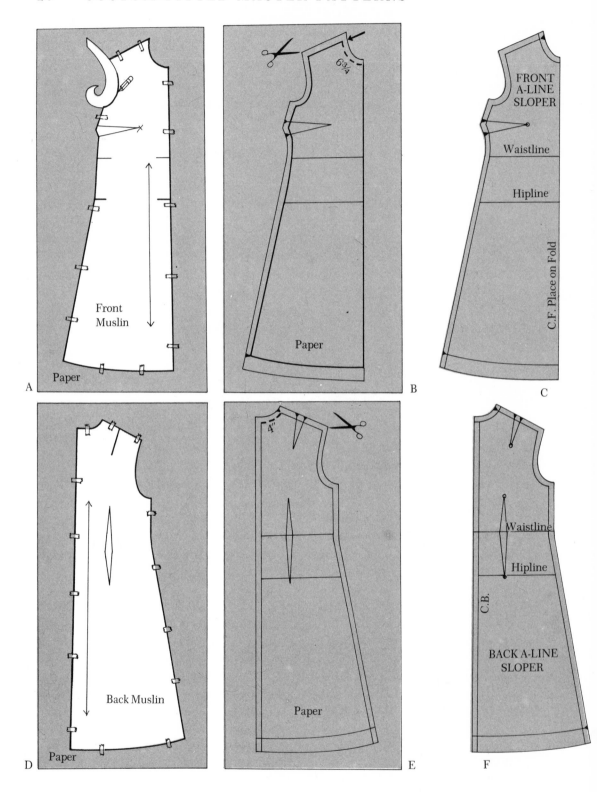

Figure 12

Follow the same general steps in making the front sloper as you did in making the sleeve (*Figure 12A*). Cut a piece of heavy paper several inches larger than your front muslin. Place the muslin on the paper face up and tape it to the paper. It is very important to keep the muslin smooth and flat and not stretch it. When the muslin is taped, draw around it using your ruler and curve rule. Use your French curve to follow the shape of the neckline and armhole accurately. Use your tracing wheel to trace the darts and waistline and hipline marks. Mark the grain line with your ruler and tracing wheel. Carefully clip the tape so the muslin can be removed from the paper. Using a red pencil and your ruler, add 5/8″ seam allowance. Use the French curve to smooth your seam-allowance lines at the neckline and armhole. Using your tape measure on its edge, measure the finished neckline from shoulder to center front (*Figure 12B*, dotted line). Mark this amount on the neckline of your pattern. You will use it when making collar patterns.

Make a V notch at the finished hemline and add 3″ allowance for the hem. Make a V notch where the shoulder seam meets the neckline (shown by arrow). Draw the bust dart on the traced line. With your ruler, connect the waistline and hipline marks. Your front sloper should now look like *Figure 12B*. Mark your center-front grain line and label the sloper. Cut out your sloper on the cutting line. Remember to fold the dart and tape it closed before you cut the side seam. Your finished sloper should look like *Figure 12C*.

To trace the back sloper, follow the same steps as you did for the front (*Figure 12D*). Tape the muslin to your paper in the same way and draw around the muslin with your ruler and curve. With your tracing wheel, mark the grain line and hipline and waistline marks. Trace the shoulder and waistline darts the same way as you did the bust dart in front. Clip the tape and remove the muslin (*Figure 12E*). Add 5/8″ seam allowance all around, including the center back. Add 3″ hem allowance. Draw in the darts and connect the waistline and hipline marks.

On the finish line, measure the back neckline from the finished shoulder to the center back (as shown by the dotted line). Mark this amount on the sloper. Mark a notch at the shoulder as you did on the front. Mark a notch at the hemline. Cut out the sloper. Be sure to fold the shoulder dart closed when cutting the shoulder seam. Label the sloper. The finished back sloper should look like *Figure 12F*. Now you have your complete A-line master pattern.

Using the basic sloper as a pattern, you can create many new styles by using various collars, necklines, sleeve styles, trimmings, pockets, and so on. Information on this is covered in chapters 8 thru 11. Turn to Chapter 12 for directions on making new patterns from this sloper.

CHAPTER 3

BASIC-SKIRT SLOPER

Please read Chapter 1 before you begin this chapter.

The A-line-skirt sloper is used to make many different skirt styles and combined with the bodice sloper to make innumerable dress and jumper designs. The basic bodice is covered in Chapter 4.

The pattern needed to make this sloper should have a fitted bodice, with underarm bust darts and waist darts in front, shoulder and waist darts in back, a jewel neckline, short sleeves, and an A-line skirt with front- and back-waist darts (*Figure 13*). Select the size pattern with the bust measurement closest to your own. The bodice and skirt are available together in one pattern. The best patterns are Butterick Personal Fit Pattern (⚸3002 in misses sizes) or Vogue Basic Fit Pattern (⚸1002 in misses). Both are available in a number of size ranges. Each of these patterns includes a straight skirt and an A-line skirt; be sure you work with the A-line-skirt pattern. Directions on altering and fitting are included in the patterns. You can refer to them as well as to the fitting directions here. If you do not plan to make the bodice sloper, then you can use any A-line-skirt pattern that has darts at the waistline in front and back and a center-back seam. If you're making only the skirt sloper, follow this chapter all the way through. If you are going to make the entire dress, follow the steps in this chapter up through fitting the muslin skirt. Then go on to Chapter 4 and make the bodice.

To make your muslin skirt, you will need only the front- and back-skirt pattern. Iron the pattern pieces with a warm iron. Straighten the grain and press the muslin. Lay out the pattern and pin the pieces, making sure the grain line is correct. Mark 1″ seam allowance at the side seams for extra leeway in fitting. Cut out your skirt. Mark the darts and grain-line arrows with your tracing wheel and carbon.

To put the skirt together, first sew the darts and press them toward the side seams. Close the center-back seam, leaving about six inches open at the top, then stitch the side seams, and press the three seams open. Use a long stitch, with contrasting thread and loose tension for easier ripping.

Now you can try on your skirt and fit it.

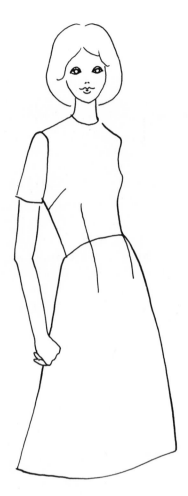
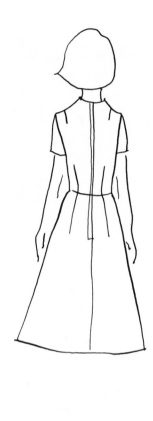

Figure 13

Pin the back opening closed and, standing in front of a full-length mirror, turn sideways and check the hips. As with the A-line dress there should be no cupping under the fanny, and you should be able to pinch an inch of fabric at the side seam at the fullest part of your hips. Take in or let out the skirt at the side seams or center back if necessary to achieve a good fit. Check the waistline. It should be loose enough so that you can slip two or three fingers between the skirt and yourself, but not so loose that it stands away from your body. If it does, take in either the front or back darts, whichever place fits poorly, or both if necessary. If the waist is too tight, let out the darts or the side seams or both at the waistline.

Sometimes the waist and hips will fit, but you may still have a problem with pulling or bubbling out around the darts. When this happens, the dart is the wrong shape for your figure and needs to be reshaped. If there is pulling, with the skirt on, clip a few stitches at a time to open the darts. When the strain is released, repin the darts so they fit smoothly. Take off the skirt, mark the correction with tailor's chalk, and stitch the darts again. When making alterations on darts, work on both darts together, not just the right or left side. If there is bubbling, pin the darts in more, to achieve a smoother fit, and continue as explained above for pulling.

The next place to mark is your natural waistline. Do this only after you have made any adjustments to the darts and side seams and have checked them. To find your true waistline, tie a piece of string snugly around your waist. Using tailor's chalk or a colored pencil; mark your waistline where the string is tied.

If you're going to make the bodice sloper, stop here and go to Chapter 4. After you have made and fitted the muslin bodice, and fitted it to the skirt, turn back to this page to make your skirt sloper. If you're making just the skirt sloper, you can continue with this chapter.

Have the hem marked with a skirt marker. Be sure to have a hem mark across the side and center-back seams. After you take off the skirt but before you take it apart, the stitching lines should be marked. Since you need only the right side of the skirt to make your sloper, you need only to mark the right side. Use the soft chalky kind of tailor's chalk rather than the harder waxy type, in a color which contrasts with your tracing-wheel marks (*Figure 14*). With the skirt right side out, beginning at the side seam, draw the chalk along the seam so you have a narrow line marking each side of the seam. Be sure both sides of the seam are marked. Follow the same procedure to mark the center back and the

Figure 14

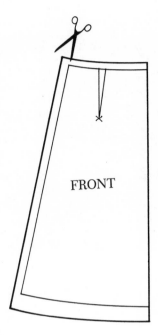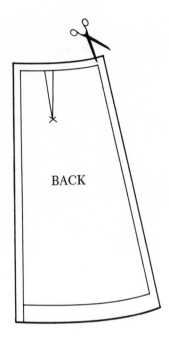

Figure 15

darts. Mark an X at the point of each dart. If the hemline is marked in pins, mark the pin locations with tailor's chalk and remove the pins. Write F on the front and B on the back so you can tell the two pieces apart. Your muslin should look like *Figure 14.*

Next, using a seam ripper, carefully open the side seams and center-back seam. Discard the left side of the back skirt—that should be the unmarked one. Open the darts and press the two pieces flat. Fold the front skirt in half carefully and press the fold to form a crease. Open up the skirt and press it flat lightly but don't press out the crease. Cut your skirt in half on the crease line and discard the unmarked half.

Using your yardstick, French curve, curve rule, and soft black pencil, blend the chalk line, including the hem, to form a smooth outline of the front patterns as in *Figure 15.* Use your curve rule or ruler to make the dart at the waistline. Follow the same steps for the back, including trueing the chalk line at the center back (*Figure 15*). Pin the dart on the front muslin closed, being sure to have the fold of the dart toward the side seam. Cut out your front muslin on the outline. You now have two muslin pattern pieces with no seam allowance.

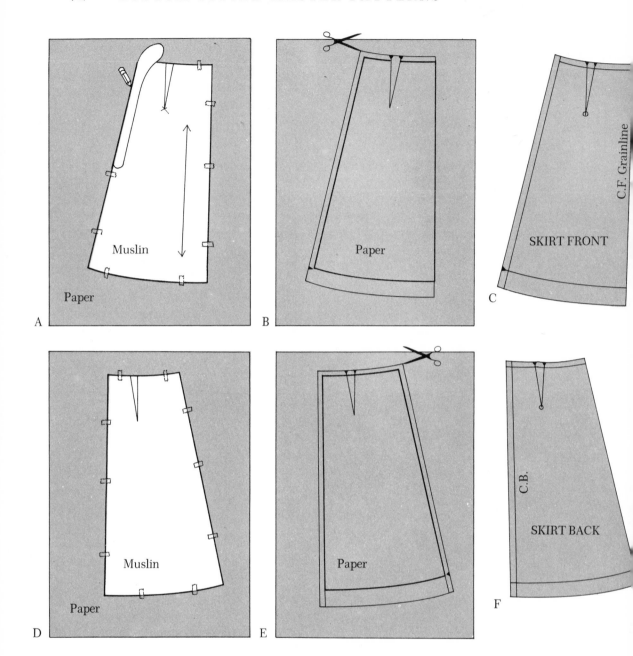

Figure 16

The last step is to transfer your muslin pattern onto heavy paper to make a permanent sloper. Press your muslin pieces again if they need it, being careful not to stretch them out of shape. Cut a sheet of heavy paper several inches larger on all sides than the skirt front. Place your front muslin face up on the paper. Be sure you have several extra inches of paper on all sides for adding your seam allowance and hem. Put some paperweights down on the muslin and carefully tape the muslin to the paper, taking care not to pull or stretch it. Now draw around the muslin like a stencil. Use your yardstick and curve rule to keep the line smooth (*Figure 16A*). Use your ruler and tracing wheel to mark the grain line. Trace the darts, using the wheel and curve rule or ruler. No carbon is needed to mark on paper. When you have finished tracing, clip the tape and remove the muslin. The line on your paper is called the finish, or stitching, line. To complete your sloper, ⅝″ seam allowance and hem allowance must be added. Using your ruler and a contrasting color pencil, measure out from your stitching line and mark your seam allowance at the waist and side seams. Measure down 3″ from the hemline to add your hem allowance. Use your ruler or curve to draw in the dart lines (*Figure 16B*). Draw the grain line with your ruler. Before you cut out your pattern along the waistline, you must have the dart closed so the top part of the waistline will be the right shape. Crease dart closed and tape in place. The pattern won't lie flat. Cut the waistline. Continue cutting the rest of the pattern. Be sure you cut on the cutting, not the stitching, line. Cut a V notch at the end of the dart lines and at the hemline. Use your heavy needle to punch a hole at the point of the dart. Label the pattern piece. Your completed front-skirt sloper should look like *Figure 16C*.

To make the back sloper, follow the same steps as you did for the front. Because of the center-back seam, you'll need to add ⅝″ seam allowance (*Figures 16D and E*). Your finished back-skirt sloper should look like *Figure 16F*.

See Chapter 13 for directions on making waistbands and skirt patterns, using your sloper. You can also create many skirt styles by adding trims, pockets, flaps, and so on to your basic skirt. (See chapters 8 and 9.)

CHAPTER 4

BASIC-BODICE SLOPER

Please read Chapter 1 before following this chapter.

The basic-bodice sloper is used to design most waistline dresses. It can be combined with the A-line-skirt sloper and other skirt patterns and is used to make empire styles as well. Begin with Chapter 3, which covers the pattern requirements and explains how to make the skirt sloper. Then continue with this chapter.

If you made the A-line sloper and needed more than minor alterations at the shoulder or bust line, use your A-line sloper to correct the bodice tissue pattern before cutting it in muslin. The neckline and bust line are the same in both the A-line and bodice of the Vogue and Butterick basic fitting patterns. For the muslin pattern, you will need only the front, back, short sleeve, and neckline-facing patterns. Straighten the grain of the muslin and press it and the pattern pieces. Pin your pattern pieces, being careful that the grain of the muslin follows the grain line on the pattern. Add 1″ seam allowance at the side seams instead of the usual ⅝″ for extra leeway in fitting. Cut out the muslin pieces. Use your tracing wheel and dressmaker's carbon to mark the darts, grain-line arrows, and the ease line on the sleeve cap. Unpin the pattern pieces.

Now you're ready to sew the muslin bodice together. Use a long, loose stitch and bright-colored thread. First stitch around the neck to keep it from stretching, then sew all the darts. Press the waist darts toward the center, the bust darts down, and the shoulder darts toward the armhole. Next, join the shoulder and facing seams, and press them open. Attach the neckline facing and press. Stitch the side seams and press them open. Try on the bodice right side out and have someone pin the back closed. Standing in front of a long mirror, stand sideways and check the bust darts. The point of the dart should be in the middle of your bosom at the fullest part but should end 1″–1½″ before the apex. If the bust darts are not in the right place, see Chapter 2, page 19, where fitting the darts is explained. After you have the bust darts corrected, you can check the waistline. The point of the waistline darts should be at least 1″ below the apex of your bosom for the best appearance. Make the darts shorter if they come up too high. When you make alterations on darts, always work on both the right and left side together, to get a good fit. The waistline itself should fit snugly but you should be able to slip several fingers between the muslin and yourself. If the waist is too tight or too loose, take in or let out at the darts, or side seams, or both. If you have trouble with the midriff not fitting smoothly, the darts probably need to be pinned in more, to shape the bodice in under the bust. If there is pulling at any place along the darts, rip out a few stitches at a time until the strain is released, then repin the darts. Mark the corrections with chalk, and sew along the new lines. The top of the darts at the back waistline should end below your shoulder blades or the back will be uncomfortable. See Chapter 2, page 20, to fit the neck and armhole areas. When you are satisfied with the way your bodice fits, you can make the sleeve.

Run a stitch along the ease line on the cap. Use button thread in the bobbin to pull on if you have trouble with the thread breaking. Stitch the seam and press it open. Pull the thread to put ease in the cap. I think the easiest way to set in a sleeve is to pin your sleeve at the armhole, first matching the seam of the sleeve with the side seam of the bodice. Be sure to have the back of the sleeve at the back of the bodice. Next pin the notch at the center of the cap to the shoulder seam. With only the two pins holding the sleeve, tighten or loosen the easing thread until the sleeve fits into the armhole neatly. Then pin the rest of the sleeve. Set in both sleeves and steam the seam allowance very lightly toward the bodice. Try on the bodice again to check the sleeves. If the cap isn't smooth, see Chapter 2, page 21, to correct this. The bottom of the sleeve should fit fairly snugly around your arm for the best ap-

pearance. Take in the sleeve seam if necessary. If the bottom of the sleeve pokes out or looks awkward, you can often make a better-looking sleeve by curving up the bottom line into a slight arch instead of having a straight line. When you are happy with the way the bodice looks and fits, mark your natural waistline by tying a string snugly around your waist and marking with tailor's chalk as you did with the skirt muslin.

For the last step, take off your muslin bodice and pin it to the skirt, matching the waistline marks of the skirt with the waistline marks of the bodice and the side seams and darts of the skirt and bodice. Stitch them together on the lines and try on the whole dress. Pin the back closed. The waistline seam should be at your waistline. The natural waistline is lower in the back than in the front, often by one or two inches. Once the dress fits correctly, mark the hem with a skirt marker.

When you've finished checking the dress, take it off and mark all the seams and darts on the right side with tailor's chalk. Since you will use only the right (not left as you wear it) side of the dress to make your sloper, you'll need only to mark the right side. Use the soft chalky kind of tailor's chalk, rather than the harder waxy kind, in a color which contrasts with your tracing-wheel markings (*Figure 17*). With the dress right side out, beginning at the waistline seam, draw the chalk along the seam so that you have a narrow line marking each side of the seam. Remove the bodice from the skirt at the waistline. Draw the chalk along the bodice side seam the same way as at the waist seam. At the armhole, draw a crossmark across the seam to indicate exactly where the side seam ends. Follow the same procedure to mark the armhole seam, sleeve seam, and shoulder seam. Be sure to mark the exact beginning and end of each seam with a crossmark.

Figure 17

Mark the darts with chalk the same as the seams, and draw an X at the point of each dart. Rub the chalk around the edge of the neckline. Mark the back of the sleeve with a B. Your marked muslin should look like *Figure 17*.

If you are going to make the long fitted- or shirt-sleeve sloper to go with the basic bodice (instead of making the entire A-line or blouse sloper), remove the short sleeve after the dress is marked, and set in and fit your new sleeve as explained in Chapter 2 (long) and Chapter 5 (short). Then continue. Once the seams and darts are marked, you can take the muslin apart. To make the skirt sloper from the muslin, turn back to Chapter 3, page 30.

To continue with the bodice, first remove the sleeves and neck facing. Open the shoulder seam on the left (unmarked) side only and open the side and right-sleeve seam. Open up the darts except at the shoulder. Pull out the easing stitch in the sleeve and press the sleeve and the front and back bodice. Discard the left sleeve and back. Before you separate the right-shoulder seam, the neckline and armhole must be trued. Using your French curve and soft pencil, blend the chalk marking at the armhole to form a smooth line. You will have to position your French curve several times in order to mark the entire line. Follow the same steps to mark the neckline (*Figure 18A*). Once you have marked the neckline and armhole, open the shoulder seam and dart. Then press each piece. Fold the front bodice in half carefully and press a crease along the center front. Open it up and lightly press flat. Cut the front muslin in half along the crease line and discard the left side. Using a soft black pencil, French curve, curve stick and ruler, true the chalk lines. Mark the darts the same way. The lines should be smooth and even with no jogs or wiggles.

When you have finished marking the front muslin, it should look like *Figure 18B*. Before you cut the muslin, the darts must be pinned closed. Pin the waist dart so the fold is toward the center front and the bust dart so the fold is down. Cut out your front muslin along the outline. Follow the same steps to mark the back muslin. The marked back muslin should look like *Figure 18C*. Before you cut out the back, be sure you have the shoulder and waist dart pinned closed.

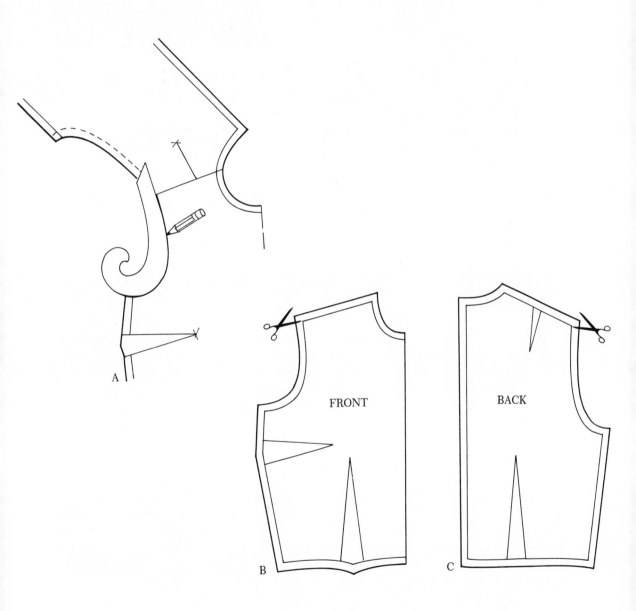

FRONT

BACK

Figure 18

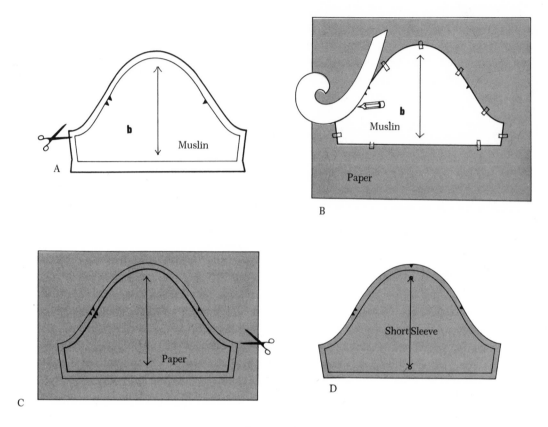

Figure 19

Use the same method to mark the muslin sleeve. At the cap, blend the chalk lines with your French curve. Mark notches at each end of the ease line, two notches at the back of the sleeve and one at the front so that your sleeve muslin looks like *Figure 19A*. Cut out your muslin sleeve.

Now your three muslin pieces are ready to be made into permanent slopers. Press the pieces if they need it.

To make your sleeve sloper, cut a piece of heavy paper several inches larger on all sides than the sleeve itself. Place the sleeve muslin on the paper and tape it in place, leaving a margin of paper around the muslin. Be sure to keep the muslin smooth and flat and not distort the shape as you tape. Using your French curve and ruler, trace around the edge of the muslin as you see in *Figure 19B*. Mark notches at each end of

the ease line on the cap, two notches at the back and one notch at the front. Use your tracing wheel to mark the grain line. You don't need carbon to mark on paper. Once you have finished tracing the muslin, clip the tape and discard the muslin. Your sloper now shows the stitching, or finish line. To finish the sloper, use your ruler to add ⅝" seam allowance (*Figure 19C*), draw in the grain line and mark the cap notches on the cutting line. With your awl, punch a hole at each end of the grain line. Cut out your sleeve pattern. Be sure to cut on the cutting line, not on the finish line. Cut V notches at the cap. Lightly fold the sleeve in half to locate the center of the cap. Clip a notch at the center to indicate where the sleeve meets the shoulder seam. Label the sloper. Your finished sleeve sloper should look like *Figure 19D*.

Making the front sloper follows the same general steps as making the sleeve. Cut a piece of heavy paper several inches larger than the muslin. Place the muslin face up on the paper and tape in place. Keep it smooth and do not stretch it. Use your French curve to follow the shape of the neckline and armhole. Use your ruler and curve stick to mark the rest of the outline. Trace the darts with your tracing wheel. Clip the tape and discard the muslin.

with pencil and ruler or curve stick. Using your tape measure on the edge, measure the finished neckline from the finished shoulder line to the center front (dotted line in *Figure 20B*). Mark this measurement on the neckline of your pattern. It will be used later in making collar patterns. Label the sloper. Cut out the neckline, shoulder, and armhole on the cutting line. Before you cut the side seam and waistline, tape the dart closed with the fold in the

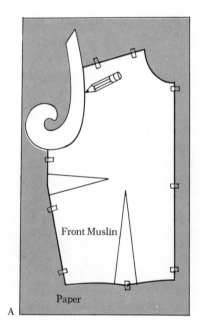

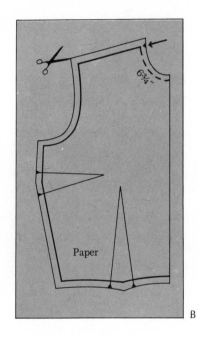

Figure 20

Using a colored pencil and ruler, add 5⁄8″ seam allowance. Blend the seam-allowance lines at the neckline and armhole, using the French curve. Mark the darts

proper direction. Your sloper will not lie flat with the darts closed. Untape the dart after you finish cutting out the sloper, and clip V notches at the end of the dart lines.

Use your awl to punch a hole at the point of each dart. Your finished sloper should look like *Figure 20C*.

Make the back sloper, following the same steps as the front, except that you also add ⅝″ seam allowance at the center back. Trace the grain line from the muslin onto the sloper with your tracing wheel. The steps in making the back sloper are shown in *Figures 20D, E,* and *F.*

Now you have your complete master pattern for making waistline dresses and skirts. See Chapter 14 for instructions on making new styles from this sloper. Also see Chapter 11 for sleeve styles made from the short-sleeve sloper.

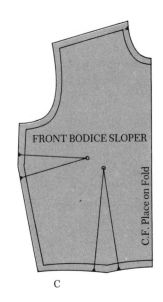

C

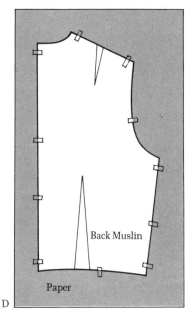

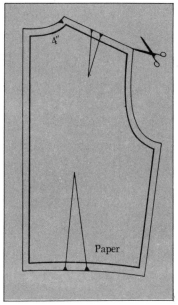

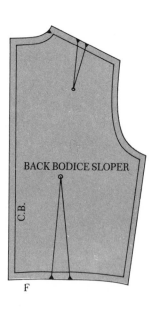

D   E   F

Figure 20

CHAPTER 5

BASIC-BLOUSE SLOPER

Please read Chapter 1 before you begin this chapter.

The basic-blouse sloper is used to make a great many different blouse styles, as well as vests and long-waist dresses. The shirt-sleeve and collar slopers are also used to make numerous designs that are used with the A-line and basic-dress slopers. The tissue pattern you will need to make this sloper is shown in *Figure 21*. It should contain a long sleeve with gathers at the wrist but not at the cap, a button cuff, underarm darts at the bust in front and at the shoulder in back, and a simple Peter Pan-type collar. It should not have a separate front placket. To make your muslin, you will need the front and back, collar, sleeve, and cuff. No separate facings are necessary.

Press your muslin and straighten the grain. If you have made either the A-line shift sloper or the basic-bodice sloper, you will want the neckline and armhole of your blouse sloper to be the same measurement as the neckline and armhole of the other sloper so that you can use sleeve and collar patterns interchangeably. If you do

Figure 21

not plan to make the A-line or bodice slopers, you can cut your muslin from the tissue pattern as you would usually. To compare the sloper with the blouse pattern, place the tissue pattern on top of the sloper so that the pattern armhole is directly aligned with the sloper armhole. Compare the shape and length of the stitching line of the pattern armhole with the stitching line of the sloper armhole. If the tissue-pattern armhole is a little longer or shorter, you can add or subtract at the side seam. If the armhole is the same measurement, but the shape of the curve is slightly different, that's all right. If the pattern armhole is really off, you should use another pattern. You are best off using a blouse pattern made by the same company that made your dress and/or A-line pattern, since one company's patterns won't vary too much. Do the same for the back as well as the front armhole.

Compare the neckline the same way. Be sure you compare the stitching line from the center front to the center back. Since the blouse pattern has a button extension at the center front and the sloper has seam allowance at the center back, it is easy to make a mistake here and work with the wrong part of the neckline. If the pattern neckline needs to be adjusted, you can make it a little larger or smaller by raising or lowering the neckline at the center front and blending a new neckline with your French curve. You can also add to, or take a small amount from, the neckline at the shoulder seam, and blend a new neckline from there.

Pin your pattern pieces to the muslin, being careful to match the grain of the muslin with the grain line on the pattern. Cut out the muslin pieces. Before unpinning the pattern, use your tracing wheel and carbon to mark all the darts and grain-line arrows. On the front, trace the center-front line and the fold line of the front facing. On the sleeve muslin, mark the ease line of the cap and the slash line for the placket. Mark the fold line of the cuff.

Now you can stitch your muslin together. Use a long, loose stitch and a bright-color thread. First stitch around the neckline to keep it from stretching, then stitch the darts. Press the shoulder darts toward the armhole and the bust darts down. Stitch the shoulder and side seams and press them open. Press the front facing under, along the fold line. Try on your muslin right side out and pin it closed along the center-front lines. Read Chapter 2, page 20, to check the fit of the neckline, shoulders, and armhole. Check the bust darts. They should be at the fullest part of your bosom and should not poke out or pull. See Chapter 2, page 19, if you have any problem with the darts. Check the length of your blouse. Many manufacturers try to economize by cutting their blouses too short. It should come to the top of your thighs, after the hem is turned up, to keep from pulling out of your pants or skirt. If the blouse is too short, draw an arrow at the bottom front and back to remind you to add more length to your sloper. You can curve in the side seams at the waistline if it seems a bit baggy there.

Next, stitch and turn the collar. Place the collar on the right side of the blouse and pin it first at the shoulder notches and the center front. The stitching line of the collar neckline should meet the center front of the blouse. Then pin the rest of the collar. Stitch the collar in place. If your shoulder notches on the collar do not match your shoulder seams on the blouse, mark new notches on the collar in the right place. If the end of the collar does not come to the center front of the blouse, measure how much it is short and let out the collar the necessary amount. When the center front of the collar extends beyond the center front of the blouse, mark the place where the collar should end and take the collar in.

Now you can work on the sleeve. Run an easing stitch along the line you traced on the cap and a gathering stitch at the bottom of the sleeve. You don't need to use a facing at the slash at the bottom of the sleeve. Stitch the sleeve seam closed and press it open. Make the cuffs and attach them to the sleeves, then set the sleeves in at the armholes, being sure you have the back of the sleeves at the back of the blouse. See Chapter 4, page 35, for a good way to pin and stitch a set-in sleeve. Lightly steam the cap so the seam allowance goes toward the blouse. Try on the blouse again. See Chapter 2, page 20, to check the fit of the cap. Pin the cuff closed. Let your arms hang at your sides and check the length of the sleeves. The end of the cuff should be at the wristbone. Lengthen or shorten the sleeve to correct the length if necessary. To shorten, take off the cuff and remove the gathers. Cut the excess length from the bottom of the sleeve, following the original shape of the sleeve bottom. Put in a new gathering stitch and put the cuff back on. You need to do this only on the right sleeve. To lengthen, remove the sleeve and open up the sleeve seam down to the cuff. Cut the sleeve in half crossways and set in a strip of muslin which is wide enough to add the needed length to the sleeve. After you have made an alteration in the sleeve, set it into the blouse again to make sure it is correct. To check the cuff, bend your arm at the elbow. The cuff should be loose enough to allow free movement of your arms. Adjust the cuff if needed.

When the blouse is fitted to your satisfaction, take it off and mark the stitching lines on the right side (*right* not left side

as you wear it). Use a soft chalky kind of tailor's chalk in a color which contrasts with your tracing-wheel markings (*Figure 22*). With the blouse right side out, beginning at the side seam, draw the chalk along the seam line so that you have a narrow line marking each side of the seam. At the armhole, draw a crossmark across the seam to indicate exactly where the side seam ends. Follow the same procedure to mark the armhole seam, sleeve seam, and shoulder seam. Make crossmarks at the end of each of the sleeve and shoulder seams.

Lift up the collar and draw a line along the seam that attaches the collar to the neckline. Chalk along the seam where the cuff is attached to the right sleeve. Rub the chalk along the bottom edge and sides of the cuff and around the edge of the collar. Mark the darts the same as the seams and draw an X at each dart point. Mark the back of the sleeve with a B. Your marked muslin should look like *Figure 22*.

Figure 22

If you are going to make either the long fitted- or short-sleeve slopers to go with the blouse (if you're not making the entire A-line or basic-bodice sloper), remove the shirt sleeve after the blouse is marked, and set in and fit your new sleeve as explained in Chapter 2 (long) or Chapter 4 (short). Then continue here.

Once the muslin is marked you can take it apart with your seam ripper. First take out the sleeves and discard the left sleeve. Remove the collar. Open the side seams and the right-bust dart. Open the left-shoulder seam only. Discard the left (unmarked) front. Remove the cuff from the sleeve and open the sleeve and cuff seams. Remove the ease from the cap, being careful not to stretch it. Take apart the collar and discard the upper (partially marked) collar. Press the muslin pieces. Before you separate the right-shoulder seam, the neckline and armhole must be trued. Using your French curve and soft pencil, blend the chalk line at the armhole to form a smooth line (*Figure 23A*). You will have to position your French curve several times in order to mark the entire line. Follow the same steps to mark the neckline. Once you have marked the neckline and armhole, open the shoulder seam and dart, and press flat.

You will need only the right side of your blouse back and collar. Press the blouse back and carefully fold it in half along the center back. Press the fold lightly. Unfold the back and cut along the center-back crease. Fold the collar in half at the center back, press the crease and mark it C.B. Cut along the crease. Discard the left (unmarked) side of the back and collar. You will also need only half of the muslin cuff.

Cut the cuff in half along the fold line. Discard the partially marked half.

Using your French curve, curve stick, and ruler, blend the chalk lines on the front muslin with a soft black pencil (*Figure 23B*). The lines should be smooth and even, with no jogs or wiggles. Blend the dart line the same way. When you finish marking the front muslin, it should look like *Figure 23B*. Before you cut out the front muslin, the dart must be pinned closed and the facing folded under. Pin the dart so the fold is down. Crease the fold line of the facing and pin it under, then cut along the outline of the muslin so there is no seam allowance. Mark the back muslin as you did the front except you will have one center-back line. When completed, the back should look like *Figure 23C*.

Use the same method to mark your muslin sleeve as you used to mark the front and back. Use your French curve, curve stick, and ruler to blend a smooth line at the cap, sides, and bottom of the sleeve. The chalk line at the sleeve bottom will be quite jagged because of the gathers. Mark notches at each end of the ease line on the sleeve cap, two at the back and one at the front. Your sleeve should look like *Figure 23D*. Cut out the sleeve along the outline.

Use your ruler and French curve to blend the chalk line at the outer edges and the neckline of your collar. Be sure the shoulder notch is clearly marked. The collar should look like *Figure 23E*. Cut out the collar along the neckline and the outer edges. Use your ruler to straighten the chalk lines on the cuff. It should look like *Figure 23F*. Cut out the cuff.

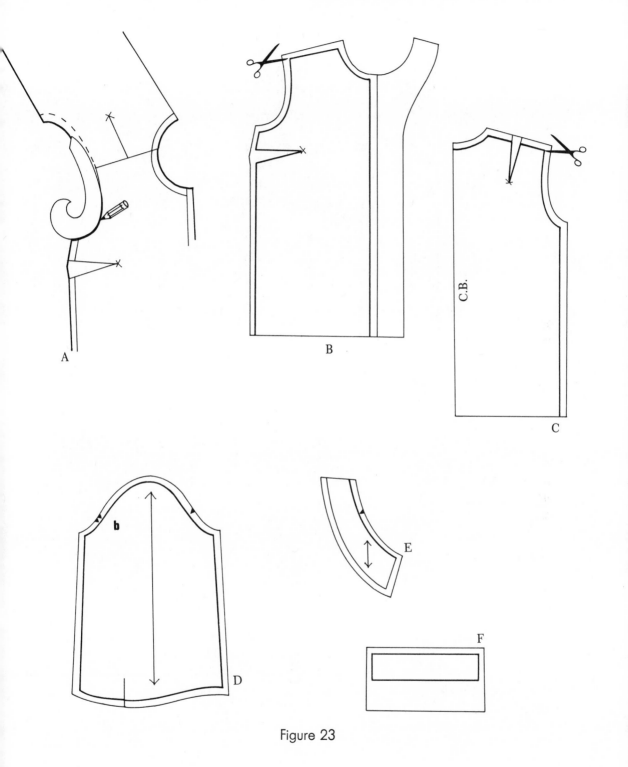

Figure 23

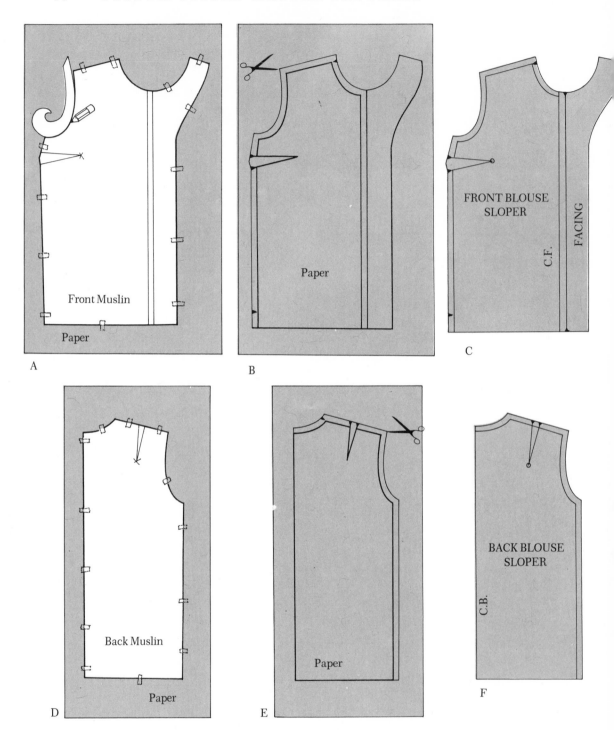

Figure 24

Now you are ready to make your permanent sloper. Cut a sheet of heavy paper several inches larger on all sides than the front muslin. Put some paperweights on the muslin if you like, and carefully tape the muslin to the paper. Be sure you leave several extra inches of paper on all sides for seam and hem allowances. Keep the muslin smooth and be careful not to pull or distort it. When you finish taping, trace around the muslin like a stencil, using your ruler, curve stick, and French curve to keep the lines smooth (*Figure 24A*). Trace the dart center-front line and fold line with your tracing wheel and ruler. No carbon is needed. Clip or peel off the tape and remove the muslin. The outline on your paper is the finish (stitching) line. To complete the sloper, you must add ⅝" seam allowance (*Figure 24B*). Using your ruler and contrasting colored pencil, measure out from your stitching line and mark your seam allowance. If your muslin was too short, you'll need to add to the bottom of your sloper. With your curve or ruler, mark the dart lines extending them to the cut line. Measure along the side seam up 1¼" from the bottom and mark a notch to indicate the hem. Using the yardstick, draw your center-front and fold lines where you marked with the tracing wheel. If you've made the A-line or bodice sloper, mark the neckline measurements, written on either of these slopers, on the blouse sloper. If you don't have the other slopers, see Chapter 4, page 39, for measuring the neckline. This is used in making collar patterns. Label the sloper as shown in *Figure 24C*.

Now you can cut out the sloper. BE SURE TO CUT ON THE CUTTING LINE, NOT ON THE SEAM-ALLOWANCE LINE. Crease along the fold line and fold the facing under before cutting the neckline. After cutting neckline, open the facing and cut the shoulder and armhole. Before you cut the side seam, the dart must be closed so that it will be the right shape. Tape the dart closed with the fold down. The sloper won't lie flat. Cut along the side seam to below the dart, then clip the tape on the dart and continue cutting the rest of the sloper. Clip V notches at the end of the dart lines and at the hem notch. Also cut V notches at the top and bottom of the facing fold line. Use your awl or a heavy needle to punch a hole at the point of the dart. Your finished front sloper should look like *Figure 24C*.

The back sloper is made following the same general steps as in making the front. Cut a piece of paper larger on all sides than the back muslin. Place the back muslin on the paper, leaving enough paper around the muslin to add seam and hem allowance. Tape the muslin as you did with the front (*Figure 24D*). Following the same procedure as for the front, trace the muslin and mark the dart and grain line. Remove the muslin and add seam allowances, notches, and marks as on the front. Label the sloper (*Figure 24E*). Tape the shoulder dart closed, with the fold toward the armhole, when you cut the shoulder seam. Remember there is no extension or seam allowance at the center back. The center back is placed on the fold of the fabric. Your finished back sloper should look like *Figure 24F*.

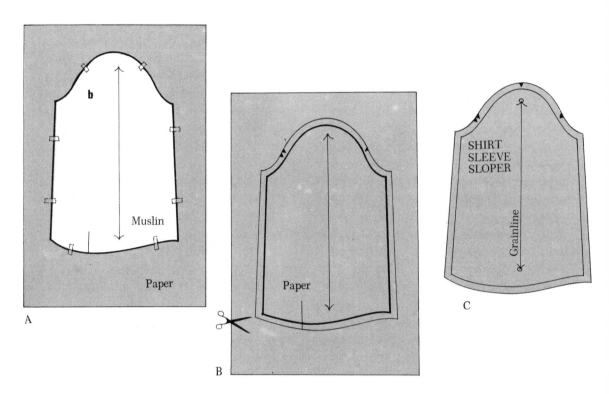

Figure 25

To make the sleeve sloper, you need a third piece of paper which is slightly larger on all sides than the muslin. Tape the sleeve to the paper. Using your French curve and ruler, trace around the muslin. Mark the notches at the ease line on the cap, and mark the placket slash line. Use your tracing wheel to mark the grain line (*Figure 25A*). Clip the tape and remove the muslin. With a contrasting colored pencil and ruler, add seam allowance of ⅝″ all around. Mark the cap notches on the seam-allowance line. Mark the grain line with your ruler and pencil. Label the sloper (*Figure 25B*). Cut out your sloper along the cutting line. Cut V notches at the cap, two in the back and one in the front. Lightly fold the sleeve in half longways, to locate the center of the cap. Clip a V notch at the center. This notch on the cap

should match the shoulder seam on the blouse when you set in the sleeve. The finished sleeve sloper should look like *Figure 25C*.

To make the cuff sloper, you will need a piece of paper a little more than twice the size of the muslin. With your ruler, draw a line across the middle of the paper and write FOLD on the line. Place the edge of the cuff longways on the fold line of the paper as shown in *Figure 26A*. Tape the muslin in place and mark around the three sides with a ruler. Remove the muslin and mark ⅝″ seam allowance except on the fold line. Crease the paper along the fold line. Use a few paper clips along the fold to keep the paper from slipping (*Figure 26B*). Cut around the three sides of the folded paper on the cutting line. Remove the paper clips and open up the cuff. The side seams of the cuff should be perfectly straight. If there is an angle going in or out, straighten the line with a ruler and cut on the corrected line. Label the cuff sloper as shown. Your finished cuff sloper should look like *Figure 26C*.

To make the collar sloper, you will need a piece of paper larger than the collar muslin. Tape the muslin in place and trace around it using your French curve and ruler (*Figure 26D*). Before you remove the muslin, label the center-back line of the collar. Remove the muslin and add ⅝″ seam allowance except at the center back.

Mark the shoulder notch on the cutting line. Label the sloper (*Figure 26E*). Cut out the collar on the cutting line and cut a V notch at the shoulder. Your finished collar sloper should look like *Figure 26F*.

Now you have completed your master pattern for making blouses. See Chapter 15 for instructions on making blouse designs from this sloper. Also see Chapter 10 on neckline and collar styles and Chapter 11 on sleeves. Sleeve or collar patterns made from the blouse sloper can be combined with the A-line dress or basic bodice as well.

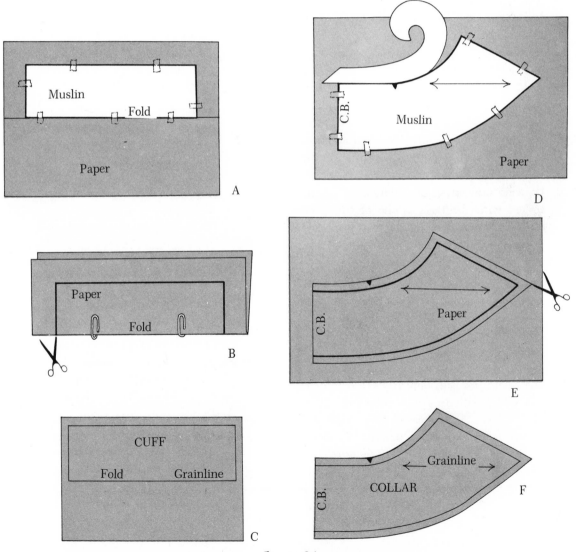

Figure 26

CHAPTER 6

BASIC-PANTS SLOPER

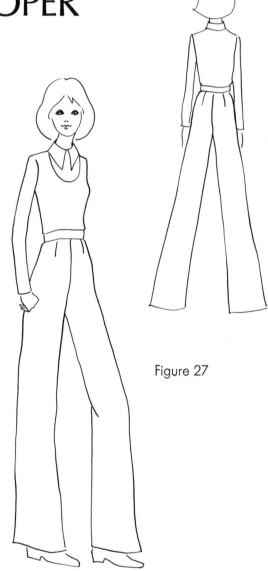

Figure 27

Please read Chapter 1 before beginning this chapter.

The pants sloper is used to make pants of any length from shorts to slacks and any width from tapered to widely flared. It is also used to make pants-skirts and jumpsuits. For this sloper select a simple straight-leg pants pattern, with two or four front and back darts, a natural waistline, and a waistband as shown in *Figure 27*. It should have no cutaway-pocket details which interfere with the basic shape of the tissue pattern. A side-zipper opening is preferred. Measure your hips at the fullest part and buy your pants pattern in the size closest to your hip measurement.

Since pants have little margin for error once they are cut, you may need to make some adjustments on the tissue pattern before cutting in muslin. First check your crotch length. To do this, sit on a hard chair and measure up from the seat to your waist with a ruler as shown in *Figure 28A*. Check this measurement with the crotch length on your pattern as shown in *Figure 28B*. The pattern should measure your crotch length plus 3/4". Shorten or lengthen the pattern front and back if necessary. This adjustment should be made above the crotch but below the bottom point of the darts. Next check the pants-leg length. Measure along your side where the side seam would be on the pants from your waist to pants hem. Now measure the side seam of the pants pattern. If adjustment is needed, lengthen or shorten the tissue pattern midway between the knee and hem of the pants leg. Once you have made the necessary adjustments you can cut your pants in muslin.

You will need only the front and back pattern pieces. Straighten the grain of your muslin and press it and the two pattern pieces. Pin the pattern, making sure the grain line is correct. For extra margin in fitting, use your red pencil to mark 1″ seam allowance at the side, center-front, and back seams. Cut out the pants. Trace the darts and the grain lines with your tracing wheel and carbon. Mark the two front pieces with a large F and the backs with a large B, to avoid a mix-up.

To sew the pants together, use a long, loose stitch and contrasting thread. First stitch all the darts closed and press them toward the side seams. Join each front and back at the side seams. Press the seams open. Join each inside-leg seam and press them open. (A sleeve board is helpful at this point.) You should now have two separate pants legs. Join at the crotch by putting one leg inside the other, right sides together. Pin at the crotch so the right and left inner-leg seams meet, then pin along the center back and part way up the center front. Leave an opening of 5 or 6 inches at

the center front. Press this seam to one side. Although this is a curved seam, it should never be clipped because that weakens the seam and makes it likely to pull open.

Now you can try on your muslin pants. First check the fit of the waistline. It should not be too tight when you sit down and should have enough room to tuck in a shirt if you want to. If the waistline is too tight, let it out by letting out each dart by an equal amount. If the waistline is too loose, take in each dart up to ¼″. If you still need to take in more at the waist, do so by taking in the side or back seam. If you take in the darts too much, they will tend to poke out at the point.

If you have a sway back or curve at your center back, you will need to take in the center-back seam and possibly the back darts also. You may want to curve the darts to achieve a better fit in the rear. You can also curve the front darts for better fit if your tummy sticks out a bit. On some com-

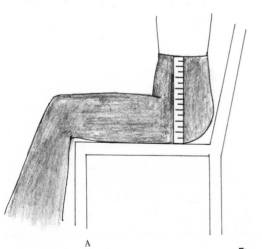

A

Figure 28

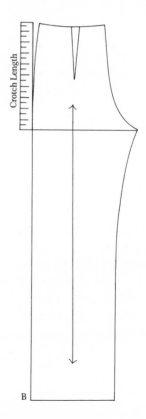

Crotch Length

B

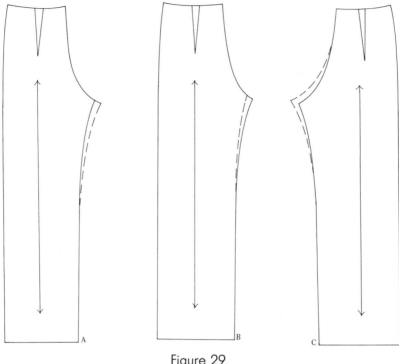

Figure 29

mercial patterns the point of the dart is too long and causes pulling across the rear or the stomach. Do not make your darts too long because they usually do not achieve a good fit and they look unprofessional. If the darts poke out or pull, they are not shaped correctly for your body. With the pants on, clip a few stitches at a time until the problem is released, then repin the darts to fit smoothly. When fitting darts, always work on the right side and the left side together. Don't pin all on one side first then the other side, or the darts may not be equal.

The seat and crotch areas are usually the most troublesome to fit. When you make any alteration in these areas, check the fit both sitting and standing, as well as walking around. A good pants pattern should be comfortable for moving and sitting and not bunch at the crotch in front or back when you stand straight. Wrinkles at the crotch will occur if that area is too tight or too loose or incorrectly shaped for your figure. The adjustments shown for this area apply to either the front or the back, whichever needs it. In fitting pants, generally, try to achieve a smooth fit which still allows enough ease for comfort. If there is pulling or binding at the crotch or the thigh is too tight, the inner leg needs additional width at the front and/or back (*Figure 29A*). If the crotch is too loose and looks bunchy, it needs reshaping. Take in the inner-leg seam at the front or front and back as shown in *Figure 29B*. If the seat is tight, add to the inner-leg seam and center seam in back only (*Figure 29C*). If the stomach and crotch are tight in front, make the adjustment shown in *Figure 29C* on the front muslin. You may need to try several different adjustments until you have a good fit.

To find your natural waistline, tie a string around your waist and mark with tailor's chalk. The marks should cross the side, center-front, and center-back seams. The natural waistline is lower in back than in front. Last, check the length of the pants legs. Wear shoes and have someone mark the length for you. Be sure you have a hem mark crossing each leg seam. Generally the wider the pants leg, the longer the length should be. Before taking off your pants, draw a line across to indicate the position of your knee, front and back. This will be a guideline for short pants.

Once your pants are fitted, take them off and mark the stitching lines. Have the pants muslin right side out and mark only the right (not left) side. Use the soft chalky kind of tailor's chalk, rather than the hard waxy kind, in a color which contrasts with your tracing-wheel markings (*Figure 30*). Beginning at the side seam, draw the chalk along the seam so that you have a narrow, continuous line marking each side of the seam, from hem to waist. Mark the inner-leg seam, center front, and center back the same way. Draw an X at the point of each dart and mark the darts the same way. If your hemline is marked with pins, mark the pin locations with chalk and remove the pins. Your marked muslin should look like *Figure 30*.

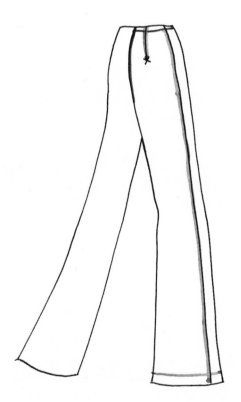

Figure 30

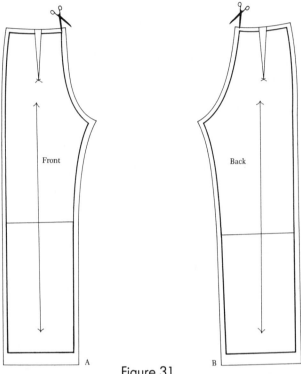

Figure 31

Using a seam ripper, carefully rip open the center-front and back seam, separating the right and left side. Discard the left (unmarked) side. Open the side seam, inner-leg seam, and the darts. Press the two muslin pieces, being careful not to stretch them out of shape. Using your French curve, curve stick, ruler, and soft pencil, blend the chalk line, including the hem, to form a smooth outline of the pattern (*Figure 31A*). Make a smooth curved line at the waistline. If you have made alteration marks, be sure you follow the correct ones. Pin the dart closed, with the fold toward the side seam. Cut your front muslin on the outlines so that you have no seam or hem allowance.

Follow the same steps in marking the back muslin (*Figure 31B*). Pin the dart closed on the back as you did on the front and cut out on the outlines.

Now you can transfer your muslin pattern onto heavy paper to make a permanent sloper. Press your muslin pieces again if they need it. Cut a sheet of heavy paper several inches larger on all sides than the front-pants muslin. Place your muslin face up on the paper. Remember to leave extra paper all around the muslin for adding your seam allowances and hem. Put some paperweights on the muslin and carefully tape it to the paper, using the tape at right angles to the edge of the muslin. First tape along the side seam, then along the other three sides, taking care not to pull or distort the shape. Now draw around the muslin like a stencil, using your yardstick, curve stick, and French curve to keep your lines even (*Figure 32A*). Using your tracing wheel, without carbon, mark the dart, grain line, and knee line. Clip the tape and remove the muslin, which can be discarded. The outline on the paper is the finish line, or stitching line. To complete your sloper, seam and hem allowances must be added. Using your ruler and a contrasting color pencil, measure out from your stitching line and mark ⅝″ seam allowance at the seams and waist. Add three inches at the hemline for hem allowance. Use your ruler to extend the dart lines to the cutting line at the waist. Label the sloper as shown. Your sloper should look like *Figure 32B*.

Now you can cut out your sloper. BE SURE TO CUT ON THE SEAM-AL-LOWANCE LINE, NOT ON THE STITCHING LINE. First cut the side seam, hem, inner leg, and center front. Before you cut the waistline, the dart must be closed. Crease the dart so that the fold of the dart is toward the side seam, and

tape the dart closed. The pattern won't lie flat. Cut along the waistline, then clip or peel off the tape. Cut V notches at the end of the dart lines and at the hemline. Use your heavy needle or awl to punch a hole at the point of the dart. Your finished front-pants sloper should look like *Figure 32C*. Follow the same steps in making your back-pants sloper as in making the front.

Read Chapter 16 for directions on making pants styles from your sloper. Making waistband patterns for the pants sloper is also covered in Chapter 16. See Chapter 9 to learn how to make patterns for pockets, flaps, tabs, and other design details that you can add to the basic-pants sloper or new pants patterns.

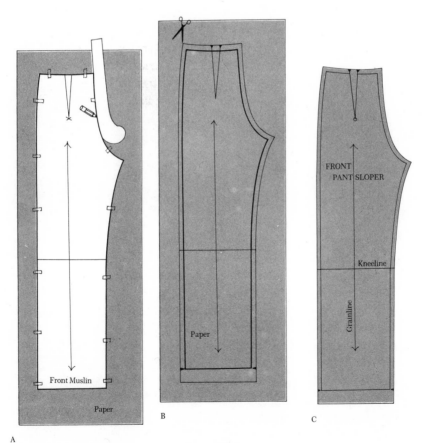

Figure 32

PART II

DESIGNING YOUR
OWN CLOTHES

CHAPTER 7

FABRICS

The more you know about fabrics, the better the results you'll have with your sewing. Knowing about fabrics will enable you to decide what will be cool in summer or warm in winter, what can survive being stuffed in a suitcase, which fabrics are easy to work with and which require special care. The more you know about fabrics, how they are made, the different fabrics that are available, and the way they perform, the better you'll be able to pick just the right fabric for your requirement.

HOW FABRICS ARE MADE

There are many steps involved in the making of fabric. Fabric begins with fibers, either man-made or natural. The fibers are spun into yarn and the yarn is knitted or woven into cloth. The final steps are called finishing. Each of these steps can be carried out in different ways. The way a fabric looks, handles, and performs is the result of the way these steps have been carried out.

FIBERS

The fabric begins with the fibers. Fibers are the main ingredient of a fabric and so the characteristics of the fiber will determine, to a significant extent, the characteristics of a fabric. Fibers have two major categories—natural, such as cotton and wool; and synthetic, or man-made, such as polyester and acrylic. Each type of fiber has advantages and disadvantages. Fibers are often blended to make a fabric that has the good qualities of each of the fibers. Once you know the characteristics of the important fibers, you know a lot about the fabric. The construction of the fabric, and the finishing processes, can change the look, drape, and feel of a fabric, but generally the main characteristics of the fibers will remain. Cotton will have the characteristics of cotton, whether it's made into double knit or corduroy, and nylon will have the characteristics of nylon whether it's made into tricot or organza. The characteristics of a fiber are also the same if that fiber is made into rugs, blankets, upholstery, or camping tents. We use so many textile products that being informed about fibers is useful in other areas too.

There are only four major *natural fibers*: cotton, wool, linen, and silk. Below is a chart showing the natural fibers, some common uses, and the advantages and disadvantages of each.

NATURAL FIBERS

FIBER NAME	USES	ADVANTAGES	DIS-ADVANTAGES
COTTON	Many different fabrics Knits: single, double raschels Wovens: broadcloth, denim, muslin, percale, sateen, duck, corduroy, velvet, voile, batiste	Strong Absorbent Takes color well Comfortable Economical	Wrinkles easily Shrinks
LINEN	Most often made into plain weave fabrics of medium to sturdy weight. Also twill and damask, fine handkerchief linen, coarse textured crash	Attractive and distinctive texture Strong Absorbent Comfortable	Wrinkles very easily Shrinks
WOOL	Many different fabrics: single and double knits, coat and suit fabrics, tweeds, twills, flannels, challis, crepe, worsteds	Molds and tailors well Warm Good shape recovery Absorbent	Shrinks Careful pressing required Attracts dirt
SILK	Can be light to fairly heavy weight. Chiffon, crepe, single knit, satin, surah, shantung, tussah	Luxurious feel Very strong Takes color well	Water spots Usually requires dry cleaning

Man-made Fibers are more confusing to deal with because they are known by both their generic names and trade names. This means the same fiber can be known by as many as eight or ten different names. The generic name is the official name and by law must appear on the label. The trade name is the brand name given by the fiber company for the fiber it produces and which is promoted in their advertising. Sometimes a fiber company will have several trade names for variations of the same fiber. For example, nylon is a generic name. DuPont makes nylon fibers which are called Antron and Qiana, and American Enka Company makes nylon fibers which are called Enkalure. The same confusing situation holds true for the other man-made fibers. Learn about fibers based on the generic names. Polyester is polyester whether it is called Dacron, Kodel, or Fortrel.

Below is a chart of the major man-made fibers, showing their generic and trade names, the most common uses, and the advantages and disadvantages of each. The main general difference between man-made fibers and natural fibers is that natural fibers tend to be absorbent and man-made fibers tend to be non-absorbent. This means fabric made of an absorbent fiber will be more comfortable to wear because it breathes, but it will also wrinkle more easily and take longer to dry. Fabric made of a non-absorbent fiber does not breathe but will wrinkle less easily and will dry quickly.

MAN-MADE FIBERS

FIBER NAME	USES	ADVANTAGES	DIS-ADVANTAGES
ACETATE Acele Avisco Chromspun Estron Celera	Silklike fabrics: taffeta, satin, brocade, single knits, tricot, crepe	Luster, good color, drapes well, economical	Hot Can feel clammy Not too durable
ACRYLIC Acrilan Creslan Orlon Zefran	Wool-like and furlike fabrics Double and single knits	Soft, warm Lightweight	Can pill
MODACRYLIC Dynel Verel	Deep-pile fleece and fake-fur fabrics	Warm, mothproof Luxurious Resists stains and mildew	Can melt if iron is too hot

NYLON

Caprolan Antron Enkalure Qiana	Tricots, jerseys, stretch knits, lace, skiwear fabrics	Strong, elastic Wrinkle resistant Easy care	Can feel hot and clammy

POLYESTER

Dacron Avlin Fortrel Kodel Trevira Vycron Encron	Many different fabrics: double knits, raschel knits, permanent press fabrics, often blended with cotton	Wrinkle resistant Retains shape Strong Easy care	Can pill Can feel hot and clammy

RAYON

Avril Coloray Cupioni Zantrel	Linenlike fabrics Cottonlike fabrics Linings	Takes color well Economical Drapes well Can feel soft and silky	Low strength

TRIACETATE

Arnel	Knit velour Tricots and single knits Sharkskin	Wrinkle resistant Easy care Drapes well Takes color well	Can feel hot and clammy

YARN

There are two ways of making fibers into yarn. The most common is *spinning,* where short fibers are twisted into long yarns. Man-made fibers and silk may be made into *filament yarns* which are long continuous yarns. Fabrics made from filament yarns are smooth and sleek.

A term you have probably come across referring to yarn is *yarn dyed.* This means that the yarn is dyed before it is made into a fabric and is usually an indication of good quality. Yarn-dyed fabrics have a deeper, richer color and tend to be more colorfast than fabrics that are dyed after they have been woven. Dyed yarns of various colors are woven to make ginghams, checks, plaids, stripes, and chambray. Another word you have probably seen referring to yarn is *combed,* such as combed cotton. This means that the yarn is literally combed with a fine-tooth comb, which makes it smooth and silky. Combed yarn is an indication of good quality.

WOVEN FABRICS

The two major methods of constructing fabric are weaving and knitting. The design and appearance of a fabric can be the result of the weave used to make the fabric. (See *Plate 2.*)

1. The basic weave is called the *plain*

Plate 2

weave. It is the simplest kind of construction and the weave you are all familiar with in such everyday fabrics as broadcloth, muslin, and homespun. Plain weave is used extensively in fabrics that are printed. Design effects may be achieved in the weaving by varying the textures of the yarn and by using yarns of contrasting colors.

2. *Twill-weave* fabrics have a diagonal rib. Sometimes the diagonal is very hard to notice and sometimes it is a prominent design feature. Do not attempt to use the diagonal as true bias because they are not the same. Depending on how prominent the twill is, the pattern may have to be placed with each piece running in the same direction as you would with a nap fabric. When you are working with a prominent twill pattern, it is best to avoid designs that have a lot of seams, especially a center-front seam. Twill-weave fabrics are good for sportswear because they are sturdy and durable and have good shape retention. Some well-known twills include denim and gabardine.

3. *Satin weave*—The luster and smoothness of satin fabrics is the result of the weave. Because of the way the yarns lie across the surface of the fabric, they reflect light and give satin its sheen. But since the yarns are not held firmly, the fabric is not durable and the yarns can snag. This is why satin fabric is usually restricted to dressy clothes. Sateen is cotton fabric which is made with a satin weave and is usually more durable than satin. Satin-weave fabrics should be treated like nap fabrics and cut with all the pattern pieces in the same direction.

4. *Pile weave*—In this weave some of the yarns form loops on the surface of the fabric. The loops may be left as is, cut open, or sheared. Fabrics with the loops cut include velveteen, velvet, and corduroy.

In terrycloth the loops are left uncut. Pile-weave fabrics have a direction and must be cut with the pattern pieces going all one way. For more information on dealing with pile-weave fabrics, see Nap, page 68.

5. *Leno-weave* fabrics have a lovely openwork lacy look. Leno is often combined with stripes of plain weave and is usually found in lightweight fabrics.

6. The *Jacquard weave* is by far the most elaborate method of weaving. Complicated designs of flowers, and other figures, and varying textures are woven into the cloth. Brocades and damask are made by the Jacquard method.

KNIT FABRICS

Knits are made of a series of interlocking loops which allows the fabric more stretch and flexibility than woven fabrics. There are two common knitting methods: circular knit, also known as weft knit, and warp knit.

Circular, or weft, knits are constructed similarly to hand knitting. Circular knits have stretch in both the width and the length. The best-known circular knits are double knits and single knits.

7. *Double knits* are made with a double set of needles and look similar on the right and wrong side. Because their construction makes them more stable (less stretchy) than single knits, they are good for tailored styles.

8. *Single knits* are also called jerseys. They have a definite right and wrong side, are lightweight, drape very well, and have a good deal of stretch. Single knits are best suited for tops, blouses, soft dresses, and other non-tailored styles.

Do not use the crease in a circular knit as the fold when placing the center front or center back of a pattern. It is often discolored and the line will not wash out.

Warp knitting is a more rigid construction and the fabric will stretch in only one direction. The best-known warp knit is *tricot* (10). Another warp knit is *raschel* (9), which produces an openwork, lacy fabric.

Single and warp knits are a little harder to handle than double knits. In handling knits, especially single knits, be sure that they don't stretch out of shape. (Polyester or nylon organza is a good interfacing to use with the lighter weight knits.)

PRINTED FABRICS

Printing on fabrics can be done in a number of different ways. The most widely used method is *roller printing*. Another method is *screen printing*. This is a slower method, done partly by hand. It is used to print large colorful and elaborate designs which could not be done by roller printing. Screen-printed fabrics are usually more expensive and may be of a better design quality than roller-printed goods.

When you buy fabrics that have printed designs, check to see that the designs are in register. When a design is not in register, the colors and lines of the designs will not meet together properly. For example, the center of the flower will not be in the center or the outline of a design will not outline the shape as it should. This is an indication of poor quality. Printed design is also sometimes used in a less expensive imitation of a woven design. For example, the best gingham checks are yarn dyed and woven, but imitation gingham checks can be roller printed. The same holds true of stripes and plaids. Printed designs that imitate woven designs may be of poor quality and printed off grain. If you are buying a printed stripe or plaid, be sure it is on grain, otherwise you'll have trouble working with it.

Another method of printing fabric is *flocking*. With this method, very short, fuzzy fibers are glued to the fabric in the shape of dots, stripes, or other designs such as flowers. This gives the printed design a different texture from the background fabric. Good-quality flocking will not wash off. To check the flocking, scrape it with your fingernail or rub the fabric. If it comes off easily, forget it. Flocking is also used to completely cover a fabric, making imitation velvet or suede.

Other methods of printing are done by hand. You might consider printing some of your own fabric. Batik, tie dye, and block print are well-known hand-printing methods.

FINISHES

There are a number of finishes used to give a fabric a distinctive appearance. A *moiré* finish causes the fabric to reflect light in a certain way, which gives moiré its unusual watery look. A *ciré* finish is a wax applied to the fabric which gives it a very shiny, almost patent-leather look. *Glazing* is another shiny finish. *Embossing* is used to give fabric a three-dimensional surface design. Figures such as dots or flowers are raised on the fabric. Poor-quality embossed designs will wash out quickly. To see if the embossing is well done, stretch a corner of the fabric tightly, then let go. If the design stays flattened out, it is not very good quality.

Cotton fabrics usually have a starch applied to them called *sizing*. A certain amount of sizing is all right, but too much is often used to make poor-quality fabric look better. The sizing fills in the openings in the weave and gives the fabric an appearance of being woven more closely. You can see if a fabric has too much sizing in it by rubbing the fabric between your hands. Excess sizing will come off as a fine powder. *Napped or brushed finish* is produced by brushing the fabric with wire brushes. Sometimes brushing is used to cover up a badly woven fabric. Brushed denim and flannelette are well-known napped fabrics.

The most popular of the practical finishes is *permanent press*. This is a plastic resin applied to the fabric, usually a polyester and cotton blend. Permanent-press fabric can present some problems in handling. If it is off grain by much, it cannot be straightened. Because it has a certain amount of stiffness, it does not drape particularly well. Seams sewn on the straight grain tend to pucker and you cannot press pleats into it. When using permanent-press fabrics, keep your design simple, and make sure your thread and trimming are permanent press. Other finishes are used to make fabric soil resistant, water repellent, waterproof, or flame retardant. These finishes can change the feel of the fabric, usually making it somewhat stiffer.

FABRIC GRAIN

During the various finishing processes, woven fabric can be pulled out of shape so that the yarns are no longer perfectly at right angles. Then the fabric is said to be off grain. If your fabric is off grain it must be straightened before you make your garment. A garment sewn with off-grain fabric will not hang right. As *Figure 33A* shows, the lengthwise grain is the same as the warp and runs parallel with the selvage. The cross grain is the same as the filling and runs from selvage to selvage. The lengthwise grain is the strongest and most stable. True bias is a 45-degree angle from the length or the cross grain. To locate true bias, place your drafting triangle so that one short side runs along the length grain and the other short side runs along the cross grain. The long side of your triangle will be the true bias.

Knitted fabrics also have a grain.

The easiest way to see if the grain of your fabric is straight is to place it on a rectangular or square table so that the selvage lines up with one side of the table.

If the cross grain of the fabric lines up with the second side of the table, then your fabric is straight (*Figure 33C*). If it doesn't line up, you can see which way it's crooked (*Figure 33B*). Another easy way to see whether the grain is straight, if you have a fabric that can be torn, is to tear across the fabric at each end, then fold the fabric so the selvages are parallel and the torn edges meet as you see in *Figure 33D*. If the fabric is on grain, it will fold smoothly and flat. If the fabric is off grain, there will be ripples and waves at the fold and it will not fold flat.

You can straighten fabric by pulling on the bias or by ironing. Washable fabric will sometimes go back on grain if you trim off the selvage, then wash the fabric. Even if the fabric is on grain, it is a good idea to wash it before making up your garment. This will remove excess sizing, return it to its original shape if its been stretched, and shrink the fabric so you won't have any disasters after you have sewn it.

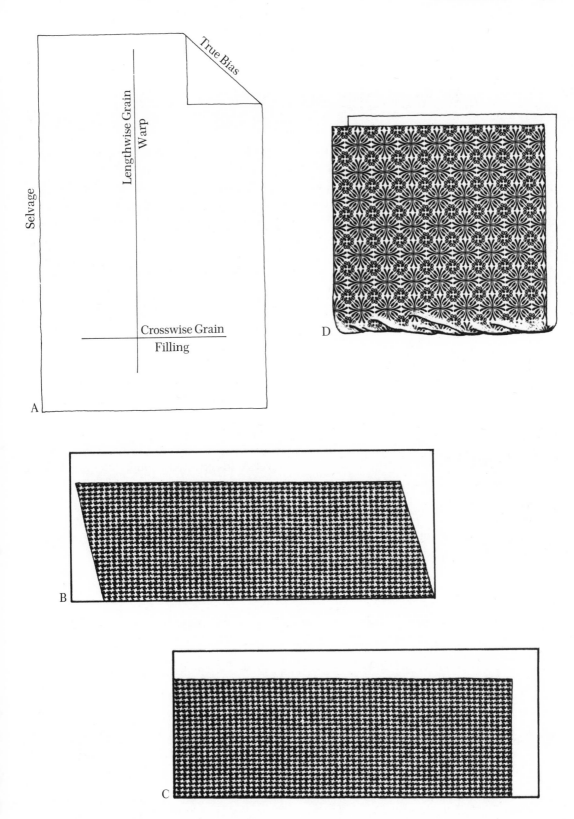

Figure 33

NAP AND ONE-WAY DESIGN FABRICS

There are a number of fabrics which must be cut with all the pattern pieces in the same direction. Sometimes a one-way fabric is referred to as a fabric with nap, and sometimes the word nap is used to refer to a pile weave such as velvet or corduroy.

A fabric must be cut in one direction, either because the way it reflects light causes the color to appear a different shade in each direction or because it has a printed or woven design which runs in one direction.

Plaids and cross-way stripes can be made this way as well as printed designs (*Figure 34*). To see whether your fabric is one way, use the fabric-direction test below.

FABRIC-DIRECTION TEST

(See *Figure 34*.) Take two skirt hangers and clip one on each end of the fabric at the cut ends, not at the selvage. Hang both hangers next to each other, on a door. One side of the fabric will be running up and the other side will be running down. Stand back and look at the fabric. If one side appears different in color, shading, or design, then the fabric is one way. If you have a one-way print, you will see the design doesn't look the same running up and running down. With a one-way stripe or plaid, you can't match the stripes or the plaid where the selvages meet. Decide which direction the fabric looks best and mark an arrow along the selvage to indicate which way to place the pattern.

Some fabrics which must be cut in one direction include velvet, velveteen, velour, fake fur, corduroy, suede cloth, satin, sateen, some twill-weave fabrics, some unbalanced plaids and stripes, one-way prints, and some brocades and laces. Corduroy, velvet, and velveteen should be cut with the pile running up, to give a rich color. Panne velvet and fake fur usually look best with the pile running down. In some cases the direction that looks best depends on the individual fabric.

FABRIC CONVERSION CHART

Fabric Width	35"-36"	39"	41"	44"-45"	50"	52"-54"	58"-60"
	1¾	1½	1½	1⅜	1¼	1⅛	1
	2	1¾	1¾	1⅝	1½	1⅜	1¼
	2¼	2	2	1¾	1⅝	1½	1⅜
	2½	2¼	2¼	2⅛	1¾	1¾	1⅝
	2⅞	2½	2½	2¼	2	1⅞	1¾
Yardage	3⅛	2¾	2¾	2½	2¼	2	1⅞
	3⅜	3	2⅞	2¾	2⅜	2¼	2
	3¾	3¼	3⅛	2⅞	2⅝	2⅜	2¼
	4¼	3½	3⅜	3⅛	2¾	2⅝	2⅜
	4½	3¾	3⅝	3⅜	3	2¾	2⅝
	4¾	4	3⅞	3⅝	3¼	2⅞	2¾
	5	4¼	4⅛	3⅞	3⅜	3⅛	2⅞

Courtesy of Cooperative Extension Service, Rutgers University, The State University of New Jersey

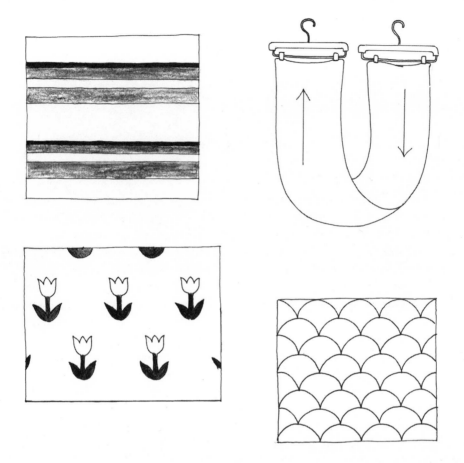

Figure 34

YARDAGE INFORMATION

There are several ways to figure the yardage for a pattern you've made. You can lay out the pattern on a piece of fabric you already have, and measure how much it takes. If you don't have a piece of fabric large enough, you can also use a sheet folded to measure the same width as the fabric. Save the pattern envelopes that come with the tissue patterns you buy to make your basic slopers since the yardage information given there can also be help-ful in determining how much you need for your new pattern. Another way to figure yardage is to look in a pattern catalogue and find a style that is similar to the pattern you've made. Allow about ½ yard extra for a nap fabric. If you are matching a very large plaid or print, you may need as much as an extra yard of fabric. The fabric-conversion chart opposite shows the equivalent amount of fabric in various widths.

LACE

Lace was originally made by hand and the making of lace was considered a fine art. Today most lace is made by machine. Lace is available in two ways—36 inches wide or more, which is called all-over lace, and narrow lace which is used as trimming. Narrow lace is made in a number of different forms.

By the way, just like fabric, lace has a right and wrong side. On some lace, it is easy to tell the right side because the design is outlined with a cording which indicates the right side. When there is no cording, look closely at both sides. Sometimes the wrong side of the lace will be flatter and have less texture than the right side, or the wrong side of the lace will not be made as neatly as the right side.

LACE FORMS

Plate 3 shows the different ways laces are made.

1. *All-over*—Lace all-overs have no grain but the design may run in one direction. Place the pattern pieces to show off the design of the lace to its best advantage.

2. *Edge*—A lace edge has a scallop on one side. Depending on the kind of lace, it may be gathered into ruffles or used flat. Edges are commonly used to trim necklines, collars, sleeves, cuffs, hemlines, and so on. The straight edge can be inserted into a seam such as a yoke seam.

3. *Picot Edge*—A picot edge is a very narrow edge made of little loops or points. It is most often used around collars and necklines or on cuffs. Most picot edges are flexible, so they can be used on a curved neckline or collar.

4. *Insertion*—An insertion has a straight edge on both sides. It is commonly used flat, around the hem of a skirt or around the end of a sleeve, for example. It can also be inserted with a seam at the top and bottom edge. This gives an openwork look because there is no fabric in back of the lace.

5. *Galloon*—A galloon has a scallop on both sides and is not usually gathered. However, there are some galloons with a plain strip along the middle so it can be gathered into a double ruffle. A galloon can also be used around the hem of a skirt, around sleeves, and across yokes among other places.

6. *Beading*—Beading has a series of little holes through which a ribbon can be laced. The ribbon can be drawn up like a drawstring or left flat. For an interesting effect, instead of a plain ribbon, use a flowered ribbon or braid. Beading can be made as an edge, galloon, or insertion.

7. *Medallions or Motifs*—These are individual designs or figures. They can be bought individually or clipped from an all-over lace. Medallions are usually used on lingerie and sleepwear, evening clothes, and bridal gowns. They can be placed wherever you like and stitched by hand or machine.

Plate 3

TYPES OF LACE

(See *Plate 4*). The best-known light-weight laces are Alençon, Chantilly, and Val (Valenciennes). These laces are named for the part of France where they were originally made.

1. *Alençon lace*—has a design, usually a floral pattern, on a fine net background. The design or figure of the lace is outlined in a heavy cord. Alençon is also called re-embroidered lace.

2. *Chantilly lace*—looks somewhat similar to Alençon, also being a figure on a fine net background. The difference is that in Chantilly lace the design is not usually outlined in a cord. If there is a cord outline, it is much finer than the cord found on Alençon lace.

Alençon and Chantilly laces are made in all-overs and narrow laces. Because of their delicate look they are most often used for lingerie, evening and bridal dresses, and dressy blouses.

3. *Val lace*—is made only in narrow lace and is probably the most common lace of all. It is a small design on a net background. It can be gathered or used flat. For a designer touch, use Val lace instead of seam binding at the hem. Val lace is most often used on blouses, dresses, and sleepwear.

The heavy laces include Cluny and Venice.

4. *Cluny lace*—is made of fairly heavy yarn and looks as though it had been crocheted by hand. It can be used flat or gathered, around yokes, collars, sleeves, hems, in seams, blouse fronts, etc.

5. *Venice lace*—is the heaviest lace and is seldom gathered. It is made by embroidery and has a rich three-dimensional appearance. Venice is used in much the same way as Cluny lace.

6. *Schiffli embroidery*—Schiffli embroidery is made in the same forms as lace—both all-overs and narrow trimmings. The best-known Schiffli embroidery is eyelet. To judge the quality of Schiffli, especially eyelet, look at the stitches of the embroidery. In good-quality embroidery, the stitches will be very close together so as to give an almost three-dimensional effect, and there will be no raw edge of fabric visible at the eyelet. In poor-quality Schiffli, the stitches are spread too far apart, which causes fraying around the eyelet. Stay away from the low-priced Schiffli embroidery because each time it is washed there will be threads hanging from the badly stitched eyelets.

Schiffli embroidery has a right and wrong side. On the wrong side you will be able to see the bobbin stitches which are not as neat. Some of the finest Schiffli embroideries come from Switzerland.

Plate 4

CHAPTER 8

DESIGNING AND SEWING PROFESSIONAL-LOOKING CLOTHES

If you love to sew, you are probably a designer at heart because you select your pattern, fabrics, and trimmings and put them together to create your own style. Sewing requires skill, imagination, and creativity. Most people sew for two reasons: creative satisfaction and good value. By knowing how to make your own patterns and becoming more aware of design possibilities, you can greatly increase your creative satisfaction. By knowing how to sew and design clothes that look as professional as possible, you can get the most value for your time and money.

I studied design and became a designer because I loved to sew my own clothes. Many women have said to me, "I could never be a designer because I can't draw." Believe it or not, many designers don't know how to draw so well either! The old movies seem to have given people an image of a designer in a beautiful penthouse suite, surrounded by miles of glorious silks and satins, perched on a high stool, painting her creations. This is strictly from Hollywood. A real-life designer works at a desk or table, surrounded by swatch cards, sample garments, cost charts, hastily scribbled sketches, pages ripped from *Elle* magazine and *Women's Wear Daily*, and a jangling telephone. She is also busy running from the sample room to the showroom and out to look at fabric and trimming lines and to check the stores to see what the competition is doing. The sketches done by a designer are not masterworks but simple, detailed drawings that are used as a guide by the patternmaker and sample hand. The sketch is only a blueprint—what counts is the finished sample. In keeping with the garment center's code of doing almost everything the fastest way possible, designers usually have several basic figures over which they trace their design sketches. These figures are called "croquis" (pronounced kró-kee) and I've included one here (*Figure 35*), which you can use with tracing paper to sketch your ideas.

Don't be intimidated at the idea of designing your own clothes. Design ideas are all around you; it just takes becoming more aware of them. Professional designers are tuned in to absorb ideas from every direc-

Figure 35

tion. They are influenced by what they see around them and what goes on in the world. Fashion trends come from many places. The clothes or costumes of an important movie often have a big impact on the fashions of the next season. The styles of past decades keep recurring as fashion influences. The 20s, 30s, 40s and 50s each have their own style. Many of the styles popular then can work today with some modification. You can see good examples of clothes from these times on the late-show movies, magazines of the time, and in books. Another good source of ideas is history-of-costume books which you can find in most libraries. The clothes worn in the eighteenth and nineteenth centuries were far more elaborate than what we wear today, but one little detail can give you an idea that will make the whole design. An interesting sleeve or a new way to use embroidery or lace can become the focal points. The easiest and most popular place to look for ideas is in American and European fashion magazines. The editorial and advertising pages are filled with ideas. When you come across a picture of a style you especially like, tear out the page and keep it in an envelope; then when you want to make something, look through your collection of pictures to get some inspiration.

One of the best ways to learn about designing is to study ready-made clothes in various price ranges—from budget to couture. Study the details and decide why you like something or why you don't. Notice the way color and fabric are used, the trimmings and buttons, and how the different components relate to each other. Look at a dress that costs $10 and decide why it costs only $10. Inexpensive buttons, inexpensive trimming or no trimming, poor-quality fabric and poor workmanship are probably what you will find in a dress at this price. Then look at dresses costing $50 and $150 and notice the differences in the quality of workmanship and materials. Look at the way the dress is designed. Recognizing the differences between something of good quality and something of poor quality will make you much more able to make the best choices in designing and sewing your own clothes. A good way to look at very expensive clothes is when they are on sale. That way the salespeople won't bother you and you can have a grand time looking at all the marvelous details.

One great advantage you have in sewing is that, for a little extra effort, you can increase the value of what you are making tremendously. When you look at ready-made clothes, you may find, for example, a blouse made out of gingham checks that costs $25 and a blouse made out of gingham checks that costs $10. The difference between the $10 blouse and the $25 blouse is the care and time involved in making them. The $25 blouse should have the seams carefully stitched, high-quality interfacing in the collar, cuffs, and placket, pearl buttons instead of plastic, and the over-all look should be one of quality. The $10 blouse is likely to have plastic buttons, poor-quality interfacing in the collar and cuffs and probably none in the placket, loose threads hanging, and the over-all look not nearly so polished as the $25 blouse. You can see that if you were making this blouse, you could make the $25 blouse with only a little extra time and money than it would cost to make the $10 blouse.

BASIC BODIES

As part of designing a line, most designers have a number of favorite silhouettes called basic bodies which they use many times. A basic body could be a flared princess dress, a basic men's-wear shirt, a straight-legged pants style, etc. Basic bodies are made up in many different fabrics— plain and patterned, winter and summer weight. They are varied by design details such as collars, sleeves, necklines, pockets, and trimmings. The variations of the basic bodies often look like completely new styles. This is a good system for the home sewer. Once you have found a style you like that really looks good on you, you can make it up in many different ways.

DESIGN TIPS

Here are some things to keep in mind when designing your clothes.

CONTRAST

An important element of good design is contrast. When you look at ready to wear, you will see there is usually contrast in the design. The most obvious way of achieving contrast is by combining a number of different fabrics in one design. For example, you might combine two or three different prints, or print and pattern such as a floral print with gingham checks. You might mix smooth and textured fabrics such as satin and velveteen or light and dark colors. In ready to wear, quite often a garment is made combining two or more different fabrics. When you mix patterned fabrics, the two patterns should have something in common to relate them. For example, they could both have a color in common, or both be stripes, flower prints, or plaids. If you are unsure of combining patterns, you can buy fabrics in co-ordinated groupings that are designed to work together.

Another way to achieve contrast is using buttons and trimmings. For example, brass buttons add contrast to a navy or dark-color dress. Silver buttons add contrast to a red or black jacket. Trimmings will add contrast even if the trimming is the same color as the fabric. More information about using trimmings is found on page 92.

Another way of achieving contrast is by cutting some parts of your garment on the cross grain or bias if it is striped or checked. For more information on using fabric this way, see page 90.

Contrast can be achieved by using an unexpected fabric. For example, a man's shirt style made in satin, because you would ordinarily expect a man's shirt to be made in cotton. Making it in satin provides the contrast; it would be especially smashing if you were to add rhinestone buttons. Making a very dressy style out of sporty fabric provides contrast; for example, using wool flannel with lace to make a long evening dress or making a very sporty style in a dressy fabric provide contrast, like jeans of velvet.

FOCAL POINTS

Another thing to remember is to have a focal point in your design. The focal point is one standout feature that makes the design something special. The focal point can be simple, such as smashing buttons or a big industrial zipper. It could be a big plaid bow on a plain blouse. Often the focal point can be the trimming—a belt with a beautiful buckle or a band of wide Cluny lace. If you are using a bold-print fabric, the design of the fabric itself can be the focal point. Some of the suggestions listed above as contrast can also be the focal point. For example, a big white linen collar can be the focal point on a dark plaid dress, or a striped yoke and placket the focal point on a solid-color blouse.

Your focal point or main design feature can be used to detract from figure problems. When designing your clothes, place your design feature away from the problem area. For example, if you have a large bosom, place your focal point on the skirt or pants. Avoid sleeves that have fullness at the shoulder, yokes with gathers, etc. If you have large hips, have your focal points on the bodice such as the yoke or collar, or have focal point be the sleeves. Keep your skirt or pants smooth and simple. You can also use the focal point to play up the best part of your figure. If you have a tiny waistline, use beautiful belts and sashes, or if you have a well-shaped bosom, make your focal point an interesting neckline or an empire waistline.

USING COLOR

The range of colors today is almost unlimited because of advances in the technology of dyeing and printing. Color is an important tool for a designer. The same dress made in two different colors can have a completely different look and feeling. Although anything goes as far as color combinations, still some care must be taken. While it's true that orange and pink are terrific together, it's still possible to come up with a combination of the wrong shade of orange with the wrong shade of pink that just won't work. A helpful tool in planning the use of color is the color wheel shown in *Figure 36*. Red, blue, and yellow are called the primary colors. Orange, vio-

let, and green are called the secondary colors. Colors that are opposite each other on the color wheel will provide strong, striking contrast. Red and green or orange and blue are opposite colors on the color wheel. The three primary colors used together or the three secondary colors used together also provide strong and dramatic color combinations. For more subtle color combination, look to combination of two or three adjoining colors on the color wheel, for example, green and blue or orange and yellow. The most subtle color combination is different shades of the same color. For example, pale yellow and deep yellow, purple and lilac, red and pink, etc. The marvelous thing about color is that it doesn't cost any money.

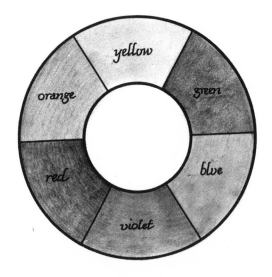

Figure 36

SELECTING FABRICS

Read through Chapter 7 for information on different kinds of fabrics and how they are made and perform.

Washable fabrics should be washed and dried before they are cut. This will remove excess sizing, preshrink them, and also help to straighten the grain. In the case of knit fabrics that have been stretched out of shape, washing will often return them to their original shape. Another reason for washing your fabric before you cut your garment is to remove excess dye. This is especially important when you are combining light and dark fabrics. If you made a navy blouse with a white collar, you would certainly hate to find the white collar streaked with blue after the first washing.

Certain designs require certain types of fabrics. Suits and tailored dresses require fairly firmly woven fabrics with body. Soft styles with gathers need soft, lightweight, or sheer fabric. Slinky or drapy styles require single knits or bias fabric. A general rule is that simple designs are best in patterned or textured fabrics. Complicated and detailed designs are best in simpler fabrics. A plain A-line dress would be best in a bold print or rich tweed. A shirtwaist dress with yoke, placket, and collar details, and topstitched would be best in a solid color or simple pattern so the details will show up. Look at ready to wear and at pictures in fashion magazines to see what fabrics are used for different designs. When you buy fabric, take the bolt over to the mirror and drape some of the fabric over yourself to see whether it hangs well for the design you have in mind.

Plaids and stripes require more care because the patterns must be matched. Light-color solid fabrics may tend to make mistakes show up. Darker colors, some knits, and all-over patterns will often minimize mistakes.

There are other places to look for new fabric ideas besides the usual yard goods department. The fabric section in the home furnishings department is one good possibility. Some of the fabrics you find there are especially good for sportswear because they are durable and often have a stain-repellent finish. If you have a custom upholstery shop in your town, it may sell remnants at bargain prices.

Another department to try for fabric ideas is linens. Sheets are printed in fabulous designs and sometimes you can buy irregulars for one half the original price or even less. Often the irregularity is so slight you would hardly notice it, or if it is obvious, you can cut around it. Also in the linens department are terry-velour towels and linen dish towels that come in beautiful designs. Either of these can be used for parts of garments.

Scarves of different sizes can be used to make blouses, sleeves, yokes, etc. Two large scarves can be used to make a long skirt. Smaller scarves like bandanas can also be very attractive for little tops, sleeves, etc.

You can also recycle fabric. If you have a garment made of suede or fine fabric but don't like the style, you can cut it apart and use the fabric again. At garage sales or flea markets you might be able to pick up some patchwork in good enough condition to make into something to wear.

Blankets, new or recycled, can be used to make coats, jackets, skirts, and other sportswear items.

Below is a list of fabric suggestions for different kinds of designs. These are only some suggestions and by no means the only possibilities.

FABRICS FOR CASUAL STYLES

Fabrics for Tailored Styles
Sportswear, Jackets, Pants, and Dresses

Piqué	Sharkskin
Double knits	Twill
Denim	Fake fur
Duck	Vinyl
Flannel	Worsted
Homespun	Woolens
Hopsacking	Tweeds
Linen	Corduroy
Poplin	Ticking
Sailcloth	Quilted fabrics
Suede cloth	Chino
Seersucker	

Fabrics for Soft Styles
Blouses, Shirts, Tops, and Dresses

Batiste	Sateen (print or plain)
Piqué	Seersucker
Broadcloth (printed and solid)	Stretch terry
	Voile
Chambray	Chintz
Dotted swiss	Challis
Dimity	Crepe
Gingham (checks and plaids)	Leno
	Raschel knits
	Tricots
Muslin	Single knits
	Knit velour

FABRICS FOR DRESSY STYLES

Lightweight

Organza	Crepe
Organdy	Taffeta
Dimity	Raschel knits
Sateen	Lace and Embroidered all-overs
Voile	
Chiffon	

Heavier Weight

Brocades	Velvet
Moiré	Velveteen
Satin	Panne

Slinky and Drapy

Matte jersey	Some raschel knits
Nylon or polyester jersey	Crepe on bias
Panne knit	Satin-back crepe

DESIGNING WITH FABRICS

Fabric is one of the most important design influences. Being aware of the different ways you can use fabric will open up new design possibilities.

PRINTED FABRICS

Printed fabrics can be knit or woven, and print designs can be either one way or two way. One-way prints must be cut with tops of the pattern pieces all going in the same direction. For more about one-way prints, see page 68.

The way you place your pattern pieces and cut a printed fabric can be an important designer touch. On better-quality ready to wear, great attention is paid to the placement of the repeat of a print on the cutting layout. In less expensive ready to wear, the garment patterns are laid out and the print repeat just falls where it may. The little extra time it takes to place your pattern to show your print to best advantage is certainly worth the results. Very often a print will look best if the repeat is centered. Look at the fabric and decide the best place to center it. In some cases, the repeat is so scrambled it doesn't require any centering, but if there is a definite, easy-to-distinguish repeat, centering will make your garment look much more professional.

Another professional look is to have the right and left sides cut so that the repeat falls in exactly the same place on each side, like a mirror image (*Figure 37A*). This can be done on the left and right side of the front if you have a front opening and on the right and left sleeve. You may have to make a center-back seam in your collar to have a repeat in the right place on both sides of the collar. Placing your pattern so the design runs down the center of a placket or along the center of a cuff is another nice thing to do. While matching prints at the side seam and center-back seam is not so important as with plaids and stripes, it really makes a much more professional look if you can do it. A really smashing look is to match perfectly all the seams of a large striking print.

Figure 37

Border prints do not have to be used only around the hem of a skirt. They can be used at the bottom of pants, sleeves, the bodice of a dress, or running up the front. *Figures 37B and C* show some ideas for ways to use border prints. The same border treatment also applies to lace or embroidery that has a border design. Read the directions given for matching plaids and follow the same steps to match prints.

USING EXPENSIVE FABRIC ON A BUDGET

Very expensive fabric can be used on a budget by using the expensive fabric for a small but important part of your design and using a simpler and less expensive fabric for the major part of the garment. For example, you could make a tiny empire bodice and short sleeves from about ¾ yard of expensive embroidered linen. Then you can make the rest of the dress out of plain linen that would cost maybe one third as much. Of course, you won't use the expensive fabric for anything that doesn't show, like facings. You can use your expensive fabric for yokes, little bodices, boleros, sleeves, jacket fronts, etc. *Figure 38* shows some ideas for ways to use a small amount of expensive fabric. None of these requires more than a yard. The rest of the garment is made using a more reasonably priced fabric. You can use this method working with lace, embroidery, suede, leather, fine wool, and so on. You can use expensive wool, tweed, or plaid for the front of a jacket or for a bolero and make the rest of your outfit from a solid color, picking up one of the colors in the plaid or tweed. Use Schiffli embroidery on voile for accent and use solid voile for the rest of your garment. Remember, contrast is an element of good design; if this is done right, it won't look as though you are skimping.

If you look at ready-made clothes, you will see that this is done all the time.

LACE FABRIC

Read about the different types of laces on page 70. If your lace has a floral design, you should place your pattern so that the repeat of the design is shown to best advantage. In the case of distinct separate motifs, you can cut out some of the motifs and use them as appliqués on other parts of the garment. This technique is often used in sleepwear, loungewear, and bridal gowns. If your lace has a floral motif, follow the same directions for pattern placement as given for printed fabrics (page 81). If your lace has a row of holes like beading, you might want to weave a ribbon through the holes for a nice effect. To keep a sheer look, use transparent organza for lining or facing. Do not turn up the hem but use organza to face the hemline, sleeve edge, etc. When lining lace, think about using a lining of a color different from the lace. The lining color peeking through the holes in the lace can look very pretty. If your lace has a very simple design, you might think about lining it in a check, stripe, or floral print.

EYELET EMBROIDERY, LENOS, AND SHEERS

Eyelet and lenos may be lined or not. For a sheer, unlined look, use organza or voile as facing and as backing for collars and cuffs, and so on. White eyelet or lenos look pretty backed in a color. You can also use the color of backing as an accent; for example, a white eyelet dress lined in blue with a blue sash. If you use a colored eyelet or leno, a nice effect is to back it in a slightly darker shade—a pink leno backed in raspberry—so that the raspberry back-

Figure 38

ing shows through the holes. If you are using a leno stripe, treat it as you would a regular stripe. See information below for designing with, and matching, stripes. Plain sheers such as voile or batiste may or may not have a backing. Transparent sheers like organza and chiffon usually do have a backing or lining. When using plain, solid-color sheers, you can achieve some attractive effects by selecting an interesting backing fabric. The backing can be a different color, a print, or a pattern. For example, pink voile over pink checks or pink floral print. Another interesting effect is to have some parts backed and some parts left sheer. A dress might have the bodice and cuffs backed and the sleeves left sheer.

If you make a double skirt, hem the underskirt one inch shorter than the overskirt so that it won't hang below. When cutting sheers and laces that are going to be backed, first cut your backing, then using your backing as a pattern, cut the lace or the sheer. This way you will be sure that the two pieces fit together exactly. When using printed sheers, your facing should be a solid-color sheer so the design of the fabric doesn't show through.

BIAS

Fabric is cut on the bias for two reasons —to achieve a beautiful fluid look, using soft fabric, or to achieve interesting design effects when using plaids, stripes, checks, or other patterns. When you use bias for a fluid look, choose a simple design that has a fairly easy fit and a flaring skirt. It should not be tight at the hips because it will stretch out. Good fabrics for bias are drapy, such as satin-backed crepe and panne velvet. When you make a dress or skirt on the bias, let it hang overnight before marking the hem. Bias is not good for pants because it will lose its shape. Lining and facing for bias-cut garments must be cut on the same grain as the garment, otherwise you will have pulls and ripples.

See Plaids and Stripes below for using bias plaids and patterns.

PLAIDS AND STRIPES

STRIPES

Stripes may follow the cross grain or the lengthwise grain. Stripes on the lengthwise grain are easier to work with because they don't require perfect matching at the side seams. Plaids may be even or uneven (*Figure 39*). An even-stripe design is the same on both sides of the dominant bar. You can check to see if you have an even stripe by folding on the dominant bar. If it is even, the lines to the right and left of the bar will match up (*Figure 39A*). An even stripe is easier to work with. An uneven stripe is not the same on either side of the dominant bar. If you fold this kind of stripe on the dominant bar, the lines will not line up (*Figure 39B*). If you want

your garment to look symmetrical, you cannot use an uneven stripe with a fabric that
has a one-way nap.

Stripes may be woven or printed. A
woven stripe that has no right and wrong
side is easier to work with. When buying a
printed stripe, be sure it is printed on the
grain.

STRIPE PLACEMENT

Stripe placement requires careful pattern placement so that your garment will
look balanced and symmetrical. If you simply let the stripes fall where they may, your
garment can look lopsided and poorly
made. For a real designer look, aim to have
the right and left sides of your garment
perfectly symmetrical. In *Figure 40A,* notice that the dominant stripe falls in the
same place on the right and left front of
the blouse and in the same place on the
right and left sleeves. The right and left

Figure 40

cuffs are cut with the same stripe centered. The total effect of well-placed stripes
is one of good design and good quality.

Small, simple stripes like pinstripes or
mattress ticking are easier to work with because they don't require special pattern
placement. Some print and woven designs
are arranged like stripes (*Figure 39*). For
best results, treat this kind of design as you
would an ordinary stripe. When using a
bold stripe, keep to a fairly simple design so
the over-all garment won't look too
chopped up. You will probably need about
a half yard of extra fabric for matching
your stripes. To match a striped fabric and
to have the left and right sides of your
garment the same, follow the system for
cutting and marking plaids described on
page 91.

Figure 39

When using an even stripe, center the space between the dominant bars of the stripe for the best effect. You have probably been advised to use the dominant bar as the center, but I don't think this looks nearly so professional or attractive as centering the space between the bars as you see in *Figure 40B*. When dealing with uneven stripes, you can use your eye to center the dominant group of bars. For a symmetrical effect, you may need a center-front seam (*Figure 40C*). In that case, cut the left side with the top of the pattern facing one way and the right side with the top of the pattern facing the other way (*Figure 40D*).

When cutting pants with even stripes, you can center the space between the dominant bar along the middle of the leg or you can center the dominant bar itself at the middle of the leg. When using an uneven stripe, to have the right and left legs symmetrical, lay your pattern with the right leg one way and the left leg the opposite way, the same as the bodice in *Figure 40C*.

HORIZONTAL STRIPES

To match the side, center, and front plus back seams, follow the directions for cutting and matching plaids (page 91). When using uneven stripes, the pattern pieces must all be placed with the top in the same direction. If your design has a set-in sleeve, it looks professional to match the stripes on the sleeves with the stripes on the bodice.

BIAS STRIPES

You can create many new designs by using the bias and cross grain of a striped fabric for detail. Yoke, pocket, sleeves, cuffs, bodices, placket, and collar can all look well cut on the bias, or cross grain, in contrast with the rest of your garment cut on the straight grain. The design technique works well with ribbed fabric such as corduroy or ottoman. See page 90 for ideas.

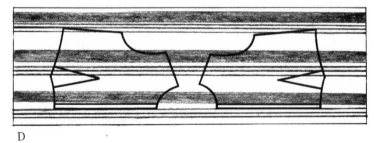

D

Figure 40

CHEVRONS

Figure 41. A chevron is formed when a stripe is cut on the bias and joined with a center-front and center-back seam. For this to work, you must fold the fabric on the straight grain, not on the bias. This style is best for simple A-line dresses and skirts. The stripe indicates the grain line of the fabric. To form chevrons, mark and cut the two fronts, then the two backs, following the directions given for plaids on page 90. Chevrons are easier to make when a balanced stripe is used.

Fold

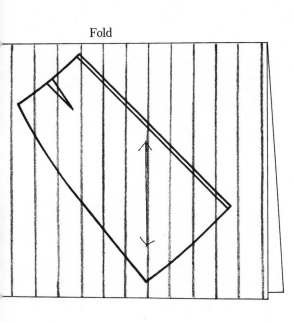

Figure 41

PLAIDS

Plaids are stripes which run in a lengthwise and crosswise direction. Because the stripes run in two directions, plaids are more difficult to work with than stripes. If you are not used to plaids, begin with a simple garment with a minimum of seams and details.

As with stripes, there are two kinds of plaids—even and uneven (*Figure 42*). In an even plaid, the plaid design is the same lengthwise and crosswise and forms a perfect square. An even plaid is easier to work with. To determine whether a plaid is even, fold the fabric on the bias and match the lengthwise design with the crosswise design. In an even plaid, the lines will match in both directions when the fabric is on grain (*Figure 42A*). There are three different kinds of uneven plaids, uneven on the cross grain (*Figure 42B*), uneven on the lengthwise grain (*Figure 42C*), and uneven in both directions (*Figure 42 D*). Uneven plaids are easier to work with if the fabric has no right and wrong side. A plaid which is uneven in both directions cannot be cut symmetrically unless it is reversible. Some plaids may look even at first, but once you make the fold test you will find that they are really uneven. Plaids may be woven or printed, but woven plaids are usually preferable. If you are considering a printed plaid, make sure it is printed on the grain.

Very large plaids work best with a simple design and require the most careful placing and matching. They also need more extra yardage in order to match. Medium or small plaids are easier to match and can be used in styles with more details. The placement of your plaid block is important for the over-all design and good looks of your garment. In working with plaid you cannot haphazardly place your pattern and hope for the best. The cutting layout and placement of your pattern must be considered carefully, but the results will be worth the extra effort. A garment made of perfectly matched and well-placed plaids looks expensive and very professional, and will show you off as an accomplished sewer.

When using an even plaid, it looks most attractive to center the block of the plaid rather than the dominant stripe (*Figure 43A*). If the plaid is unbalanced only along the cross grain, you can still center the dominant block of the plaid (*Figure

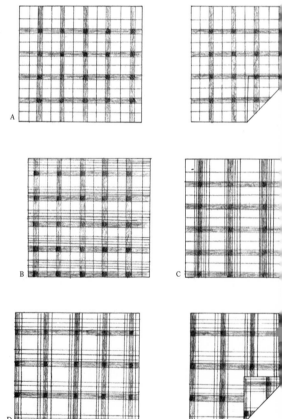

Figure 42

A

B

43B). For a plaid that is unbalanced on the lengthwise grain, use your eye to decide the best place for the center. If you want symmetry, the garment will need a center-front seam (*Figure 43C*). For symmetry, you will have to cut the right side with the pattern facing in one direction, and the left side with the pattern facing the opposite direction, the same as for an uneven stripe (page 86, *Figure 40*).

USING PLAID ON THE BIAS

Some decidedly unbalanced plaid may look peculiar cut on the bias. Be sure to look at your fabric on the bias before cutting it. Design details using plaid cut on the bias can be very attractive. These same ideas also will work for checks and stripes. A yoke, pocket, collar, cuff, or bodice can

C

Figure 43

look attractive cut on the cross grain or bias, with the rest of the garment on the straight grain. An even plaid will look the same on the cross grain or the straight grain, so you won't gain anything by using the cross grain. However, an uneven plaid can look quite different cut on the cross grain and you can create some interesting design effects that way. *Figure 44* shows some other ideas for using plaids and stripes on the bias and cross grain. To cut chevrons, see page 87. When you look at ready to wear, you will note that using a plaid or stripe cut on different grain lines is a popular design technique. Using fabric this way gives a professional look.

Figure 44

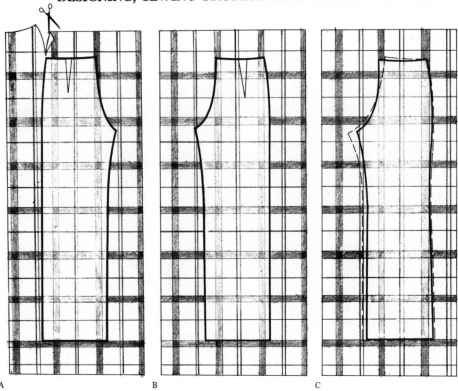

A   B   C

Figure 45

CUTTING AND MATCHING PLAIDS

The easiest way to match plaids is to mark and match one piece at a time. This way each cut piece is used to make sure the next piece is properly matched.

CUTTING STYLES WITH A CENTER-FRONT SEAM

Plaid pants:

1. Using one thickness of fabric, place your front-pants pattern on your plaid and position the pattern so the block of the plaid is centered.

2. Trace around your pattern and cut the one leg (*Figure 45A*).

3. With your fabric right side up, place the cut leg face down on your plaid. Move the pants leg around until the lines of the plaid on the pants leg and the fabric coin-cide in both directions (*Figure 45B*). (If you can't get the lines to coincide, you have an uneven plaid and your pants leg is facing in the wrong direction.)

4. Using the cut leg as a pattern, cut your second leg. Be sure you work with the right sides together, or wrong sides together. Otherwise, you will end up with two right legs or two left legs.

5. To cut your back, place one of the cut front legs on the plaid. Position the leg again so that the lines of the plaid and the lines of the cut leg coincide the same as in Step 3. This is your guide to placing the back pattern.

6. Now place the back-pants pattern directly on top of the pants leg so the side seams coincide (*Figure 45C*).

7. Trace around your back pattern. If

any of the front leg extends beyond the back pattern, fold it under so it is out of the way.

8. After you have traced your back pattern, remove the back pattern and the front leg and cut out the back leg.

9. To cut the second back leg, follow the same procedure as you did to cut the second front leg in Step 4.

By cutting each pattern piece one at a time, you can be sure your plaid will match in both directions. Use the same method when cutting skirts or dresses with center-front and center-back seams.

CUTTING STYLES WITH NO CENTER-FRONT SEAM

To cut plaid garments that have a center front on the fold:

1. Fold the plaid along the center of a block or along the line you select for the center. Be sure the crossways stripes of the plaid line up on the top and underlayer of fabric. To check this, pin through a stripe of the plaid. Turn the plaid over to see that the pin goes through the same stripe on the bottom layer of the plaid. The fabric grain must be perfectly straight to do this.

2. Once you have the plaid properly pinned, position your pattern so that the block of the plaid falls in the most attractive way.

3. Trace around your pattern.

4. Remove your pattern and cut out the front.

5. Keep the pinned front folded. Cut each side of the back separately, following the same directions given above and using your folded front as if it were only one side. If your front has a dart at the side seam, the part of the seam from the dart to the armhole will not match the back. Match from the dart to the hem.

To cut a garment with a front opening, and the center back on the fold, follow the same steps beginning with the back.

DESIGNING WITH TRIMMINGS

There seems to be an almost endless number of trimmings. For simplicity, I have grouped them into three categories. Soft trim, such as lace and braid; hard trim, such as buckles and buttons; and fabric and stitchery trim, such as ruffles and embroidery. Fabric and stitchery trims are covered in Chapter 9.

The way you use trim can make or break a look. Poor trim selection can make your garment look homemade, and good use of trim can make it look professional. To think of ways to use trimming, look at ready to wear in stores and in fashion magazines. Notice what trims are used with what fabrics and how different trimmings are combined in one garment. You will probably see combinations you wouldn't have considered but which look right. There are also illustrations using trim in the design chapters which follow.

In less expensive ready to wear, trimming is often the first place where cost is cut. You should use good-quality trimming, which doesn't necessarily mean the most expensive. Narrow, well-made lace costs less than a wide, poorly made lace. Simple buttons of pearl can cost less than some gaudy plastic ones. Learn to be discerning in selecting trim. There are too many gimmicky and garish trims that will cause anything you make to look terrible. For the most part, avoid ready-made ruffles. They really are too skimpy and often are made of poor-quality lace or fabric. Ruffles made with little pleats and doodads are the worst.

When you go to the store to select trimming, always have a good size swatch of the fabric it is going to be used with. Sometimes you will see something that goes with your fabric that you wouldn't expect to work. If you are buying trim by the yard, unwind the trimming and place it on the swatch to see if they look well together. When you are buying buttons, place some buttons on the fabric, or if the buttons are on a card, stick an edge of the swatch under the buttons so you can see how they look. When using a permanent-press fabric, be sure your trim is also permanent press or made of a synthetic that won't wrinkle when you wash it. If you are using a washable fabric, make sure your trimming is also washable. You can also recycle trim. If you have clothes that don't fit or are out of style, they might still have attractive buttons, lace, or braid in good condition, which you might use again.

SOFT TRIMMINGS

Soft trims include laces, braids, ribbons, rickrack, soutache, fringe, and knit trim. They are bought by the yard ready made and can be as narrow as $\frac{1}{8}''$ or as wide as $4''$–$6''$ or more. It is very important to wash most soft trimming before stitching your garment. Some trims of this type can shrink enormously—as much as 10 per cent—and often the dyes will run. Washing isn't necessary with polyester and nylon trim since they don't shrink.

Depending on the style and the width of the trim, soft trim can be used almost anywhere; around necklines and collars, yokes, sleeves, cuffs, at front openings, and around the hem of a skirt or pants leg are all possibilities (*Figure 46*).

When the trimming is the focal point of your design, it is usually best to stick with simple, classic fabrics. This does not mean that the fabric must be plain, however. Gingham checks and eyelet are a classic combination, so are calico prints and rickrack. A leno-weave fabric looks beautiful with Cluny lace or eyelet. Patterned braid trim combined with simple patterned fabric can look very attractive. For unity, have a color in common in the trim and in the fabric. For example, a nautical trim of red and blue stars could be used with red, white, and blue stripes. A pink and green floral-design braid would be nice with pink dotted swiss. Red and white strawberry-design braid could be combined with red gingham checks and so on. You can combine more than one trim on the same garment. A delicate floral-design braid goes well with lace. A sophisticated heavy braid could be combined with fringe. Rickrack and eyelet can work well together, or rickrack of different sizes.

You will sometimes see, in expensive

ready to wear, a style that is a very simple dress or skirt with bands of a number of different trims around the hem. To make a similar style, select a very basic fabric such as white piqué or gray flannel and select trims that co-ordinate with each other in color and feeling. For example, a long gray flannel skirt could be trimmed with a band of wide black-and-white patterned braid at the hem, next a band of black Cluny lace, a band of narrow black-and-white braid in a different pattern, a band of white Cluny lace, and a band of black grosgrain ribbon. Bring along a long swatch of fabric and work out your trim combinations in the store before you buy anything. Keep

pulling out the trims and laying them on the fabric until you get a fabulous combination. When you stitch the rows of trim, be sure to measure accurately and keep the rows straight.

For some styles, your trimming may cost more than your fabric. There are some terrific combinations of basic fabrics with good trimmings. One of my favorites is unbleached muslin with ecru Cluny lace. On a budget, you can use an expensive trim in a place that takes only a small amount of trim. You need less than ½ yard of braid to go across the front of a yoke; also about ½ yard will trim two cuffs.

Figure 46

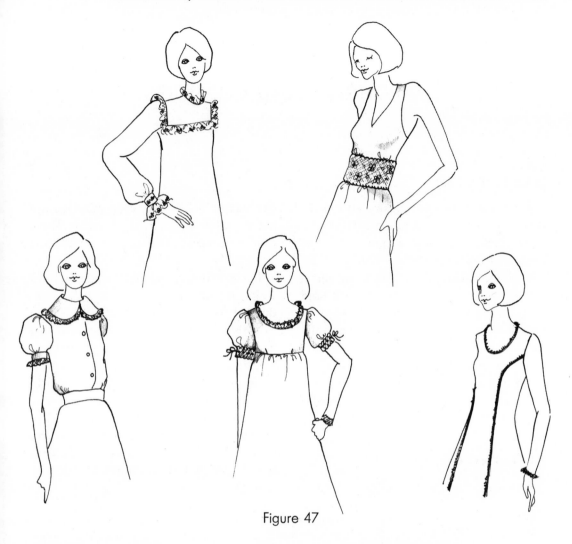

Figure 47

LACES

Read about laces in Chapter 7, page 70. When using laces, it is best to stay with white, ecru (off white), or black. Avoid brightly colored and multicolored lace for the most part. If you have white lace made out of cotton, you can make it off white by dipping it in a pot of strong tea. Test a scrap of your lace and dry it first, to make sure it comes out the color you want. *Figure 47* shows some suggestions on ways to use lace. For information on making lace ruffles, read about ruffles on page 106.

FLEXIBLE TRIMS

When you are trimming a curved shape such as a neckline or collar, the trim you use must be flexible in order to conform to the shape of the curve. Flexible trims include gathered lace, picot edges, bias fold-over trims, ribbed knit, piping, cording, soutache, and rickrack.

HARD TRIMS AND CLOSINGS

HARD TRIMS

Hard trims include buckles and rings, studs and gromets, decorative clips and zipper pulls, beads and sequins. Many of the hard trims work well in sportswear designs. The smoothness of wood or metal provides an interesting contrast when used with the texture of wool, corduroy, or suede. Beads and sequins are generally used with dressy fabric. However, they should be used with moderation to avoid a Las Vegas look. Most hard trims are made of woods, metal, or plastic. (See *Figure 48* for some ways of using hard trims.)

CLOSINGS

Closings include buttons, zippers, decorative snaps, hooks and eyes, toggles, and metal eyelets with lacing. A front closing can be the focal point of a design (*Figure 49*).

For sportswear, consider a zipper in front with contrast topstitching, or a bold industrial zipper with the teeth exposed. You can also use an ordinary zipper with a decorative zipper pull. Or use a contrasting zipper, stitched so the zipper tape is on top of the outside instead of hidden in the seam. A front closing is an ideal way to show off beautiful buttons. If you like antique or very expensive buttons, you can make a garment that opens only part way, so you need to buy only three or four buttons.

Figure 48

Figure 49

WORKMANSHIP

Workmanship can distinguish between a homemade garment and a professional one. Good workmanship does not mean that everything must be finished like a couture garment. That would be very nice, but few of us have the time or patience to do that except for the most special designs. Good workmanship simply means that what you do, you do well. When your time is limited, it is much better to make a very simple dress and sew it well than to try a complicated style that will have mistakes. It is better to omit a collar than to use one that is badly made. Work at having seams that are straight, sleeves that are well set in, collars with even points, matched plaids,

even gathers, straight topstitching, and so on. Relate the cost of your fabric and trim to the amount of time you put into your garment. Very expensive fabric should be given your best treatment if the result is to be worth while for the money spent.

In the sample room (designer's workroom), each sample hand may make as many as four or five garments a day. She must sew well, efficiently, and quickly. Some of the techniques used in the sample room can also be used by the home sewer to save time. One of the best ways to save time is to train your eye to measure distances and to recognize the shape of patterns. It's so much quicker to stitch 5/8″ by eye without using a guide, or to stitch bands of trimming in straight rows without guide marks. In the sample room, very few marks are made on the cut garment pieces. Tracing wheel and carbon are seldom used, to save time and avoid the risk of having marks left on the garment where they would show. Darts are marked by a pin or a tiny dot at the point of the dart and a notch at the end of each of the dart lines. If you train your eye to be familiar with the shape of a dart, you should have no trouble stitching from the point to the seam without having it marked in carbon or tailor's chalk. Carbon doesn't wash out and tracing marks can make a garment look handled and homemade. In the sample room, pins are not used for most straight stitching. The friction of the fabric holds the pieces together. Two or three of the same garments are often cut in different fabrics and sewn at the same time. You might want to try this sometime if you are in a hurry, sewing up several pairs of pants to go on vacation, for example. Sewing two of the same thing assembly-line style goes a lot faster than sewing two things separately. You can layer the two fabrics and cut two of the same garments together if the fabric is not heavy.

Use your sewing machine attachments for doing various jobs, such as gathering or making narrow hems. The attachments will do the job more quickly and neatly.

In the sample room, unit construction is used. This means that each part of the garment is sewn as completely as possible before being attached to another part. For example, a sleeve cuff and placket are completed before the sleeve is set into the armhole, and a bodice is completed before it is joined to a skirt. It is efficient to do as much stitching as possible before you get up to press. Following the unit system, you would stitch all the darts—front, back,

shoulder darts, etc.—then get up and press all the darts. This is far more efficient than sewing the front darts and pressing them, sewing the back darts and pressing again, and so on.

You can also save time by feeding pieces into the machine without stopping and cutting the thread. Usually, when you get to the end of a seam, you stop, raise the presser foot, pull the fabric out of the machine, and cut the thread. In many cases, this is not necessary. When you get to the end of a line of stitching, take another piece that needs stitching and stick it right under the presser foot, without lifting the presser foot up and without cutting the thread, then continue sewing. Another way to save time is to use a minimum of hand sewing, when hand sewing is not necessary. In some cases of course, hand finishing is very nice; but in other instances, it is not necessary and, in fact, is less durable than machine sewing. In most cases, french piping, waistbands, and shirt collars are best sewn completely by machine. You can also save time by learning to handle fabrics without stretching them. Once you do this, you can omit the step of stay stitching around necklines and armholes in many cases.

An important part of good workmanship is good pressing. Pressing is not the same as ironing. Pressing should be done always following the grain of your fabric. The best kind of iron is the "shot of steam" type, which is closest to the kind used in the sample room. When using medium and heavyweight fabrics, don't place the full weight of the iron on the seams or hem. If you do, the weight of the iron will make an impression of the seam or hem allowance, which will show on the right side. If you have a "shot of steam" iron, hold the iron above the fabric, push the steam button, and let the steam do your pressing.

Test your iron temperature and amount of steam on a scrap of fabric before pressing your garment.

Another important part of good workmanship is a well-done hem. A bad hemming job will make a garment look homemade immediately. When you do a blind hem, you should pick up only one thread of the fabric with your needle. Different fabrics need different kinds of hems. You might need to try several until you see which looks best on the kind of fabric you are using. Your hem should not show as a thick ridge at the bottom of your garment.

Another sign of good workmanship, which is found on expensive clothes, is pockets hidden in the side seams of a dress or skirt. An attractive design touch you can use is contrasting fabric for the lining or facing of your garment. It also looks nice to use a different fabric for an undercollar or cuff backing.

CHAPTER 9

DESIGN DETAILS

GOOD USE OF DESIGN DETAILS

Good use of design details can make the difference between whether what you sew looks professional or homemade. These details should, however, be used in moderation. Too many can look badly designed and cheap. Most of the details in this chapter can be used to make any of the basic slopers into a new style with no change in the sloper itself. Add big patch pockets with flaps to the basic pants and you have a new pants style. Add a belt and tabs to the basic skirt and you have a new skirt design. Add a ruffle at the neck and sleeves of the A-line and you make a new dress, and so on. Of course these design details can be used with other patterns you make or buy.

POCKET FLAPS AND TABS

PATCH POCKETS

A patch pocket is one which is stitched on top of the garment. When using patch pockets, unless part of the pocket will be stitched into a seam, make your entire garment first, including the hem. This way you can see exactly how large or small your pockets should be and where to place them. Designers often work this way on a first sample. Pocket-placement marks on commercial patterns do not take into account individual variations in height and body proportions.

First decide what size you want your finished pocket. You can judge this by cutting several different pockets from scraps. Leave the raw edge. You will just use these pieces to see the effect. Try on the finished garment and stand in front of your full-length mirror. Pin on a pocket where you think you might want it. Stand back and look. Try moving it around to see if it looks better higher or lower. If it looks too small or large, try another of your test pockets. Once you decide where you want your pocket, leave it pinned and carefully take off your garment. Before removing the test pocket from your garment, place a line of pins on the garment along the top edge of the pocket. This will show you where to place your finished pocket. If your fabric shows pin marks, then place two pins just inside where the top two corners of the pocket will go. You can cover these marks when you stitch on your pocket. There are two kinds of patch pockets, lined and unlined. The one you use depends on the style of your pocket and the fabric. Sheer or loosely woven fabrics and sometimes bias should be lined. A pocket of unusual shape must be lined, also. A simple square, U-shaped, or V-bottom pocket, using fairly sturdy woven or double-knit goods, need not be lined. When lining a pocket, use a lightweight fabric such as batiste or silk, or it will be too bulky. When lining a sheer print, use a solid color for the lining.

UNLINED POCKET

Figure 50. Square, U-shaped, or V-bottom:

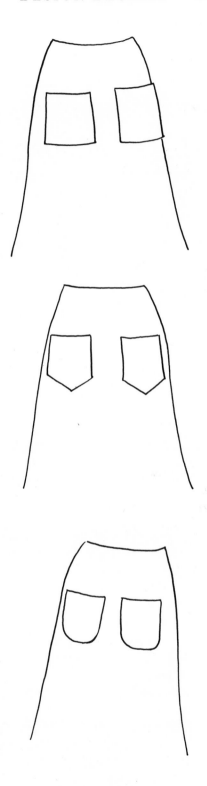

Figure 50

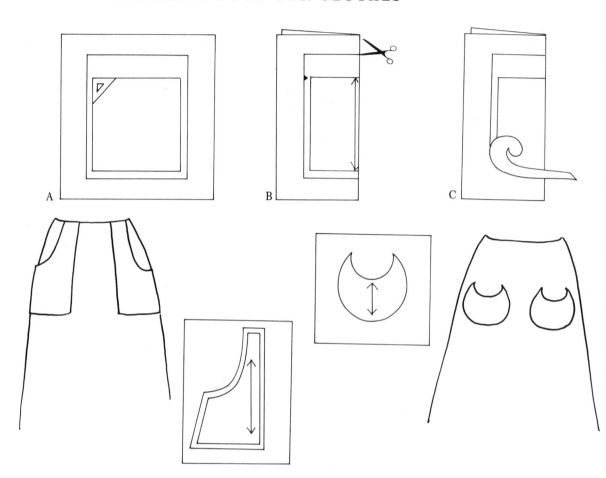

Figure 50

1. Measure the length and width of your test pocket.

2. On your pattern paper, draw a rectangle the length and width of your test pocket (*Figure 50A*). Use your triangle to be sure your corners are square.

3. Add ⅝″ seam allowance at the sides and bottom and 2″ allowance on top. This 2″ will be folded down to form a facing for the top of the pocket.

4. Fold the pattern in half lengthwise and cut it out along the cutting line (*Figure 50B*). Cut V notches at the finish line at the top of the pocket.

5. If you're making a U-shaped pocket, use your French curve to shape the bottom (*Figure 50C*). If you're making a V-bottom pocket, shape the bottom of the pattern with your ruler while the pattern is folded to be sure both sides of the pattern are the same. Add seam allowance and cut on the cutting line.

6. The center crease forms the grain line unless you want your pocket on the cross grain or bias.

To achieve a smooth curve at the bottom of a U-shaped pocket, run an ease stitch along the curve and pull the thread, just as you would in making a set-in sleeve.

To make unusually shaped pockets, follow the directions for flaps (*Figure 51A*, page 104).

LINED POCKET

Make your pocket pattern the same way as the unlined pocket except mark ⅝″ seam allowance on the top instead of the 2″ facing. If you make a bias pocket, the lining should also be cut on the bias.

STITCHING POCKETS

You can apply patch pockets by hand or machine. By machine, topstitch carefully with matching or contrasting thread, using a straight or zigzag stitch. By hand, use blind stitch or saddle stitch. Pockets applied by hand are found on the best-quality ready to wear.

If your fabric is easy to work on, you can eliminate the step of making a paper pattern and mark the pocket directly on the fabric if you wish. You can also mark it on the lining and use the lining as a pattern.

FLAPS

Figure 51. Flaps can be used alone or combined with pockets to create many designs. Flaps are easy to make and, except for a fancy-shape flap, once you have made a few, you can probably eliminate the step of making a paper pattern and mark it directly on the wrong side of the fabric.

To make a pattern for a flap, follow the directions for patch pockets, marking the size of the flap on paper and adding the seam allowance. Flaps must be lined. A rectangle flap can be made on the fold like a shirt cuff instead of having a separate lining. Once the flap is sewn to the garment, if it won't lie flat, tack the flap lining to the garment by hand, or use a decorative button to hold it down. You can also topstitch along the top of the flap after it is pressed down to keep it in place.

If you're using a flap with a patch pocket, stitch the flap on first, then stitch the pocket. Press the flap down last.

Figure 51

Flaps can be trimmed with lace, ruffles, embroidery, braid, or buttons. When using hand or machine embroidery, stitch the design on a large piece of fabric first, then cut the flap, centering the design. When you apply braid trim, stitch it to the top flap before you stitch the lining so that the ends of the braid will be in the seam. You can trim a flap with a ruffle (see page 106 for making ruffles) of gathered lace or fabric.

Flaps and pockets can also be made with scalloped bottoms or unusual shapes. When you make a pattern for this kind of flap, you will have better results if you omit the seam allowance from the pattern. After you make your pattern, cut a square of fabric and lining larger than your pattern and trace the flap outline onto the lining (*Figure 51A*). Stitch directly on the outline, leaving an opening to turn right side out. Trim away excess fabric, leaving ¼" seam allowance and ⅝" at the top. This way

TABS

Figure 52. Tabs are really the same as flaps except they are long and narrow. They can be used alone or with pockets, collars, or as belt loops.

Follow the directions for making a patch-pocket pattern when making a tab. Like a flap, it must be lined. A tab can be topstitched to the garment or just the top edge caught in the seam and the bottom held in place by one or more buttons. It can be trimmed with lace, braid, or embroidery, the same as a flap. Follow the same general instructions for applying trims to tabs as those given for flaps.

COMBINATION POCKETS

You can design some interesting pockets by combining a patch pocket with a flap or tab as you see in *Figure 53*.

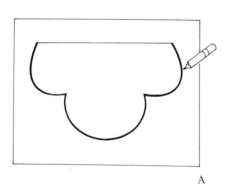

A

you will have a guideline to keep your scallops or curve even and accurate. You can use this method of omitting seam allowance and stitching on a guideline whenever you have a complicated shape line to stitch on such as a pocket, tab, collar, and so on.

Figure 51

Figure 52

Figure 53

RUFFLES

Ruffles may be made of the same fabric as your garment, contrasting fabric, or of lace. You can read about lace in Chapter 7, page 70, and about using lace trims in Chapter 8, page 95. Ruffles made of fabric cost a good deal less than those made of lace. Fabric ruffles can be trimmed with narrow lace, rickrack, braid, cording, and so on. Ruffles can be used almost anywhere —necklines, sleeves, sleeveless armholes, collars, front openings, skirt hems, and around yokes, to name a few places. Ruffles are made in different ways, depending on the kind of fabric you're using and the look you want. The three basic types of ruffles are bias, straight grain, and flared.

The length of fabric or lace you need for a ruffle is between two and three times the measurement of the place where the ruffle will be used, depending on the weight of the fabric and the amount of fullness you want in the ruffle. When you are using a fabric or lace of medium weight, or if you don't want the ruffle too full, then use twice the measurement. If you are using a lightweight fabric or lace and want quite a bit of fullness, then use three times the measurement. For example, suppose you want to make a ruffle to go around the hem of a skirt that measures 54″ all around. If you want to make a ruffle of Cluny lace (which is a fairly heavy lace), you will need twice the measurement of the hemline, or $54″ \times 2 = 108″$, or 3 yards of lace. If you want to make the ruffle of voile (which is lightweight), you would need three times the measurement

of the hemline, or $54″ \times 3 = 162″$, or $4\frac{1}{2}$ yards.

SEWING RUFFLES

When you sew a ruffle to the garment, stitch on top of the gathering stitch. If you stitch below it, you will have tucks and pleats in the ruffle which will look awful. If you are using a facing, pin the facing in place, then turn the garment over so the stitching line attaching the ruffle to the garment is face up. Using the ruffle stitching line as a guide, sew the facing on the same stitching line.

FINISHING ENDS OF RUFFLES

If the ruffle ends at an opening such as the center back, you can finish the ends of the ruffle with a narrow rolled hem. A bias-fold ruffle can be finished by turning the raw edges to the inside of the ruffle and slip stitching the ends. If there is no opening in the ruffle, such as around the hem of a skirt, you can join the two ends with a french seam.

MAKING RUFFLES FROM LACE

Most lace edges have a narrow ($\frac{1}{8}″$ to $\frac{1}{4}″$) band along one side that is meant for stitching. When you gather lace, stitch carefully along this band. The finer the lace, the shorter the stitch you should use to maintain even gathers. If your lace becomes tangled in the feed dog (the teeth under the presser foot) of your machine as you sew, place a strip of tissue paper under the lace when you stitch. Tear it away when you finish.

BIAS RUFFLES

Figure 54. One of the prettiest ruffles is made of a folded strip of bias. The bias-fold ruffle works best with lighter weight knit or woven fabrics and eliminates the need of a hem. To figure the width to cut the bias, decide the width you want the finished ruffle to be, double that amount, and add $1\frac{3}{8}''$. For example if you want your ruffle $2''$ wide, double $2''$ is $4''$ plus $1\frac{3}{8}''=5\frac{3}{8}''$, which is the width to cut the bias. The fabric must be cut on true bias, or the fold will not press flat. When joining bias pieces, the seams must follow the grain line, not be on the bias (*Figure 54A*).

Once you have joined the pieces into one long strip, fold the strip in half longways, right side out, and press (*Figure 54B*). Be careful not to stretch the bias as

you press it. You can gather the ruffle with the gathering foot on your machine, or use the thread-pulling method. The secret of getting good gathers with a gathering foot follows: Keep the tension tight and the stitch fairly long. Hold the first finger of your left hand directly behind the presser foot so that the fabric bunches up behind the foot, meanwhile hold your pattern awl in your right hand and use it to help feed the bias into the presser foot while you run the machine. You really have to stuff the fabric under the presser foot with the awl to make this work. If the gathers are too tight, loosen the tension and/or shorten the stitch. If the gathers are still too loose, you can run the whole business through the gathering foot a second or even third time. The thinner the fabric the more it will gather. The other way to gather a ruffle is to use button thread in the bobbin and a fairly loose long stitch. Run two rows of stitching $\frac{1}{4}''$ apart. Gather up the ruffle by hand, pulling on the two heavy bobbin threads. Using the gathering foot is much quicker if you can get the hang of it.

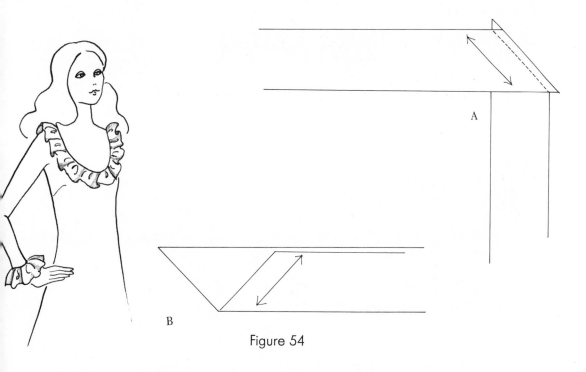

Figure 54

Sometimes you might want to make a bias ruffle with a fabric which is too heavy to fold, but where a hem would be unattractive. Velvet, velour, or wool would be in this category. In this case, you can make a lined bias ruffle. Cut the ruffle and the lining the width of the finished ruffle plus one inch. The lining should be of a thin fabric such as organza. Place the right sides of the lining and fabric together and join them with a seam 1/4" from the edge. Press, turn right side out, and press again. Then continue as for the regular bias ruffle.

You can also make a bias ruffle with a hem instead of on the fold. Follow the instructions for straight ruffle below except cut the fabric on the bias.

STRAIGHT RUFFLES

Figure 55. The straight ruffle is cut on the straight grain and hemmed on one side. (Folded ruffles do not work well on the straight grain with most fabrics.) The hem on this ruffle should be made with a hemmer foot, to be as neat and narrow as possible. The edge of the ruffle may also be finished by applying a narrow lace, picot edge, or braid before gathering. Calico prints look nice with a ruffle edged in narrow rickrack. A pastel voile is pretty with a ruffle edged in a delicate flower braid. If you want a lace look but don't want to spend a lot of money for yards of wide lace

A

B

Figure 55

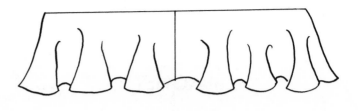

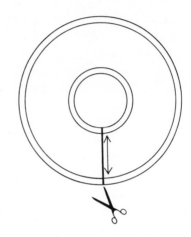

Figure 56

ruffles, cut your ruffles in white leno or dotted swiss and edge with a narrow inexpensive picot or Val (*Figure 55B*). This will give you a similar look for much less money.

To determine the width to cut your fabric, add one inch to the measurement you want the finished ruffle to be. For example, if you want your ruffle 2″, cut it 3″ wide. After hemming one side, gather the ruffle as described for bias ruffle. Another way of making a straight-grain ruffle is with a header (*Figure 55A*). A header is a tiny ruffle created by gathering below the top edge of a ruffle. To determine how wide to cut the fabric, add 1¼″ to the width you want the finished ruffle to be. This will give you a header of ⅝″. Hem both sides of the ruffle, then gather it ⅝″ from the hemmed edge. After you have gathered the ruffle, pin it in place on the

garment and topstitch it right on top of the gathering thread. Use only one row of stitching to gather the ruffle. The header may be wider on one side or narrower. You could also gather the ruffle in the middle.

FLARED RUFFLE

The flared ruffle has no gathers and is made by joining a series of circles. To make a pattern for this ruffle, see *Figure 56*. Use a compass to draw the circles. Don't forget to add seam allowance on both sides. The smaller the inside circle of the pattern, the more flare to the ruffle and the more circles you will need. The cut line of the circle is the straight grain of the fabric. Join the circles at the cut line to form the ruffle. The edge can be finished with a rolled hem, or you can line the ruffle.

SPAGHETTI, CORDING, AND PIPING

Spaghetti, cording, and piping are three decorative ways of using bias stripping. They work equally well with knit or woven fabrics. The fabric must be cut accurately on true bias or it will ripple and pucker. The bias may be pieced as long as it is joined on the straight or cross grain, but not with a bias seam. When you use a filler cord inside spaghetti or cording, you must wash the cord first, since it can shrink as much as 10 or 15 per cent. Cording is sometimes mistakenly called piping. Cording is made with cord inside, piping is not. Ready-made trims in this category are generally not good. The fabric is often poor quality, won't match your garment, and will make it look homemade.

Figure 57

SPAGHETTI

Spaghetti (*Figure 57*) is a tube of bias which can be used for ties, shoulder straps, drawstring, lacing, belt loops, and button loops among other things. It is just about impossible to turn spaghetti without a loop turner. This tool isn't expensive and is a great convenience.

For thin spaghetti (about ¼″), cut a strip of bias an inch wide. Fold it in half longways, wrong side out. Stitch one end closed and stitch along the length, using a loose stitch so that the thread won't break. Poke the loop turner inside the tube and work the little hook around the closed end of the spaghetti. When the end is hooked, hold the ring of the turner in one hand and with the other hand carefully work the bias over the hook so you can pull it right side out. This part may take some patience until you get the hang of it.

For thick spaghetti, you will have better results if you have a cord inside as a filler. Cut the bias about 1⅝″, fold and stitch as for narrow spaghetti. Cut a piece of cord the same length as the spaghetti and attach it to the closed end of the bias. Insert the loop turner as for the narrow spaghetti,

Figure 58

a cording or zipper foot. To figure how wide to cut your bias, add $1\frac{1}{4}''$ for seam allowance plus $\frac{1}{4}''$ for thin cord or $\frac{1}{2}''$ or more for thick cord. For example, if your cord is thin, add $1\frac{1}{4}''+\frac{1}{4}''=1\frac{1}{2}''$ wide bias. Upholstery departments sell a thick filler cord for slipcovers, which can be used very successfully on clothing. Cording can be used to trim necklines, waist and yokelines, collars, tabs, pockets, sleeveless armholes, and collarless necklines among other places. It should be used with a facing. You can use the same fabric as the garment, a contrasting color, or a solid to co-ordinate with a patterned fabric. You can use cording in combination with ruffles and other trims.

Spaghetti and cording are often used together. For example, you might have cording at the neckline and armholes and a spaghetti tie at the waist, both made of the same fabric.

FRENCH PIPING

Figure 58. French piping is a bias strip used instead of a facing to clean finish a raw edge such as a neckline or armhole. Piping can also be used to trim collars, pockets, hemlines, jacket fronts, or any other edge. Piping fabric may match or contrast, but will not work well if it is too bulky. Cut your bias four times the finished width of the piping. The seam allowance of the piping should be the same amount as the finished width of the piping. For example, for $\frac{1}{4}''$ piping cut the bias $1''$ wide ($\frac{1}{4}''$ seam allowance). The piping can be applied with a machine attachment. If you use piping around the basic jewel neckline, trim away the neckline seam allowance first or the neckline will be too tight.

and pull the bias right side out over the cord. Plushy fabrics like velvet do not need a filler cord.

CORDING

Figure 58. Cording is bias stripping folded over a filler cord and stitched with

SCARVES, BELTS AND SASHES, BOWS AND TIES

Each of these design details are easy to make and most are essentially a variation on a theme. Except for the scarves, they may be made of trimmings or of fabric.

SCARVES, STOLES, AND SHAWLS

Figure 59. A scarf can be square or rectangular. A square scarf is usually hemmed with a hand-rolled hem or a very closely stitched zigzag stitch. It should be made of soft fabric which will drape well. A rectangular scarf can be stitched and turned or hemmed at the edges with a hemmer foot. A stole is a large rectangular scarf. A shawl is a large triangular-shaped scarf. Scarves, stoles, and shawls are often trimmed with braid, fringe, or lace. You don't need to make a separate pattern for any of these. Figure the size you want your scarf, add seam allowance, and mark directly on the wrong side of your fabric with your yardstick. Use your triangle or an L square to keep the corners square.

Figure 59

BELTS AND SASHES

Figure 60. Belts may be made from self or contrast fabric, suede, ribbon, braid, and other trimmings. There are many good-looking buckles available. A belt can be made to button onto the buckle so you can use an expensive buckle with several belts. Avoid self-covered belts and buckles unless you can do a superb job of covering.

There are two kinds of sashes. The first is a long separate sash which encircles the waist and ties in front or back. The second is two shorter ties which are attached to the garment, one at each side seam, princess seam, or waist dart. Sashes may be hemmed at the edge or stitched and turned. They can tie in a bow or a middy knot. A wide bias sash (which must be stitched and turned, not hemmed) forms lovely soft folds and bow. To prevent the weight of the bow from causing the sash to droop, attach a thread loop to the waistline where the bow will be tied. Pull the sash through the thread loop before you tie the bow.

Figure 60

BOWS AND TIES

These are most often used at the neckline with a collar. They can be made three ways: as a separate bow which pins or buttons on at the neckline, as one long tie which encircles the neckline and ties in front, or as two ties, one stitched into each shoulder seam. The separate kind should be used when the bow fabric is not washable or if the dye might run. Bows and ties can be made of the same or contrasting fabric, braid, ribbon, and so on. Small bows can be made of spaghetti.

To determine the length needed for a sash, tie, or bow, use a piece of seam binding or ribbon, tie it the way you want, then measure it. As with the scarves, you can mark directly on the wrong side of the fabric without making a pattern.

Figure 60

STITCHERY

Many different types of stitchery can be used to create your own designer touches.

QUILTING

You can buy quilted fabric ready made, or make your own. If you buy ready made, check the quality since some ready-made quilting may be done very cheaply. See that the backing fabric is something better than cheesecloth and that the stitching is not breaking and pulling out. If you make your own quilting, you can use a traditional diamond pattern or, for an extra-special look, use hand-guided quilting on a patterned fabric following the shape of a motif, such as a flower or a paisley. The quilting can be contrasting fabric or the same fabric as the rest of your garment. If you are quilting your own fabric, you will probably only want to do enough for accents, such as a yoke, pockets, cuffs, waistband, or bands around the hem and collars (*Figure 61*.)

Another kind of quilting is Trapunto, sometimes called Italian quilting. This can be done as one motif placed on the front of a garment, or as bands, stitched around the hem, sleeves, neck, and so on.

APPLIQUES

Figure 61. The ready-made Schiffli type of appliqué has become a bit tiresome, having been overused in recent years. However, appliqués are by no means limited to decorating blue jeans. You can make your own appliqués, some of which can be quite sophisticated. One interesting kind of appliqué is made by cutting a motif from the

Figure 61

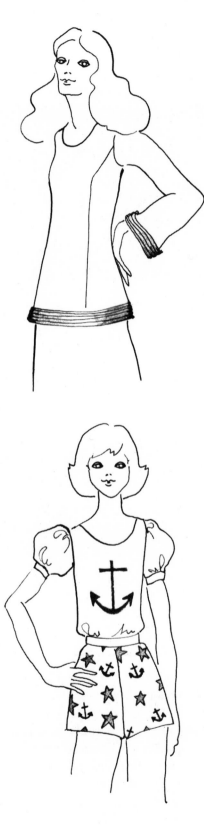

Figure 61

design of a printed fabric. For example, you may make a dress with a paisley bodice, then select a plain fabric for the skirt. Cut out a number of the paisley motifs from your fabric and apply them to the skirt as appliqués. If you apply an appliqué by machine, it's best to use the zigzag stitch. Appliqués applied by hand can be held in place with an invisible stitch on the back or by using embroidery stitches like the blanket stitch as part of the over-all design. You can also apply appliqués with your iron and a fusable bonding fabric, such as Stitch Witchery. Another way of using appliqués is to make an appliqué to co-ordinate with a design of a print. For example, for a summer sportswear outfit, you might make pants out of a nautical print, with stars and anchors, then make a top from a solid fabric and appliqué an anchor design.

SMOCKING AND SHIRRING

Figure 62. Smocking and shirring add a soft feminine look to a design. They work best on lightweight or very soft fabrics. Shirring can be done with elastic thread in the bobbin. Experiment with the size of your stitch and your tension to get the look you want. There are many different smocking designs. The easiest way to keep your

Figure 62

smocking straight is to use a woven stripe or check and follow the lines on the fabric. Smocking and shirring can be used on bodice fronts, yokes, cuffs, midriff bands, and so on. An attractive ruffle can be made by using one or two rows of smocking to gather the ruffle.

head tacks, which can be used at the top of pleats and to reinforce the ends of pockets (*Figure 62*). Saddle stitching is very attractive used on sportswear. It can be used around necklines, armholes, belts, and to accent design seaming, such as the center-front seam or princess seam. Hand stitching can be done using embroidery floss, pearl cotton, or washable crewel or Persian yarn.

Figure 62

OTHER HAND STITCHERY

You can use embroidery stitches such as blanket stitch, feather stitch, or herringbone stitch as trimming around collars, necklines, cuffs, blouse fronts, and so on. Another nice-looking hand stitch is arrow-

CHAPTER 10

NECKLINES AND COLLARS

NECKLINES

Changing the neckline is one of the easiest ways to vary a style. The different necklines shown in this chapter can be made using the A-line, bodice or blouse sloper, a commercial pattern, or a pattern you've made. When you use the blouse sloper, crease the front facing of the pattern on the fold line and fold it under before you cut the new pattern neckline. This must be done so that the facing will be the same shape as the neckline.

Below is a detailed explanation of the scoop-neck pattern. The method for making this pattern applies to any variation in neckline shape, so once you understand how to make the scoop-neckline pattern, you can make any other neckline designs which follow, as well as new ideas of your own. Once you have made a few patterns and become more confident, you can leave out the step of making a paper pattern and simply mark the new neckline directly on the wrong side of the garment after it has been cut, if you like.

SCOOP NECK

Figure 63A. 1. Take whichever sloper or pattern you are using and trace around it on a new piece of paper.

2. Using a colored pencil, mark the new neckline where you want it. You can draw the neckline freehand, then use your French curve to make the line smooth and even. When making low necklines, use the bust-dart lines as a guide to know how low to cut the neck.

3. Use your ruler and black pencil to add ⅝″ seam allowance.

4. You will also need a facing line so that you will know where to cut the facing for your new neckline. At the center front, measure 3″ down from the cutting line of the neckline and mark. The side of the facing follows the shape of the armhole (*Figure 63B*). When you sew your garment, stitch the side of the facing to the seam allowance of the armhole and it will not stick out of the neckline. The facing must not extend below the bust dart. If you have a very low neckline, your facing will be narrower than 3″, to avoid the bust dart.

5. Cut out your front pattern. Be sure to cut on the cutting line of the new neckline (*Figure 63C*).

6. When you make the back-neckline pattern, the front and back patterns must be joined at the shoulder seam so that the neckline can be blended in one continuous line, the same way you trued the front and back neckline of the muslin while the shoulder seam was joined. Trace around your back sloper on a new sheet of paper and cut out the pattern.

7. Use your ruler to draw the shoulder-seam stitching lines on the front and back pattern. The stitching line is parallel to the cutting line ⅝″ below it as you see in *Figure 63D*. You can ignore the back-shoulder dart for this step.

8. Crease along the stitching line of the front-shoulder seam and fold the seam allowance under.

9. Place the front pattern so that the stitching line (edge of the fold) on the front shoulder is lined up against the stitching line of the back shoulder as you see in *Figure 63E*. Tape together.

10. Now you can continue the front neckline onto the back pattern. Keep the line from the front to the back neckline flowing smoothly over the shoulder seam. Blend the line with your French curve (*Figure 63E*). When the neckline is shaped so that it eliminates more than half of the shoulder dart, you may leave out the shoulder dart entirely. If the neckline is only slightly larger than the original neckline, then the shoulder dart should remain.

11. Separate the front and back by cutting the tape.

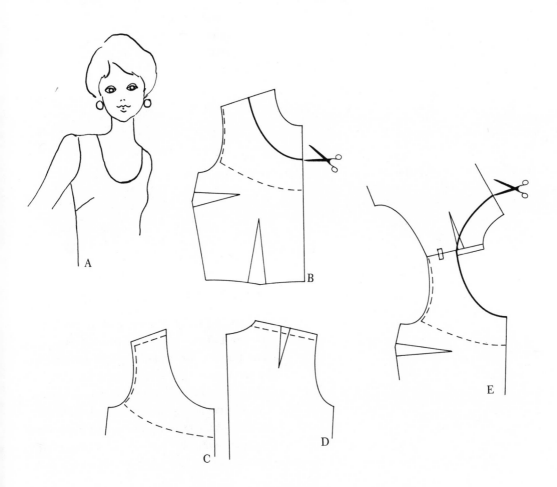

Figure 63

12. Mark the facing line as you did on the front pattern. If your pattern has shoulder darts, your facing should also have them. When you make your garment, press the dart on the facing toward the armhole and the dart on the garment toward the center back.

13. Your finished front and back patterns should look like *Figure 63F*. When you cut your facing in fabric, cut around the pattern at the neckline, shoulder, armhole, and top part of the side seam to the facing line. Slip a piece of dressmaker's carbon paper face down between the pattern and the fabric. Mark the facing line with your tracing wheel, remove the pattern, then continue cutting.

SQUARE NECKLINE

Figure 63G. Follow the same steps as for scoop neck, using your ruler to draw the neckline. Square the neckline from center front with your triangle.

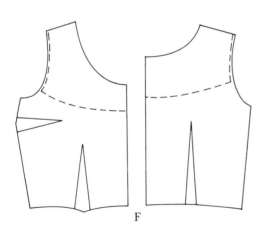

Figure 63

NECKLINE VARIATIONS

Figure 64 illustrates some other necklines and the pattern changes on the front pattern. Follow the same steps as in making the scoop-neck pattern (*Figure 63*).

If you make a pattern that has a narrow V or U neckline, which begins at the shoulder seam at the same place as the regular neckline, you do not need to make any change in the back neckline.

Figure 64

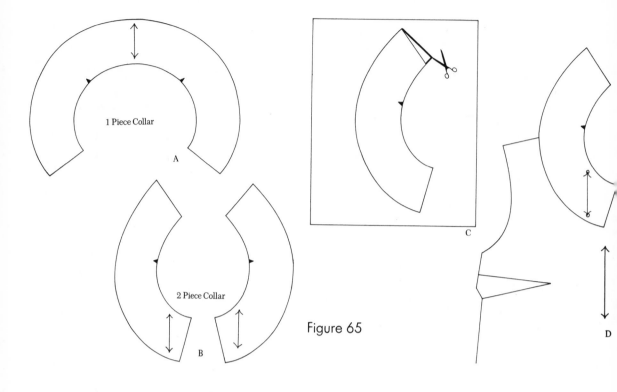

1 Piece Collar

A

2 Piece Collar

B

C

Figure 65

D

DESIGNING WITH THE COLLAR SLOPER

TWO-PIECE-COLLAR SLOPER

The collar sloper you made with the blouse sloper is called a one-piece collar and is used with front openings. For a garment which opens in the back, you need a two-piece collar. The two types of collars are shown in *Figures 65A* and *B*. If you plan to make a collar for the A-line dress, basic bodice, or other garments which open in the back, you should have a two-piece-collar sloper. This is very easy to make from your one-piece-collar sloper.

1. Place your collar sloper on a sheet of heavy paper and trace around it. Remove the sloper.

2. Extend the collar neckline ⅝″ beyond the center back of the collar as shown in *Figure 65C*.

3. With your ruler, connect the end of the ⅝″ extended line with the outside edge of the collar as shown in *Figure 65C*.

4. Cut out the collar on the new lines and cut a V notch at the shoulder.

5. Write 2-PIECE COLLAR, CUT 4 on the sloper.

6. To establish the grain line, place the collar sloper at the neckline of a front sloper as shown in *Figure 65D*. The grain line of the collar should be parallel to the grain line of the front sloper. Mark the grain line with your ruler and write GRAIN LINE. Use your awl to punch a hole at the top and bottom of the grain line.

COLLAR DESIGNS

Using your one- or two-piece-collar sloper, you can easily make many different shape collars (*Figure 66*). When you make collar patterns, the design line must not change the collar neckline. The outside edge of the collar may be whatever shape you wish, but the collar neckline must remain the same measurement or the collar will not fit the garment neckline. Because your collar sloper already has seam allowance, you do not need to add seam allowance to your new pattern.

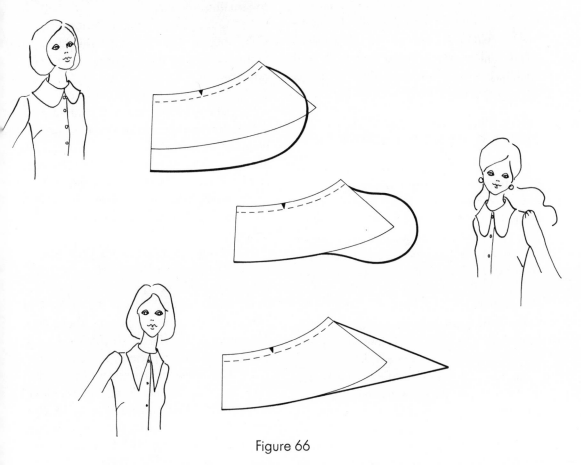

Figure 66

MAKING COLLARS WITHOUT THE COLLAR SLOPER

There are some collars which cannot be made from the collar slopers. These include convertible, man's shirt, neckband, square, and bertha collars. Also in this category are collars for necklines which have been changed from the basic sloper's jewel neckline. For example, you may want to add a round collar to a scoop neck, or a sailor collar to a V neck.

BERTHA COLLARS

The bertha collar is a large one-piece collar which is generally used with back openings. It may be round or square as shown in *Figures 67A* and *F*. To make bertha collars, as well as the other collars which follow, you can use the front and back slopers of the dress, bodice or blouse, or a commercial pattern.

ROUND BERTHA COLLAR

1. Take a sheet of paper about 16″× 24″ and place the front sloper or pattern at the bottom-right side of the paper. Trace around the center front, neckline, shoulder line, and armhole. If your pattern or sloper has a front opening, be sure you mark the center-front line and *not* the extension (*Figure 67B*).

2. Remove the pattern.

3. With your ruler, draw the stitching line of the shoulder ⅝″ below the cutting line of the shoulder (*Figure 67B*).

4. On the back pattern, mark the stitching line on the shoulder the same way. For this purpose, you can draw a straight line, ignoring the shoulder dart.

5. Place the back shoulder on the front shoulder so the stitching lines meet at the neckline as you see in *Figure 67C*. This must be done for the collar to fit the finished neckline.

6. Keeping the shoulder seams together at the neckline, pivot the shoulder at the armhole so the back shoulder overlaps the front shoulder by 1¼″. (See arrow in *Figure 67C*.) This is done to give the collar a slight roll. Be sure that you keep the

shoulder at the neckline from moving while you pivot, or your neckline will become too small or too large.

7. Once you have the back sloper in the right position, put some paperweights on it and trace around the neckline, center back, and armhole.

8. Remove the back pattern.

9. The width of the collar should be ½″ wider than the shoulder line of the garment so that the finished collar extends about ½″ over the armhole seam. Use your ruler to measure the shoulder width.

10. Mark that measurement in several places to indicate the outside edge of your collar.

11. Blend the outline with your French curve. At the center front and center back, the collar should be square (*Figure 67D*).

12. Mark center front, PLACE ON FOLD at the center front of the collar. Also write ROUND BERTHA COLLAR and CUT 2 on the pattern.

13. Cut out your pattern on the cutting line and clip the notch at the shoulder. Your finished pattern should look like *Figure 67E*. When you cut the collar in fabric, remember to trim ⅛″ from the undercollar before you sew the collar together.

SQUARE BERTHA COLLAR

Figure 67F.

1. Follow steps 1 through 9 for round bertha collar above.

2. The front of the collar can be longer than the width at the shoulder, if you like. Decide the length you want your collar.

Measure down from the neckline at the center front and square a line across as you see in *Figure 67G*.

3. At the center back, measure down the same amount plus two inches, and square a line across.

4. To form the corners of the collar, square a line up at the armhole from the bottom collar line about 2″ long in front and in back.

5. With your French curve, blend a line from front to back, following the shape of the armhole. Add 5⁄8″ seam allowance.

6. Write CENTER FRONT and PLACE ON FOLD at the center front of the collar. Write SQUARE BERTHA COLLAR and CUT 2.

7. Cut out your collar pattern and clip the shoulder notch.

8. Your finished pattern should look like *Figure 67H*.

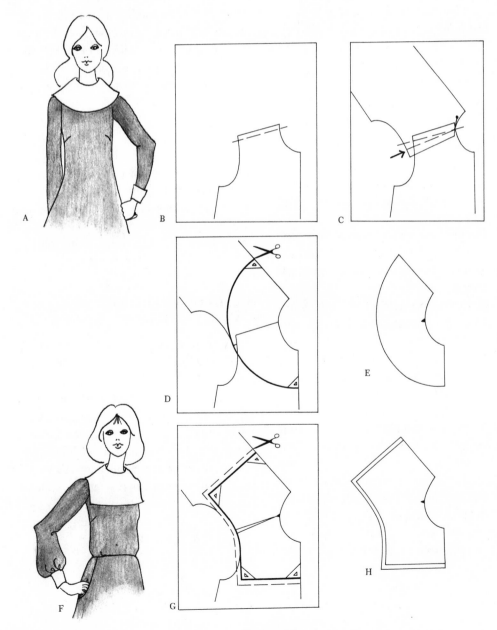

Figure 67

SAILOR COLLARS

A sailor collar can be made as a one-piece collar for a front opening, or as a two-piece collar for a back-opening garment. First you will need to make a V neckline. (See page 121, to make a V-neck pattern.) The steps in making this collar are similar to those in making the square bertha collar above.

BASIC SAILOR COLLAR

Figure 68A.

1. Make a V-neck pattern.

2. Using your V-neck pattern, follow steps 1 through 8 for bertha collar (page 124).

3. Decide how long you want your collar at the back. Measure on the center-back line down from the neckline and mark that amount.

4. Square a line across from the center back where you want the collar to end (*Figure 68B*).

5. From the collar line, square a second line up about two inches near the armhole to form the outer corner of the collar as shown in *Figure 68B*.

6. Mark your stitching line ⅝″ in from the edge of the front V neckline. (See arrows in *Figure 68C*.) Because of the shape of the collar, you must work with the finish line, then add seam allowance.

7. Beginning where the STITCHING line meets the center front (arrow), use your French curve to blend a line to the outer corner of the collar at the back as shown in *Figure 68C*.

8. Add ⅝″ seam allowance to this line.

9. If you're making a two-piece collar, you already have the necessary seam allowance at the center back. For a one-piece collar, remove ⅝″ at the center back.

10. Write the necessary information on the collar.

11. Your finished collar should look like *Figure 68D*.

A one-piece sailor-collar pattern can be used to cut a two-piece collar by adding seam allowance at the center back. The two-piece sailor-collar pattern can be used to cut a one-piece collar by placing the center-back stitching line on the fold, disregarding the center-back seam allowance.

SAILOR-COLLAR VARIATIONS

You can vary this collar by adding nautical trim such as soutache, middy braid, stars, and so on. For a snappy nautical look, make a white dress or blouse and a sailor collar in red or navy, trimmed with white braid. The sailor collar can be dressy too or left plain or trimmed with lace.

The shape of the collar can also vary by making it wide or narrow at the shoulder, long or short in the back. A middy tie or bow in the same or contrasting color can be added at the neck.

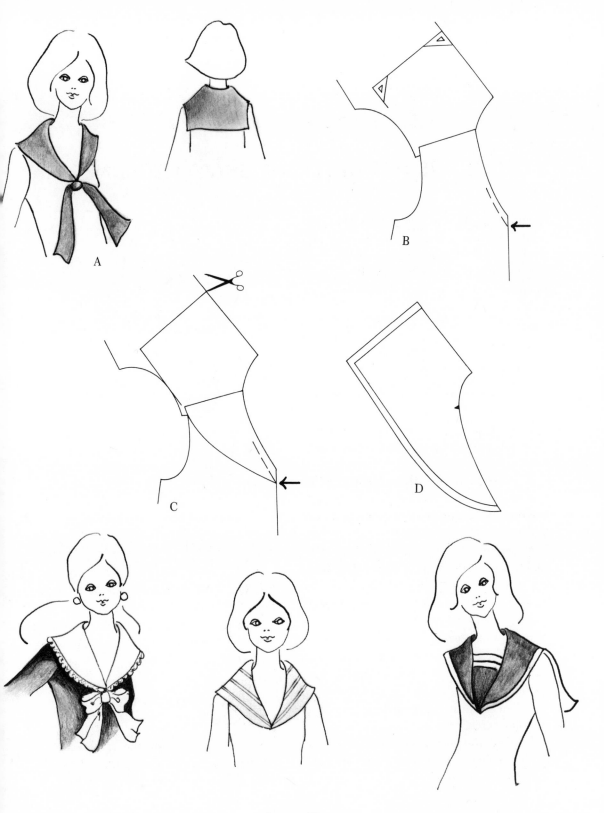

Figure 68

COLLARS FOR DIFFERENT SHAPE NECKLINES

Figure 69. If you have a scoop or other shape neckline pattern, you can also add a collar to it. A scoop neck with a round collar is shown, but the method is the same to make collars for most different shape necklines.

TWO-PIECE COLLAR FOR SCOOP NECK

1. Make scoop-neck pattern front and back.

2. Using the scoop-neck pattern, follow steps 1 through 8 for bertha collar (page 124).

3. Measure in ⅝″ from the cut neckline and mark the stitching line at the center-front and center-back neckline as shown in *Figure 69B.*

4. Beginning at the STITCHING LINE, sketch the shape of your collar, ending at the stitching line in the back, shown by arrows in *Figure 69B.* Use your French curve to blend the line.

5. Add ⅝″ seam allowance to the outer edge of the collar and mark the grain line parallel to the center front as shown (*Figure 69C*).

6. Cut out the collar pattern and the shoulder notch.

7. Write the necessary information. The finished collar pattern for the scoop neck looks like *Figure 69D.*

A

ONE-PIECE COLLAR FOR SCOOP NECK

If you want to make a one-piece collar, the collar outline is squared at the center back as shown in *Figure 69E.* The center back is placed on the fold, which is the grain line.

COLLAR FOR WIDE V NECK

Figure 69F. Follow the same steps as for the scoop neck above, then draw the collar shown in *Figure 69G.*

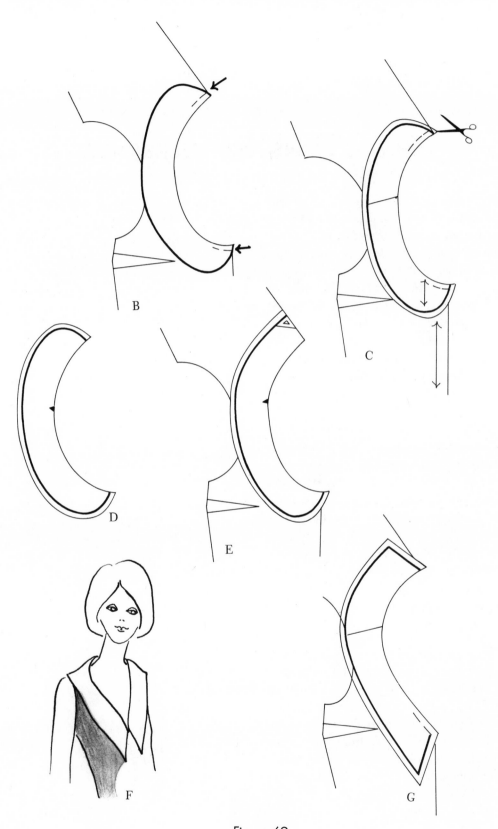

Figure 69

SHIRT COLLARS AND NECKBANDS

The basic pattern for a shirt collar and neckband is quite complicated to make but very easy to redesign. For this reason, use a commercial pattern for the basic collar. To see if the collar will fit your sloper, measure along the STITCHING line of the collar from center back to center front. Compare that measure to the measurement of the front and back neckline of your pattern or sloper. Be sure you measure only the finished stitching line of the neckline and do not include the shoulder-seam allowance. If the collar needs adjustment, add to, or subtract from, the center back.

There are two types of shirt collars, one-part, shown in *Figure 70A,* and two-part, shown in *Figure 70B.* The two-part collar has a separate neckband and fits the neck better than the one-part collar. The neckband of the two-part collar can also be used alone. The shirt-collar variations can be made using either collar.

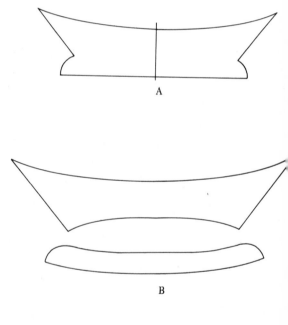

SHIRT-COLLAR VARIATIONS

Figure 70. The shirt collar can be varied by making the points longer (E) or shorter (C), or given a different shape, such as round (F) or dog eared (D). When changing the shape of the collar, be sure you do not add to, or take away from, the collar neckline, or the collar will not fit the neckline of the garment.

Figure 70

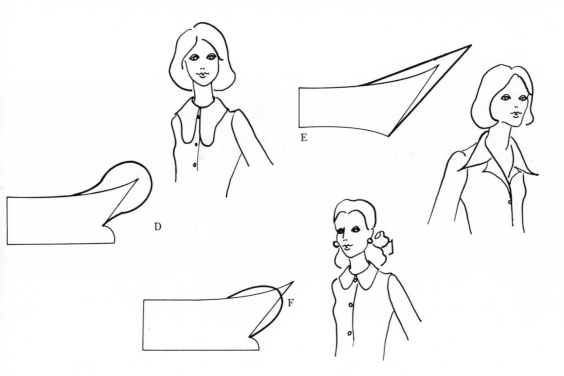

Figure 70

NECKBAND VARIATIONS

Figure 71. You can use the shirt-collar neckband by itself to make a Victorian or Chinese collar. To make the collars in *Figures 71A* and *D,* place the center front of the neckband pattern on the fold and add seam allowance at the center back.

To make the Chinese collar in *Figure 71B,* disregard the extension at the front of the pattern, add ⅝″ seam allowance to the center front, and round the top of the collar.

To make a Victorian collar (*Figure 71C*), add a ruffle of lace or fabric at the top of the neckband and at the neckline too if you like.

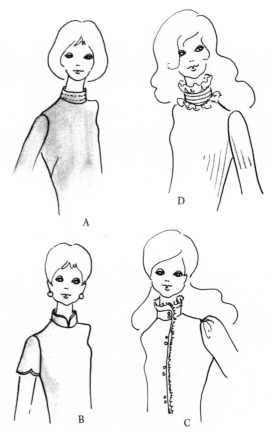

Figure 71

CHAPTER 11

DESIGNING SLEEVES

Don't forget to think about sleeves when designing your patterns. An interesting sleeve can become the focal point of your design. By adding a new sleeve to the basic sloper, you can create a completely new design without making any other changes in the sloper. You can also use the information in this chapter to redesign sleeves from commercial patterns.

In making sleeve patterns, there are only a few different methods, but these methods will enable you to make a large variety of different sleeve designs. The first part of this chapter shows styles made from the basic-sleeve slopers that are quick and easy. The second part of this chapter covers sleeves that take a little more time because they are made by slashing and spreading.

EASY DESIGNS MADE WITH THE SHORT SLEEVE

The simplest way to vary your sleeve sloper is to change the length. The steps are almost the same whichever sloper you use. Once you are used to making a paper pattern to alter the length of the sleeve, you can leave out the step of making a pattern and mark the change directly on the wrong side of your fabric.

TINY SHORT SLEEVE

Figure 72A.

1. Trace around the sloper on a sheet of paper.

2. Mark the top and bottom of the grain line by sticking the point of your

pencil in each hole. Remove the sloper and connect the two dots with your ruler. Mark the line GRAIN LINE.

3. Measure down from the cap along the underarm seam the length you want the new sleeve, and mark as shown in *Figure 72B*. Measure the same amount on the other side of the underarm seam of the sleeve. Don't make the seam less than 2" long. The line across the bottom should not be straight, but arch up as shown. You can use your curve ruler here.

4. Cut out the pattern, and cut notches at the cap.

5. Fold the sleeve pattern in half longways so that the seams meet. If the bottom of the sleeve is not the same on both sides, trim away the irregular part. Also check that the seam is the same length on both sides.

When you sew your sleeve, you will need a facing for the bottom because it is curved. The facing can be a strip of bias, or a shaped facing. If your sleeve is made of heavy fabric, use a lighter weight fabric for the facing so it won't be too bulky. A contrasting pattern or color facing is an attractive designer touch. To make a shaped facing, you will need to mark a facing line on your pattern. Measure up from the bottom edge of the sleeve 2½" and mark the measurement in three or four places, using your red pencil. Connect the lines, and write FACING LINE on your facing pattern which should look like *Figure 72C*. If you have a very short sleeve, make your facing of narrow bias. To mark the facing, when you cut out the facing in fabric, trace around the underarm seams and along the bottom of the sleeve pattern. Then place a sheet of dressmaker's carbon face down between the pattern and the fabric and mark the facing line with your tracing wheel.

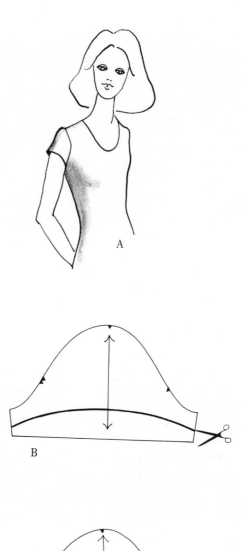

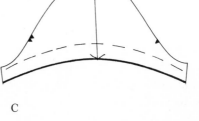

Figure 72

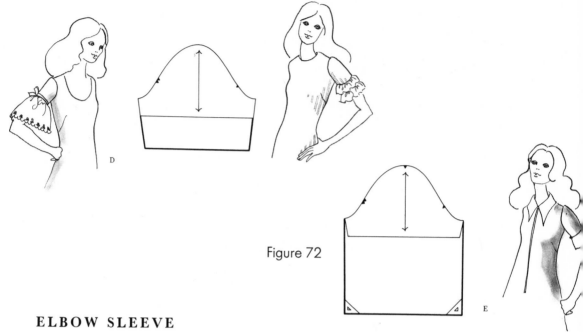

Figure 72

ELBOW SLEEVE

Figure 72D. You can lengthen the short-sleeve sloper to just above the bend of your elbow. Measure your arm where the underarm sleeve seam would be, to figure the length of your sleeve. To lengthen the sleeve:

1. Trace around the sloper on a new sheet of paper and mark the grain line as explained above (*Figure 72D*).

2. Measure down from the mark on each side of the sleeve as described above in shortening the sleeve. The bottom line of the sleeve is arched less than the short sleeve.

3. Cut out the sleeve pattern and the notches at the cap.

4. Fold the pattern in half and check the seams and bottom as explained above. Draw the facing line as explained above.

SHORT-SLEEVE VARIATIONS

You can vary the short sleeve by adding ruffles, braid, and other trims. (Read about ruffles on page 106.) If you use a trim that is not flexible around the bottom of the sleeve, you will have to make the line across the bottom of the sleeve straight instead of curved. You can also add cuffs to the sleeve. (Read about cuffs on page 153.)

ROLL-UP SLEEVE

Figure 72E.

1. Trace the short-sleeve sloper and mark the grain line.

2. With your ruler draw a line from the end of the cap straight down about 12″ (*Figure 72E*). Draw a line the same way on the other side of the cap.

3. Square the bottom line as you see in the drawing.

4. Cut out your sleeve pattern on the new lines and cut the notches at the cap.

5. Fold the pattern in half longways and check that the seams are the same length.

EASY DESIGNS MADE WITH THE LONG FITTED SLEEVE

THREE-QUARTER SLEEVE

Figure 73. You can shorten the long fitted sleeve to about 2″ below the elbow dart.

1. To shorten, trace around your sloper on a new sheet of paper and mark the grain line as explained above for short sleeve.

2. Measure up from the bottom of the sleeve along the seam the amount you want to shorten it, and mark in several places.

3. With your curve rule, connect the marks so that your new line follows the same curve as at the original bottom of the sleeve.

4. Cut out the sleeve pattern and mark the notches.

5. To make a shaped facing for a long sleeve, follow the same steps as for the short sleeve (*Figure 72C*).

OTHER LONG-SLEEVE VARIATIONS

Figure 73. You can vary the long fitted sleeve by adding ruffles, lace, braid, or other trimmings the same as with the short sleeve. You can also vary the sleeve by adding a cuff.

Figure 73

EASY DESIGNS MADE WITH THE SHIRT SLEEVE

THREE-QUARTER SHIRT SLEEVE

Figure 74A. Shorten the shirt-sleeve sloper about 4 to 5″ for a three-quarter sleeve.

1. Trace around the sloper on a sheet of paper and mark the grain line (*Figure 74B*).

2. Using your ruler, measure up from the bottom of the sleeve the amount you want to shorten it. Using your red pencil, mark this amount every 2″ or so, along the bottom of the sleeve.

3. If you want your sleeve to have a button cuff, you'll need a placket slash line. Mark it about 2½″ long as shown.

4. Cut out your sleeve pattern including the notches at the cap. When you shorten the sleeve, you must make the cuff longer because your arm has a greater circumference than your wrist. (See page 154 to make a cuff pattern for this style.)

OTHER SHIRT-SLEEVE VARIATIONS

You can make a number of variations in the shirt sleeve by using a different cuff instead of the regular cuff sloper. Read about cuffs on page 153.

You can also vary the shirt sleeve by omitting the cuff and finishing the end of the sleeve in a number of other different ways.

The sleeve in *Figure 74C* has a drawstring at the end. You don't need to make a different pattern for this. Just make an elastic casing of bias, and thread through a piece of elastic or a spaghetti drawstring. For a wrist-length sleeve, add 2″ to the bottom of your sleeve sloper.

The sleeve in *Figure 74E* does not have a separate ruffle attached to the bottom. The ruffle is made by stretching a piece of elastic the size of your wrist measurement about 2″ to 3″ above the hem of the sleeve and zigzagging the elastic onto the sleeve. The elastic will gather up the end of the sleeve into a ruffle.

The sleeve in *Figure 74F* is made the same way as the sleeve in *Figure 74E* except a longer elastic is stitched at the upper arm.

The sleeve in *Figure 74D* is a basic-sleeve sloper with flat lace stitched at the wrist.

You can also vary the sleeves by adding a variety of different lace, braid, and other trimmings to the sleeve itself or to the cuff if you use one. You can make a sleeve with a lace ruffle at the end by stitching a piece of flat lace to the bottom of the sleeve and then stretching and stitching elastic across the seam which joins the lace to the sleeve the same way the elastic sleeve in *Figure 74E* is finished.

A

B

C

D

E

F

Figure 74

SLEEVES MADE BY SLASHING AND SPREADING

To make a full sleeve, you must slash and spread. This is used to make sleeves such as puffed, leg of mutton, full bishop, and butterfly. If you haven't made a pattern that calls for slashing and spreading before, read about this in Chapter 1, page 13.

Try doing the sleeve first, using your miniature slopers before you use your full-size sloper.

PUFFED SLEEVES

BASIC PUFFED SLEEVE

Figure 75. To make your puffed-sleeve pattern:

1. Trace the back half of the short-sleeve sloper on a piece of paper. Mark the notches at the cap. If you want your puffed sleeve to be longer than the sloper, lengthen the pattern as explained on page 134.

2. *Figure 75A.* Using your ruler, draw five lines to divide your pattern into six sections as you see here. Notice that the first line begins at the notch on the cap. Number each of these sections one to six, beginning at the left.

3. Using your triangle, square a line across the sleeve as you see in *Figure 75A.*

4. Cut out your pattern. This pattern is called the working pattern.

5. Cut along each of the slash lines from the cap to the bottom of the sleeve so that you have six separate pieces.

6. Cut a sheet of paper, about 18″× 36″. Draw a straight line down the center of the paper and mark this line GRAIN LINE.

7. To make your puffed-sleeve pattern, arrange the six pieces of your working pattern in numbered order as you see in *Figure 75B.* Spread the pieces according to how full you want your sleeves. For a full sleeve, leave an inch or more between each piece of the working pattern. For a less puffy sleeve, leave between ½″ and ¾″ between each piece. When you have the pieces of the working pattern arranged the way you want, tape them in place.

8. Using the taped pieces as a guide, draw your new sleeve, adding about ½″ to 1″ at the top and bottom, as you see in *Figure 75B.* Use your French curve and curved rule to blend a smooth line. Mark V notches at the cap and bottom of the sleeve at the end of piece number 1 of the working pattern. When you sew your sleeve, gather between these notches.

9. Clip the tape and discard the pieces of the working pattern. Crease your paper along the grain line and fold it in half.

10. Cut out your sleeve pattern with the paper folded. Cut the V notches and also cut a V notch at the center cap.

11. Open up the pattern, and label it. Your finished puffed-sleeve pattern should look like *Figure 75C*.

To finish the end of the sleeve, read about cuffs on pages 153 to 155 and elastic ruffles on page 136.

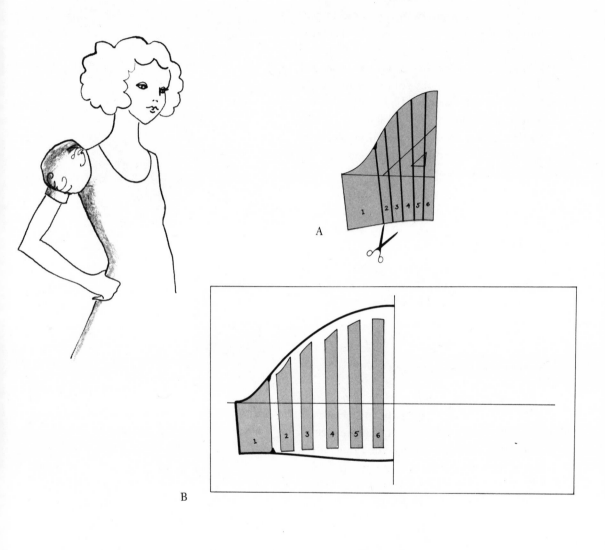

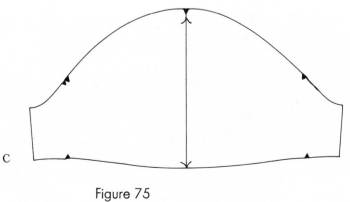

Figure 75

PUFFED-SLEEVE VARIATIONS

The basic puffed sleeve in *Figure 75* was made by placing pieces of the working pattern parallel to each other so that the same amount of fullness is added at the cap and bottom of the sleeve. You can vary the puff sleeve by adding more fullness only at the bottom of the sleeve. The puffed sleeve shown in *Figure 76A* has gathers at the bottom of the sleeve because the pieces of the working pattern are spread only at the bottom and not at the cap.

1940S SLEEVE

Figure 76B. This sleeve is made like the puffed sleeve except fullness is added only at the cap, none at the bottom.

PINAFORE SLEEVE

To make the pinafore sleeve in *Figure 76C*, make the working pattern sleeve very short. Butterfly sleeves and pinafore sleeves look nice combined with the long fitted sleeve for a double sleeve (page 151). Finish the end of the sleeve with a bias facing, french piping, or a rolled hem.

BUTTERFLY SLEEVE

The sleeve pattern for the sleeve in *Figure 76D* is exactly the same pattern as the puffed sleeve; the difference is in construction. The bottom of the sleeve is not gathered, only the cap. You can use the basic puffed-sleeve pattern or the puffed-sleeve pattern in *Figure 76A*.

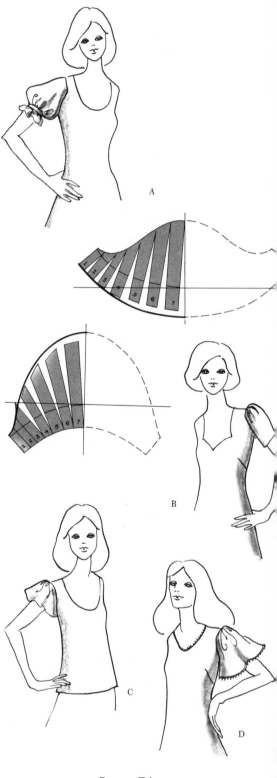

Figure 76

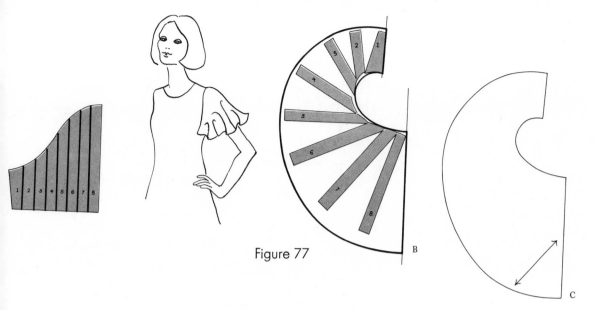

Figure 77

B

C

FLUTTER SLEEVE

Figure 77. This sleeve can be made very full by spreading the pieces very wide at the bottom so your sleeve is almost a full circle. It can also be made with less fullness by spreading the pieces less. In this sleeve, there are no gathers at the cap.

1. Trace the back half of your short-sleeve sloper. Using your ruler, draw seven or eight slash lines parallel to the grain line about ¾″ apart, dividing the sleeve into even sections. Number the sections.

2. Cut out your working pattern. Cut along each of the slash lines so there are seven or eight separate pieces.

3. Cut a sheet of paper about 15″× 20″. Draw a straight line along the right side of your paper for the grain line.

4. Place the pieces of your working pattern as shown in *Figure 77B.* In this drawing the pieces are spread very widely which will give you a very full sleeve. Spread the pieces less if you want a sleeve without as much fullness. Notice that there is more space between the pieces of the working pattern near the grain line and that the pieces are closer together near the underarm seam. Once you have the pieces arranged, tape them in place.

5. Draw the outline of your new pattern, using the working pattern as a guide. The bottom of the sleeve should dip about one inch below the working pattern, at the grain line, as you see in *Figure 77B.* Use your French curve to blend a smooth line.

6. Cut the strips of the working pattern and discard them.

7. Cut out your new pattern. Your finished pattern should look like *Figure 77C.* Because of the large shape of this pattern, it is easier to make just half of it. Place the fold on the straight grain of your fabric. The edge of the sleeve can be finished with a strip of bias, rolled hem, or shaped facing. This pattern works very well with the grain line on the bias. To mark a bias grain line, place your triangle so the short side is on the grain line. The long side of the triangle will be bias. Draw a line along the long side of the triangle and mark it, BIAS.

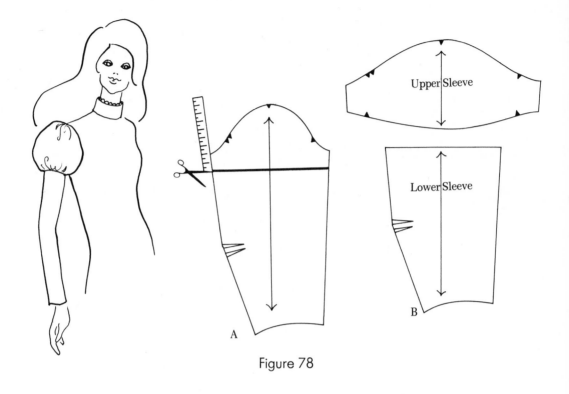

Figure 78

JULIETTE SLEEVE

Figure 78. This sleeve is made by combining a puffed-sleeve pattern with part of the long fitted-sleeve pattern. For the top of the sleeve you can use any puffed-sleeve pattern. To make the rest of the pattern:

1. Trace your long fitted-sleeve sloper.

2. Measure the underarm seam of your puffed sleeve and subtract 1¼" from that measurement. With your ruler, measure down from the cap at the underarm seam of the long fitted sleeve that amount, as you see in *Figure 78A.* For example, if the underarm seam of your puffed sleeve measures three inches, measure down 1¾" at the seam of your long fitted sleeve (3" minus 1¼"). Measure the same amount on the other side of your sleeve.

3. Connect the marks on each side of your sleeve with a straight line as you see in *Figure 78A.*

4. Cut out your sleeve pattern on this line.

5. When you sew the sleeve, gather the bottom of the puffed sleeve, if it has gathers, and join the bottom of the puffed sleeve to the top of the long fitted sleeve.

This is a very romantic-looking sleeve and looks very good in old-fashioned patterns like calico prints, gingham checks, or challis. It also works well in knits. To vary this sleeve, use a plaid or check and cut the bottom of the sleeve on the straight grain and the puffed part of the sleeve on the bias. You can also add interest to the sleeve by adding trimming at the seam, which joins the top and bottom of the sleeve, or at the wrist. You might make the top of the sleeve in one fabric and the bottom of the sleeve in a different fabric.

LEG-OF-MUTTON SLEEVE

Figure 79. Like the Juliette sleeve, this has a romantic old-fashioned look. It is very effective made in velveteen or in prints like calico, trimmed with rickrack or lace edging. To make this pattern:

1. Trace your long fitted-sleeve sloper; mark your notches at the cap.

2. With a contrasting colored pencil, draw your slash lines as follows. Measure down along the grain line from the cap and mark a point at 4″ and at 6″. On each side of the sleeve measure down from the cap and mark 1½″ and 3″. Connect the marks from the seam to the grain line as shown in *Figure 79A.*

3. Cut out your pattern. Cut along the grain line from the cap to the slash lines.

Cut each slash line to within ⅛″ of the seam.

4. Cut a new sheet of paper about 18″ square.

5. Place the sleeve cap of the working pattern on the paper, and spread as shown. You can spread from 1″ to 2″, but opposite pieces must be spread the same amount. Once you have the cap spread correctly, tape it in place.

6. Blend in a new cap line with your French curve. Extend the grain line.

7. Cut out the new part of the pattern on the new line and cut the cap notches. When you sew the sleeve, gather the cap between the notches.

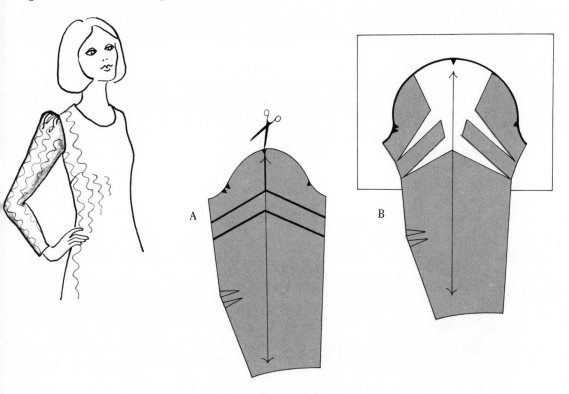

A   B

Figure 79

TRUMPET SLEEVE

Figure 80. This sleeve is fitted at the upper arm and flares out below the elbow. It differs from the bell sleeve because the bell sleeve is loose all the way up. This sleeve is actually the opposite of the leg-of-mutton sleeve. In the leg-of-mutton sleeve, you slash and spread above the elbow dart. In this sleeve, you slash and spread below the elbow dart.

To make the trumpet-sleeve pattern:

1. Trace the long fitted-sleeve sloper; mark the notches and the grain line.

2. Extend the bottom line of each elbow dart to the grain line as you see in *Figure 80A.*

3. Draw a slash line from the extended dart line to the middle of the sleeve at the wrist as you see in *Figure 80A.*

4. Cut out the sleeve pattern and cut along the slash line from the wrist up to the extended elbow dart.

5. Crease the extended lines of the elbow darts and tape the elbow darts closed. The pattern will open up at the wrist as you see in *Figure 80B.* Your darts should be taped closed so that your working pattern lays flat.

6. Mark two L-shaped slash lines below the elbow dart as you see in *Figure 80C.* Make two slash lines exactly the same on the other side of the sleeve. The slash lines must be exactly the same on each side of the sleeve or your seams of the sleeve won't fit together.

7. Cut a sheet of paper about twice the size of your sleeve sloper and place your working pattern on the paper. Spread the pieces as you see in *Figure 80D.* There should be about the same amount of space between each piece. Once the pieces are arranged, tape them in place.

8. Trace around the pattern and use your French curve or curved rule to blend a smooth line at the bottom of the sleeve.

9. Cut out the new sleeve. Fold the sleeve in half longways and check to be sure both sides are exactly the same. Make corrections, if you need to, at the seam.

10. Your finished sleeve pattern should look like *Figure 80E.*

You can finish the end of the sleeve with a facing. Measure up $2\frac{1}{2}''$ from the sleeve for your facing line. You can also finish the end of the sleeve with bias or with a narrow rolled hem.

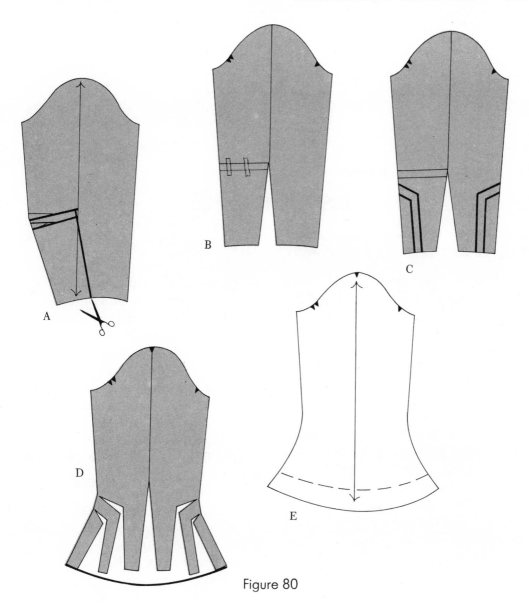

Figure 80

DESIGNING SLEEVE PATTERNS WITH
THE SHIRT SLEEVE

Making sleeve patterns using a shirt-sleeve sloper is just about the same as making patterns with the short-sleeve sloper. The main difference is that when you use the shirt-sleeve sloper, you make the entire pattern because the front and back have a slightly different shape.

BISHOP SLEEVES

BASIC BISHOP SLEEVE

Figure 81. The bishop sleeve is a full version of the shirt sleeve. To make this pattern:

1. Trace the shirt-sleeve sloper and mark grain line, notches, and placket line.

2. Make your slash lines the same as for puffed sleeves: Beginning at the grain line, with your ruler draw parallel lines about ¾″ apart to divide the sleeve into ten sections as you see in *Figure 81A.* Notice that the first and last slash lines are at the notches on the cap. You do not slash beyond the notches on the cap. Number the pieces of the working pattern.

3. Cut out the pattern and cut along the slash line from the bottom to within ⅛″ of the cap.

4. Cut a sheet of paper about 30″× 30″. With your yardstick, draw the grain line down the center of the paper.

5. Carefully place the slashed working pattern on the paper.

6. Spread the pieces of your working pattern so there is about ¾″ to 1½″ between each piece at the back and about ½″to 1″ between each piece at the front. The back should be spread slightly more than the front. Once the working pattern is spread properly, tape the pieces in place.

7. With your curve stick, blend the bottom of the sleeve, using the pieces of the working pattern as a guide. Notice that at the middle of the back of the sleeve, there is a dip of about one inch. This gives the sleeve more puffiness.

8. Mark the placket line and the notches of the working pattern in the same place on the new pattern.

9. Clip the tape and discard the pieces of your working pattern.

10. Cut out your new pattern. Your finished pattern should look like *Figure 81C.*

A

B

C

Figure 81

BISHOP-SLEEVE VARIATIONS

You can vary the bishop sleeve by adding gathers at the cap as well as at the wrist. To make this pattern, follow the directions for making the bishop sleeve in *Figure 81*, except slash each piece of the working pattern all the way through so that you have 10 separate pieces. Spread the pieces so that you have from 1/2" to 3/4" between each piece at the cap. Use your French curve to blend a new cap line. Blend a wristline the same as explained above. The pattern should look like *Figure 82A*. You can vary the bishop sleeve by changing the gathers at the cap or the wrist into tucks or pleats as you see in *Figure 82B*. After you've stitched your tucks or pleats, the cap or wrist will become somewhat jagged. Use your original sloper as a guide as to how much to take in at the cap or the wrist. After you sew in the tucks or pleats, retrace the cap and wristlines from the original sloper to smooth off the jaggedness. You can also vary the sleeve by adding different trimmings or ruffles, or by using different style cuffs.

The bishop sleeve can also be varied by adding an elastic casing at the hem of the sleeve or by adding elastic and a wide band of lace (*Figure 82C*).

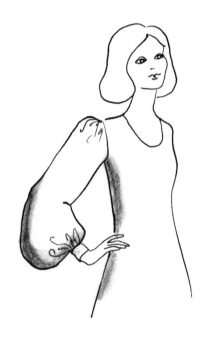

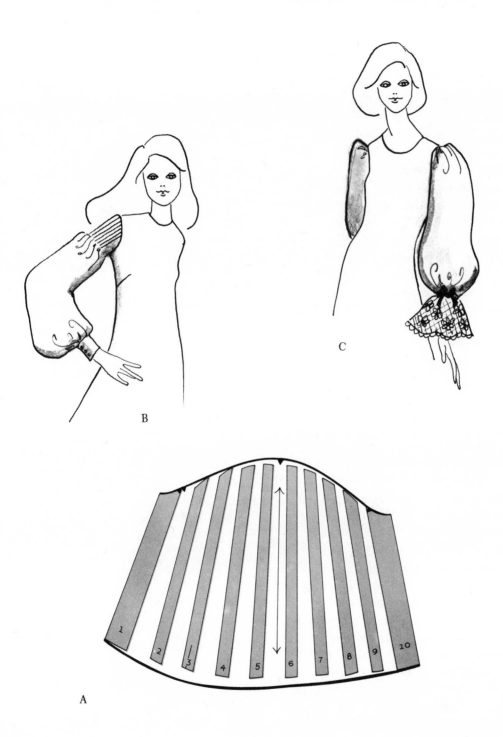

Figure 82

BELL SLEEVES

Figure 83. The pattern for bell sleeves is almost the same as for the bishop sleeve. The difference being that it has no gathers at the wrist. Because the sleeve hangs freely, it works best in soft or sheer fabric. Follow the directions for making a bishop-sleeve pattern, with or without the gathers at the cap, whichever you prefer (*Figures 83A and B*). If you want the bell sleeve wrist length, you will need to add two inches to your working pattern, because the basic shirt-sleeve sloper is shorter, to allow for a cuff.

You can finish the end of the sleeve with bias facing, a shaped facing, or a rolled hem. For a shaped facing, draw a facing line 2½″ up from the bottom of the sleeve.

BELL-SLEEVE VARIATIONS

The sleeve in *Figure 83C* is a bell sleeve with gathers at the cap. It has elastic stitched across it in a straight line about 7″ below the center of the cap. You can stretch the elastic and stitch it with a zig-zag stitch, or make an elastic casing and pull the elastic through the casing. This effect can also be achieved with a draw-string threaded through lace beading.

You can also vary the sleeve by adding different trimmings such as rows of lace, gathered or flat, braid, ruffles, etc. This sleeve looks nice made out of lace or eyelet with the rest of the garment made out of a solid fabric. Because it is loose, it won't interfere with the bending of your elbow, and it can be whatever length you want. If you are using a stripe, check, or plaid, the sleeve might look attractive cut on the bias.

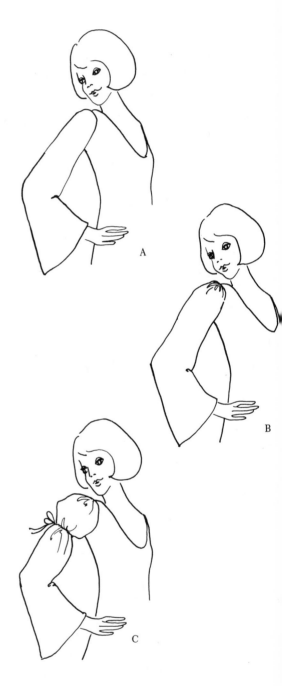

Figure 83

Figure 84

DOUBLE SLEEVES

You can make a number of new sleeve styles by combining two sleeves as you see in *Figure 84*. The long fitted sleeve works well with a short full sleeve such as the butterfly, pinafore, or flutter sleeve. You can also combine the shirt sleeve with the short full sleeve.

Another combination is two of the same sleeve, one a little longer than the other. The butterfly, bell, or flutter sleeves could work this way. Both sleeves can be made from the same fabric or one from contrasting fabric. For example, you might make the undersleeve on the straight grain and the upper sleeve on the bias. The upper sleeve could be a sheer over a different fabric undersleeve, or eyelet sleeve over a solid sleeve. The double sleeve can also be effective using the same print in two different color combinations.

Figure 85

CUFFS

CUFFS FOR FITTED SLEEVES

The cuffs in *Figure 85* are used on a sleeve that does not have gathers at the bottom. You can use them on any length sleeve: the short sleeve, long fitted sleeve, three quarter, and so on. The easiest cuff for this kind of sleeve is a bias turnback cuff (*Figure 85A*). You don't need to make a pattern for this. It is simply a folded band of bias which is, as the name says, turned back. For each cuff, cut a length of bias a little longer than your sleeve. To figure the width of the bias, double the width of your finished cuff and add $1\frac{1}{4}''$ for seam allowance. For example, if you want your finished cuff $1\frac{1}{2}''$, double that is $3''+1\frac{1}{4}''=4\frac{1}{4}''$ wide (the width to cut your bias). The easiest way to attach this cuff is to join it to the sleeve while the sleeve is still open. Then stitch the underarm seam with a french seam to hide the raw edge. You can add design interest by making the cuff out of a contrasting fabric. When using a plaid, stripe, or other patterned fabric, you will achieve contrast because the bias cuff is a different grain from the sleeve. You can also topstitch a narrow lace edging or other trim to the cuff before applying the cuff to the sleeve (*Figure 85B*).

SELF-CUFF SLEEVE

Figure 85C. This sleeve is made with the cuff and sleeve all together as one pattern piece. This works best in lightweight to medium-weight fabric. In heavier fabric it will become too bulky.

1. Trace your sleeve sloper and mark the notches and grain line.

2. With your ruler, straighten the bottom line of the sleeve as you see in *Figure 85D* (Line A).

3. Measure down from Line A the width you want your cuff and draw another line parallel to Line A (Line B).

4. Measure down the same amount again and draw a third line (Line C).

5. Measure the same amount once more and draw the hemline so that you have four parallel lines the same distance apart.

6. Crease along Line B, and fold the bottom of the sleeve under as you see in *Figure 85E*.

7. Keeping the two layers of paper together, crease along Line A and fold under as you see in *Figure 85F*. Use paper clips at the bottom of the sleeve to hold the cuff in place.

8. Cut out your sleeve at the sides and cap. Open up your sleeve and cut notches at each end of Line A and Line C as you see in *Figure 85G*. Cut along the hemline.

9. Your finished sleeve pattern should look like *Figure 85G*. When you sew your sleeve, fold the sleeve so the cuff is to the right side, matching the two notches at lines A and C. Finish with a french seam at the underarm.

CUFFS FOR GATHERED SLEEVES

You can use your basic-cuff sloper with the basic shirt sleeve and with long variations of the shirt sleeve such as the bishop.

To make the cuff narrower or wider, trace your cuff sloper on the wrong side of the fabric and then add or subtract the amount you want. Remember that if you make a cuff narrower or wider, you will need to adjust the sleeve by the same amount so the total sleeve will remain the same length. For example, if you make your cuff one inch wider, make your sleeve one inch shorter. If you make the cuff one inch narrower, add an inch to the sleeve.

You can also vary the cuff by adding gathered lace or a ruffle (*Figure 86A*). In this case a separate under and upper cuff are needed because the lace or ruffle must go into a seam. To make the pattern, fold your cuff sloper along the fold line, and trace the sloper. Measure down from the fold line 5/8″ and draw a line to add seam allowance (*Figure 86A*). Cut out your new cuff pattern. You will need to cut four in fabric instead of the usual two.

FRENCH CUFF

Figure 86B. You can use your cuff sloper as a pattern for a french cuff. Just cut four cuffs instead of two. Construct the french cuff as you would a regular cuff. A french cuff looks nice with gathered lace around three sides.

ALL-AROUND CUFF

Figure 86C. This style cuff has no opening. It can be used on a sleeve of any length—short puffed, three quarter, bishop, and so on. You can make a pattern, or mark directly on the wrong side of the fabric.

1. To figure the length of the cuff, measure the circumference of your arm where the sleeve will end. Add to this measurement 2¼″ for ease and seam allowance.

2. To figure the width of the cuff, decide how wide you want the finished cuff, double that amount and add 1¼″. For example, to make a cuff that is 1″ finished, double that is 2″+1¼″=3¼″ (the width to cut the cuff).

If you are making a wrist cuff, be sure that it is large enough to put your hand through. Measure your hand at the widest part to check.

BUTTON CUFFS FOR SHORTER SLEEVES

Figure 86D. The cuff sloper will work only with a long sleeve. For a short or three-quarter sleeve, you need a new cuff pattern because your arm is bigger than your wrist. The pattern is almost the same as for the all-around cuff above.

1. To figure the length of the cuff, measure the circumference of your arm where the sleeve will end. Add to this measurement 4¼″ for overlap, ease, and seam allowance.

2. To figure the width of the cuff, follow Step 2 given above for all-around cuff.

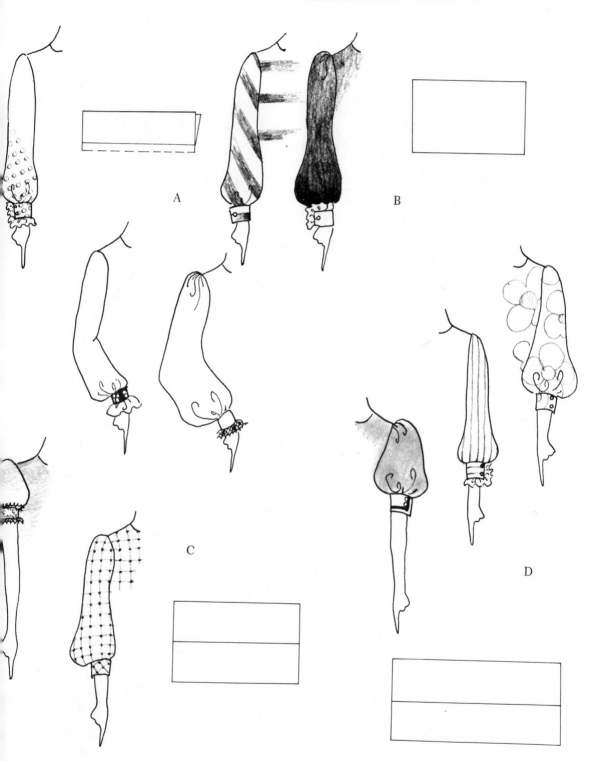

A

B

C

D

Figure 86

DESIGNS MADE FROM THE A-LINE SLOPER

The A-line sloper can be used to make a tremendous number of styles in any length. From the A-line you can make dresses with yokes, smocks, tent and flared shapes, princess line, and halter styles. Besides dresses, the sloper can be used to make patterns for jumpers, vests, coats, and jackets. You can use the croquis (page 75) to sketch your ideas and try out new patterns with the miniature slopers.

Figure 87

EASY-TO-MAKE A-LINE STYLES

You can design many new styles using the basic sloper as the front and back pattern and adding trimming, such as a row of buttons or band of lace, ruffles, a new sleeve or collar, pockets and so on. A new neckline can change the look of the sloper significantly. The styles shown in *Figure 87* are made using the basic sloper combined with patterns and design details covered in chapters 8 through 11.

ADDING A CENTER-FRONT SEAM

Adding a seam at the center front is very easy and can be an attractive design feature (*Figure 88*). The seam looks important when topstitched or saddle stitched in a matching or contrasting color thread. You can continue the topstitching around the neck and sleeves too. A center-front seam may also be used for a zipper opening. In that case remember to cut your back on the fold. You don't really need to make a new pattern if you are not making any other changes in the sloper. Just trace around the sloper on the wrong side of the fabric, then with your ruler add 5/8″ seam allowance to the center front.

Figure 88

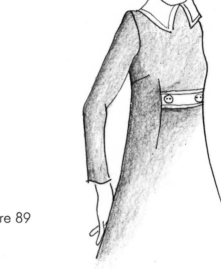

Figure 89

ADDING DARTS AT THE FRONT WAIST

You can achieve a closer fit by adding darts at the front waist the same as you have at the back waist (*Figure 89*). No pattern is necessary. After you sew the center-back and side seams of your garment try it on and pin the darts in place. Begin the darts 1½″ below the bust point, pinning a small amount of fabric to shape the dress in at the waist. The darts should be parallel to the side seam (that is, not straight up and down) to look more graceful. You can make a very pretty dress by inserting a sash or belt into the waistline darts, either at the natural waistline or under the bosom. The belt can tie or button in back. See Chapter 9 on how to make different kinds of sashes.

LONG-DRESS PATTERN

1. On a long piece of paper trace around your A-line sloper.

2. (See *Figure 90*). Figure the amount you need to add to your sloper to make it the length that you need. Don't forget to include three inches for hem allowance.

3. Extend the center-front line with your yardstick.

4. Measure down from the original hemline, and mark the added length on the center-front line.

5. Extend the side seam and measure down from the hem the same amount on the side seam as at the center front.

6. With your curved ruler, draw a new hemline the same shape as the original hemline.

7. Cut out your new pattern.

8. Follow the same steps to make the back pattern.

If you like, you can eliminate the step of making the paper pattern and mark the additional length directly on the wrong side of your fabric after you trace the A-line sloper or pattern on the fabric.

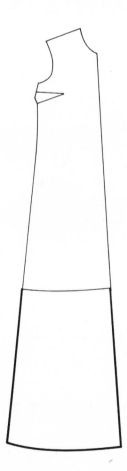

Figure 90

Figure 91

SASHED, DRAWSTRING, AND ELASTIC WAISTLINES

Figure 91. You can change the look of the basic A-line or a new pattern by adding a sash or drawstring tie at the waistline or under the bust. To make an elastic casing, cut a strip of bias the width of the elastic plus 1½″. Press the raw edge under on each side of the bias and stitch the bias strip to the wrong side of the dress. For comfort, use soft elastic.

For a drawstring waist, the ties can be stitched and turned or made of spaghetti. Cut the casing for a drawstring the same as the elastic casing above. Before you stitch the casing to the dress, make two buttonholes at the center front to pull each end of the tie through. The tie should be the measurement of your waist plus 30″. This idea works well with the flared A-line and yoke styles as well as the basic A-line.

To make sashes, see page 113.

You can achieve a similar effect using smocking or shirring at the waistline (page 116).

CHANGING THE POSITION OF THE BUST DART

The basic sloper has the bust dart at the side seam. This dart can be easily moved to the armhole, shoulder, or the neckline as shown in *Figure 92A.* When there is a center-front seam, the dart can also be moved to the center front.

MOVING BUST DART TO SHOULDER

1. Trace your sloper and cut out the pattern.

2. (See *Figure 92B.*) On your new pattern, mark a point one half inch in from the dart point. With your ruler, draw a straight line from the dart point up to the shoulder seam. This line indicates the position of your new dart.

3. Slash along the new dart line to the bust point.

4. Crease your original dart and tape it closed. A space will open up at the shoulder indicating the new dart (*Figure 92C*).

5. To finish the pattern, tape a piece of paper to the back of the pattern so that it fills in the space where the new dart opened. Your new dart must be shortened by one inch so as not to extend all the way to the bust point (*Figure 92D*). Mark a

point one inch up from the end of the slash and draw your dart as shown.

6. To arrive at the correct shape at the shoulder seam, you must close the dart before cutting the pattern shoulder. Crease the dart on the new line and close it so the fold of the dart is toward the armhole. (If the fold extends beyond the armhole, fold the dart toward the neckline.) Your pattern won't lie flat. Tape the dart closed and cut along the shoulder seam. Open the dart.

7. Punch a hole at the point of the dart with your awl and clip V notches at the end of the dart lines.

8. Your finished pattern should look like *Figure 92E.*

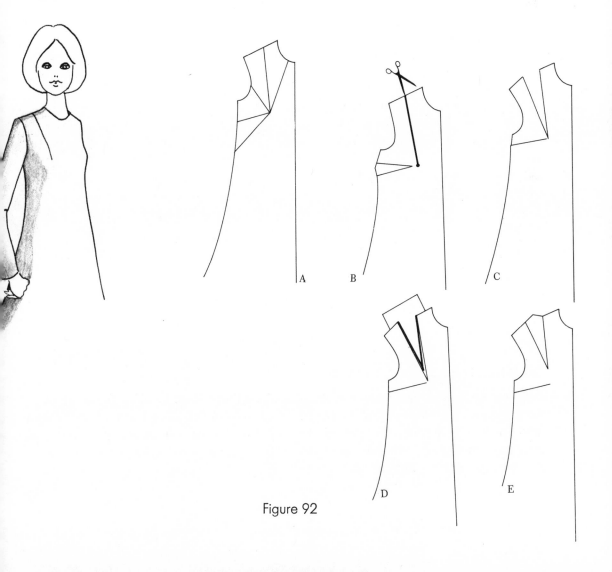

Figure 92

Figure 93

OTHER DART POSITIONS

Figure 93 shows some other dart locations. Follow the same steps to move the dart as given in moving the dart to the shoulder. Draw your dart line from the bust point to where you want the dart to end. Remember to shorten the finished dart one inch. These sketches are only suggestions; a dart can be placed anywhere in between the darts shown.

DARTLESS KNIT DRESSES

T-SHIRT DRESS

Figure 94. Because it has no darts, this style works best in stretchy knit fabrics. Trace your front sloper. Remove the bust dart, following the directions given on page 263, using the A-line sloper instead of the blouse sloper. Then change the neckline if you want. Trace your back sloper. Disregard the waistline dart. Remove the shoulder dart, following the same directions given on page 263.

If your T-shirt dress design has a crew neck, trim away 5⁄8" seam allowance at the neckline of the front and back patterns. When you sew this dress, you may want to shape in the side seam a little more at the waistline to make up for not having waistline darts. Finish the end of the sleeves and the neckline with ribbing.

If you use pockets, you can finish the tops of the pockets with ribbing also.

Figure 94

KNIT-DRESS VARIATIONS

A T-shirt dress can be made with long or short sleeves, with or without ribbing. It can be made sleeveless like a tank top. (Be sure to make the armhole adjustment for sleeveless.) If your T-shirt dress has a scoop neckline, you can omit the center-back opening and make it to pull on over your head. Cut it with the center-back stitching line of the pattern on the fold.

This style can also be made with no ribbing or facing. Turn the raw edge at the neck and sleeve or armhole 5⁄8″ wide to the wrong side. Topstitch with two rows of straight stitch or one row of zigzag. For contrast, the sleeves or collar and cuffs can be made of woven fabric in a pattern or a different color.

SLEEVELESS DRESSES

A sleeveless dress is not simply a dress with the sleeve taken out. The armhole of a dress with a set-in sleeve is larger and the shoulder seam wider to allow for ease of movement. With no sleeve, the armhole should be made smaller and the shoulder and side seams fitted more closely or your dress will have a big armhole which looks very unattractive. I know the pattern companies will show the same pattern both with a sleeve and without a sleeve, but this really is unprofessional. The armhole will be either too tight with the sleeve set in, or too loose if sleeveless. The changes needed are very simple and worth the few extra minutes. If you live in a warm climate and make a lot of sleeveless clothes, you may want to make a sloper with a sleeveless armhole.

BASIC SLEEVELESS DRESS

1. Trace your front sloper on a new piece of paper (*Figure 95A*).
2. Measure in at the shoulder seam 1⁄2″ and mark.

3. At the armhole, measure in from the side seam 1⁄2″ and mark.
4. Extend the side seam up 1⁄2″ from this mark as shown.
5. Draw a new armhole with your French curve by connecting the raised side seam with the mark on the shoulder seam.
6. Blend a line from the original side-seam line to the new armhole.
7. Cut out your pattern, following the new side seam and armhole.
8. Follow the same steps, using the back sloper.

When you make any of the design variations in this chapter as sleeveless styles, make the armhole adjustments first, then check the directions to see if you should cut out the pattern next or not. Continue the pattern steps as given in the directions for a regular armhole.

EXTENDED SHOULDER

Figure 95B. This armhole looks especially attractive on a dress with a center-front seam. Adjust the side seam and raise

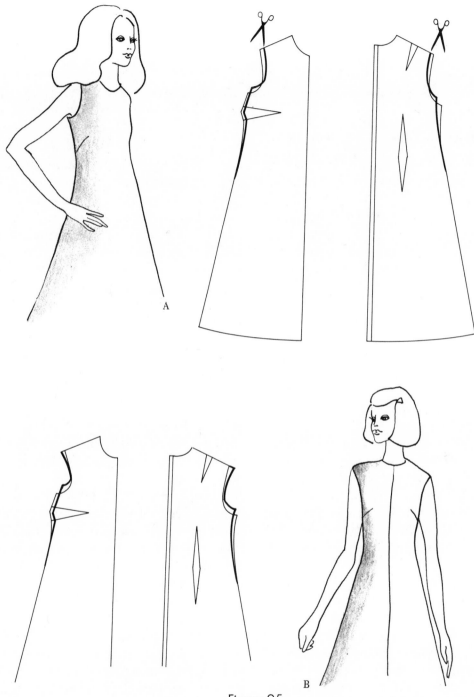

Figure 95

the armhole as described above for sleeveless. Extend the shoulder seam ½″ to 1″ instead of making it narrower as you would for a regular sleeveless dress. With your French curve, mark your new armhole. Make the same adjustments on the back pattern.

HALTERS

BARE HALTER ARMHOLE

Figure 96. This armhole is cut in, to bare the shoulders, and cut low at the underarm.

1. Trace your sloper on a new piece of paper.

2. Make the adjustment at the side seam for sleeveless armhole given in *Figure 95A.*

3. Cut out your pattern.

4. Move the bust dart to the french dart position. (See page 160 on shifting darts.) The dart is moved so that it won't interfere with the new armhole shape.

5. (See *Figure 96A.*) At the shoulder seam, measure in from the armhole from 2″ to 3½″ and mark.

6. At the side seam, measure down from the armhole from 1″ to 3″ and mark.

7. Shape your new armhole, using your French curve to join the two marks.

8. Draw the facing line as shown. Keep the facing above the point of the bust dart.

9. Cut out your pattern on the new armhole line.

If you are planning to change the neckline, do not do so until you make the back pattern. Because you have made the front-shoulder seam smaller, when you make your back pattern you must be sure the shoulder seam of the back pattern is exactly the same as the shoulder seam of the front pattern, otherwise the front and back of your garment won't fit together properly. Making the front- and the back-shoulder seams the same is called trueing the shoulder seam.

10. (See *Figure 96B.*) Trace the back sloper (shown in black).

11. Place the front pattern (shown in dotted line) face down on the back pattern so that the shoulder seam at the front neck and back neckline meet (see arrow) and the shoulder seams of the front and back line up together as shown.

12. Beginning at the shoulder seam, trace about 2″ of the front armhole onto the back pattern. Ignore the shoulder dart as it is omitted from this pattern.

13. Remove your front pattern.

Because the armhole was lowered, the side seam of the front pattern is shorter than on the original sloper. Therefore you must also true the side seam to be sure that the side seam on your back pattern is exactly the same length as the side seam of the front pattern. This follows the same steps as trueing the shoulder seam explained above. When the bust dart ends at the side seam, you must tape the dart closed before trueing the side seam. Once you tape the dart closed, the pattern won't lie flat. Let the center front curl around.

14. (See *Figure 96C.*) Place the new front pattern (shown in dotted line) face down on the back pattern so that the side seam of the front and side seam of the back are lined up together and the front hem and back hem meet. (See arrow.) Use tape or paperweights to hold the front pattern properly positioned on the back pattern.

15. Beginning at the side seam, trace

about 2″ of the front armhole onto the back pattern.

16. Remove the front pattern.

17. Using your French curve, blend a new armhole, connecting the trueing marks at the shoulder seam with the trueing marks at the side seam as you see in *Figure 96D*.

Straighten the shoulder seam if necessary, to remove the jog, at the shoulder dart. Draw in your facing line.

18. Cut out your new pattern, cutting along your new armhole line.

19. Your finished pattern should look like *Figure 96E*.

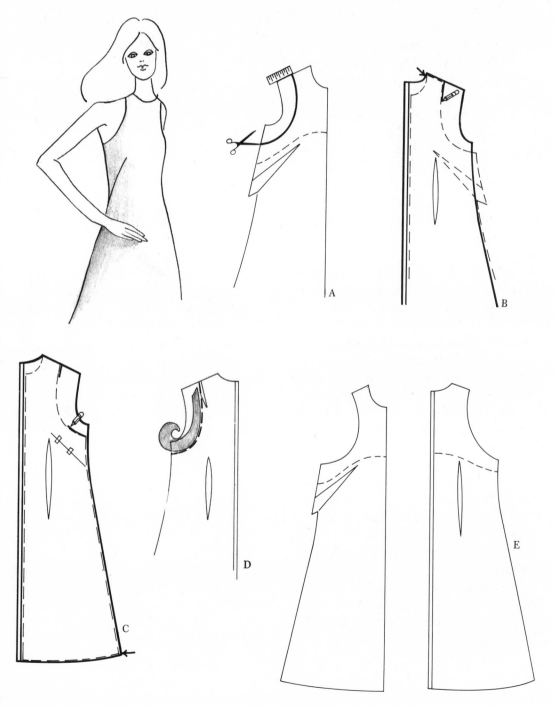

Figure 96

HALTER TOP WITH BARE BACK

Figure 97.

1. Trace the front sloper, making the adjustments at the side seam for a sleeveless pattern. You don't need to change the armhole because the armhole will be cut away in this pattern.

2. Cut out your pattern.

3. Shift down to the french dart position. (See SHIFTING DARTS, page 160.)

4. (See *Figure 97A.*) At the side seam, measure down from the armhole 1"–2" and mark.

5. With your curved rule, draw the design line from this mark to the center front at the neckline as shown.

6. Draw your facing line. Be sure your facing line is above the point of the bust dart.

7. Trace your back sloper and make the same adjustments for sleeveless on the back sloper at the side seam.

8. True the side seam so that the front and back side seams are the same length as explained for halter armhole (*Figure 96C.*)

9. After you mark the front armhole on the back pattern, use your curved rule to blend your design line from the new armhole at the side seam to the center back as shown in *Figure 97B.* Dip the line slightly from the side seam to the center back. It's all right if the top of the waistline dart is cut off.

10. Draw your facing line. When you cut your facing, close the dart on the back pattern so that you don't have a dart in the facing.

11. Cut out the pattern. Use spaghetti or ribbons for halter ties at the neckline. You'll need two ties about fourteen inches long each.

Figure 97

A-LINE DRESSES WITH FLARED SKIRTS

You can make a great many new styles with your A-line sloper by adding flare to the skirt. You can add a small amount of flare at the side seams or, for more fullness, use slashing and spreading. Flare can also be added by using godets. Any of these variations will work with a long skirt as well.

SKIRT FLARED AT SIDE SEAM

Figure 98.

1. Trace your A-line sloper.

2. At the hemline, measure out from the side seam from 1″ to 4″ and mark with a point (*Figure 98A*).

3. Blend a line from the original side seam to the new point. For a looser silhouette, begin the new side seam just below the bust dart. For closer fit in the torso, begin the new side-seam line below the waist.

4. With your curved ruler, extend the hemline to meet the new side seam. Do not make a straight line at the hemline.

5. Cut out your front pattern, following the new side-seam line.

6. Your back pattern must have the same shape side seam as the front (*Figure 98B*). Trace the back sloper (shown in black). Measure out from the hemline at the side seams the same amount as you measured at the front, and mark a point.

7. Place the front pattern (shown in dotted line) face down on top of the back pattern so that the center-front and center-back lines are parallel and the hem of the

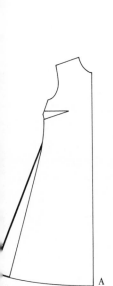
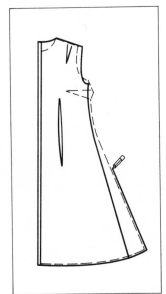

A   B   C

Figure 98

front meets the hem of the back. The center front may extend beyond the center back; that is all right as long as they are parallel.

8. Trace the side seam of the front pattern onto the back pattern.

9. Remove the front pattern.

10. Blend your new side-seam line into the original side seam. Extend the hemline to the new side seam.

11. Cut out your pattern, following the new side-seam line.

12. The finished back pattern should look like *Figure 98C.*

FLARED SKIRTS MADE BY SLASHING AND SPREADING

If you want more than a slight flare in your dress, you need to use slashing and spreading. You can vary the silhouette of your dress by the way that the pattern is spread and the way slash lines are placed. For example, for a tent type of silhouette, the slash lines extend to just below the bust line. (You should not extend your slash lines above the bust darts because your dress will get wide across the chest and won't fit nicely.) If you want a silhouette that is slim through the torso and flares out at the hips, the slash lines extend only up to the hipline. The slash lines can come up to the waist or wherever you like, to achieve the kind of silhouette you want. All the slash lines can go into the side seams, or some can go into the center front for a different shape. You can first try making patterns for various silhouettes, using your miniature slopers.

You should let a flared dress hang overnight or longer before marking the hem.

TENT DRESS

Figure 99.

1. Trace your front and back slopers and cut them out.

2. On the front pattern, draw five L-shaped slash lines with your yardstick as you see in *Figure 99A.* Number the pieces.

3. Place the front pattern on top of the back pattern so that the side seams and the hemline line up together. Use your tracing wheel, without carbon, to trace the front slash lines onto the back pattern.

4. Take your front pattern and, beginning at the hem, cut along each slash line to within $1/8''$ of the side seam.

5. Place the working pattern on a large sheet of paper and spread the pieces as shown in *Figure 99B.* The more you spread, the more fullness you will have in the dress.

6. Once the pieces are spread the way you want, tape them in place.

7. Draw around the pattern and blend a new hemline with your curved rule, smoothing out the jogs.

8. Remove the working pattern and discard.

9. Cut out your pattern and label it. The center-front line is the grain line.

10. Your finished front pattern should look like *Figure 99C.*

11. To make your back pattern, follow the same steps as in making the front. Be sure to spread exactly the same amount between the pieces as you did on the front pattern. The finished back pattern should look like *Figure 99D.*

Figure 99

Figure 100

TENT DRESS WITH CENTER-FRONT SEAM

Figure 100. This style has a different shape because there is flare added at the center-front and center-back seams as well as at the side seams. In the tent-dress pattern (*Figure 99*), the slash lines all went into the side seams. In making this pattern, two slash lines go into the side seams and two other slash lines go into the center-front seam. This gives a more swingy shape.

1. Trace your front and back slopers and cut out the patterns.

2. With your yardstick, draw two L-shaped slash lines ending at the center front and draw two L-shaped slash lines ending at the side seam. As you see in *Figure 100A,* the lines ending at the side seam and the center front should be the same length and size. Number the pieces.

3. Place your front pattern on top of your back pattern so that the side seams and hemline match. With your tracing wheel, and no carbon, trace the front slash lines onto the back pattern.

4. Take your front pattern and cut along the slash lines from the hem to within ⅛″ of the side seam and to within ⅛″ of the center front.

5. Place the working pattern on a new large sheet of paper. Spread the pieces as much as desired. The more you spread the pieces, the more fullness you will have in the dress. Have the same amount of space between each piece.

6. Tape the pieces in place and trace the new pattern including the dart notches. Blend a new hemline, smoothing out the jogs (*Figure 100B*). Discard and remove the working pattern. Add ⅝″ seam allowance at the center front.

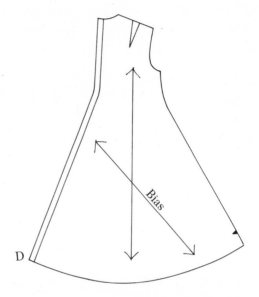

Figure 100

7. To establish the grain line, fold the pattern in half longways. Match the center-front seam with the side seam and crease along the fold. Open up your pattern and mark the crease GRAIN LINE (*Figure 100C*).

8. To make the back pattern, follow the same steps as in making the front pattern. Disregard the waistline dart. Be sure to spread exactly the same amount between the pieces as you did on the front pattern.

9. The finished back pattern should look like *Figure 100D*. This style works well cut in plaid or stripes cut on the bias.

FLARED-SKIRT DRESS WITH CENTER-FRONT SEAM

Figure 101A. This dress has a more swingy skirt than the basic A-line. Follow the same instructions given for the tent dress with a center-front seam above except mark the slash lines only to the hipline as shown here.

FLARED SKIRT WITH GODETS

Figure 101B. For extra flare, godets may be added to center front, center back, and side seams. A godet is a triangular piece of fabric. To make a godet pattern:

1. On the side seam of your working pattern, measure the distance from the hemline to the lowest slash line, or to the point where you want the godet to end.

2. Draw a line that measurement on a piece of paper. That line is one side of the godet (*Figure 101B*).

3. Draw the triangle for the godet with two sides the same length. The two sides of the triangle are sewn into the seam. The bottom of the triangle forms the hem and can be as wide as you like.

4. Add seam allowance at the two side seams and curve the triangle at the hem.

5. Cut out the pattern.

6. To establish the grain line, fold the triangle in half longways and crease. Mark the crease GRAIN LINE. After the dress is sewn, the hem should be checked by measuring up from the floor and marking carefully.

You can use godets with the A-line sloper or with a slashed-and-spread pattern. They can also be used in princess-line seams. If there is no seam, you can slash the fabric to insert godets.

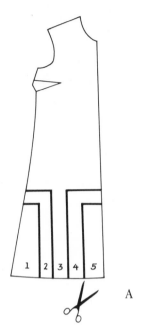

A

Figure 101

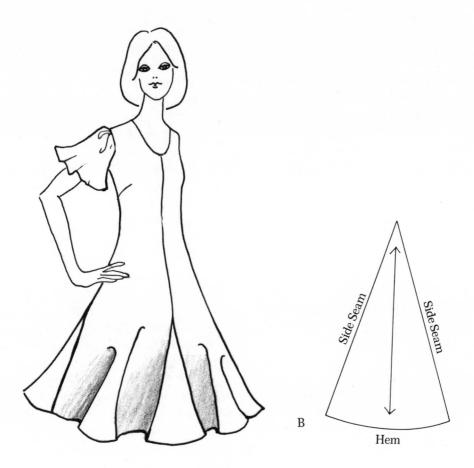

B

Side Seam

Side Seam

Hem

Figure 101

YOKES

A yoke can be a place to show detail too expensive or time consuming to use for a whole dress, for example, hand embroidery or costly lace fabric. The yoke-seam line may have gathers and is also a good place to add trim or fancy stitching. A yoke made from the same fabric as your dress can be more interesting on a different grain line. For example, a dress with stripes running up and down might have the stripes crossways on the yoke, or a plaid dress might have the yoke on the bias. A yoke dress can be long or short or tunic length to be worn over pants. You can use the regular neckline with or without a collar, or a different neckline such as a scoop or square neck.

BASIC YOKE DRESS

Figure 102.

1. Trace your front sloper on a new piece of paper and cut out your pattern.

2. (See *Figure 102A*.) Square the design line of your yoke across the front at a right angle to the center front. The yoke line should be no higher than 2″ below the neckline and no lower than 1½″ above the bust dart. The yoke line can be wherever you like between these two measurements.

3. Next you will need to add seam allowance to the yoke and the skirt of the dress pattern. Take another piece of paper larger than the yoke and place it underneath your pattern, as you see in *Figure 102B*. With your pencil, trace around the center front, neckline, shoulder, and armhole of the yoke on the new paper as shown. Use the tracing wheel without carbon paper to trace the design line of the yoke onto the paper.

4. Remove the dress pattern.

5. (See *Figure 102C*.) Using your ruler and pencil, mark the yoke line, going over where you marked with the tracing wheel. Add ⅝″ seam allowance below the yoke line as shown.

6. Cut out your yoke pattern. The center-front line is the grain line.

7. Next, take your dress pattern and add ⅝″ seam allowance above the yoke line as shown in *Figure 102D*.

8. Cut along the seam-allowance line.

9. Your finished pattern should look like *Figure 102E*.

10. To make the back yoke pattern, follow the same instructions. The yoke should not be any longer than 7 inches below the regular neckline at the center back.

11. The back pattern should look like *Figure 102F*.

If you have no collar, use your yoke pattern as the neckline facing and attach the facing at the armhole to keep it in place.

YOKE VARIATIONS

A yoke can be curved or V-shaped as shown in *Figure 103*. Draw your design line the shape you want, then continue as for the basic yoke dress in *Figure 102*.

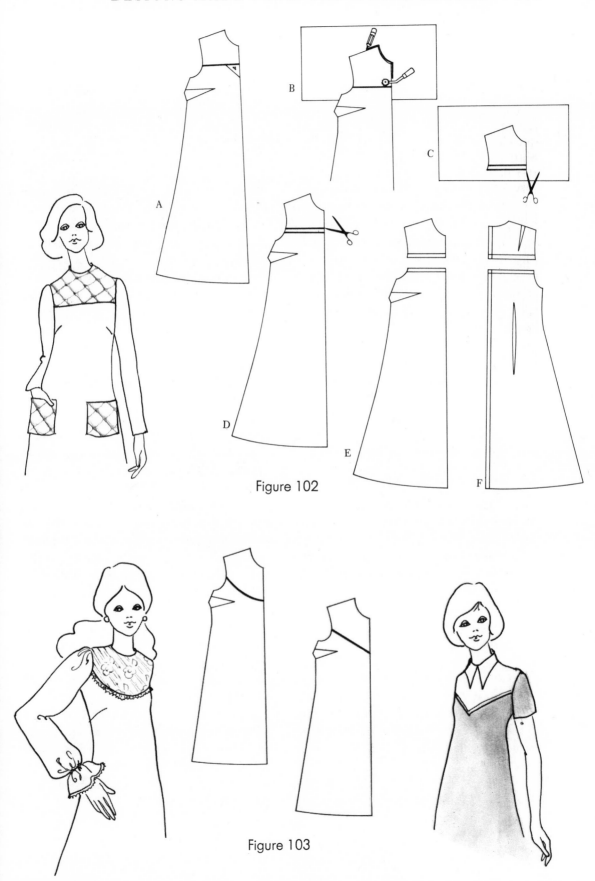

Figure 102

Figure 103

SMOCK DRESSES

A smock dress is a yoke dress with gathers added to the skirt by slashing and spreading. The smock can be very sporty worn over pants or a bikini or it can be very dressy made long, possibly with a lace yoke. A smock shape is lovely in soft, drapy fabrics like jersey, or in lightweight sheer fabrics like voile. If you make a smock out of a heavier fabric such as wool or corduroy, add only a small amount of fullness when spreading your pattern. For design possibilities, consider very full sleeves, a contrasting color collar, or fancy cuff details. A smock looks attractive with big patch pockets, with cording at the yoke, or with a square or scoop neckline.

BASIC SMOCK DRESS

1. *Figure 104.* Follow the instructions on page 176 for making the basic yoke dress.

2. Before slashing and spreading the skirt, the bust dart must be moved to the yoke seam.

3. (See *Figure 104A.*) Draw a line from the bust point up to the yoke-seam line. Slash this line to the bust point.

4. Tape the underarm dart closed as you see in *Figure 104B.* A new dart will open up at the yoke seam and the yoke seam will curve down. By moving the dart to the yoke seam, the dart fullness will be included in the gathers when you spread your pattern.

5. Divide the skirt by drawing five slash lines parallel to the center front as shown in *Figure 104C.* The first slash line should be about 1″ from the armhole.

6. Number the pieces.

7. Slash along each line from hem to yoke seam.

8. Place the pieces of the working pattern in numbered order on a large sheet of paper.

9. Spread the pieces so that each strip of the working pattern is parallel to the center front and there is the same amount of space between the pieces (*Figure 104D*). The more spread, the more fullness in the skirt. Depending on the effect you want, spread from ½″ between each piece for a slight amount of ease up to 2″ for a full smock.

10. Tape your pieces in place.

11. With your yardstick, draw a new side seam parallel to the center front as shown in *Figure 104D,* and draw the center-front line.

12. With your curve ruler, blend a smooth line at the yoke seam and at the hem.

13. Remove the working pattern and discard. The center-front line is the grain line.

14. Your finished pattern should look like *Figure 104E.*

15. To make your back pattern, disregard the waistline dart and slash, and spread the back skirt the same as the front. Be sure you spread the same amount between each piece on the back as you spread for the front.

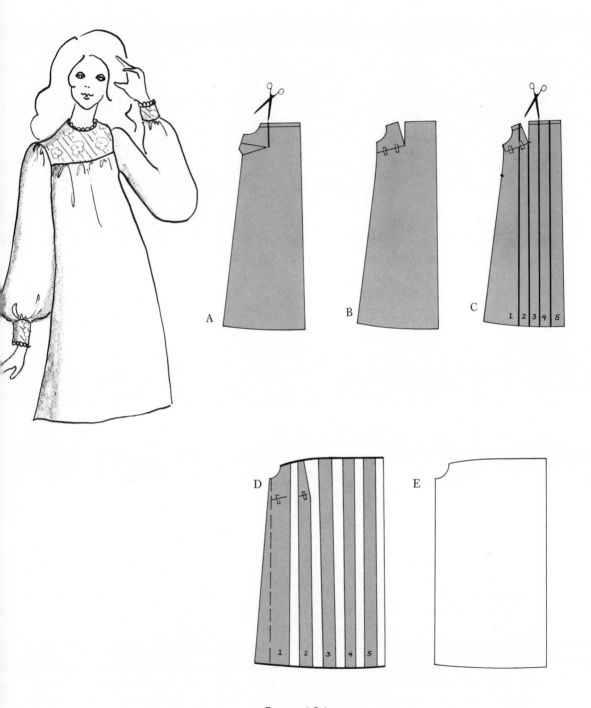

Figure 104

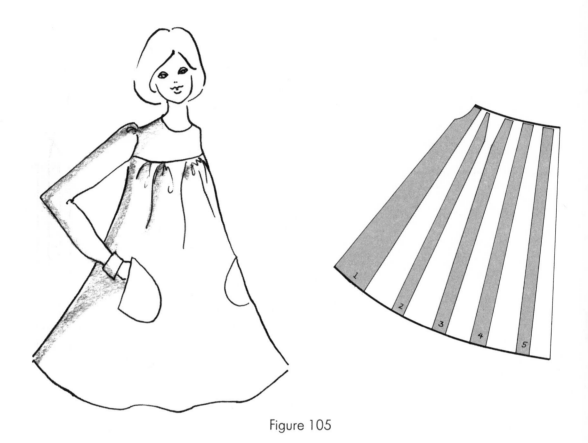

Figure 105

TENT SMOCK

Figure 105. This smock flares out at the hem because it has more fullness at the hem and less at the yoke line.

1. Follow the steps for the basic smock up through slashing the working pattern (*Figure 104C*).

2. Then spread the working pattern as you see in *Figure 105.* When spreading the pieces, leave from ½″ to 1″ between each strip of working pattern at the top and between 1″ and 3½″ at the hemline. Have the same amount of space between each strip of working pattern.

3. Straighten the side seam with your yardstick.

4. Finish the pattern the same as the basic smock.

PINAFORES

The smock can be made as a pinafore to be worn over a dress or pants. At the armhole, add a ruffle or the pinafore sleeve shown on page 140.

CHANGING THE BUST DART INTO A YOKE SEAM

LONG YOKE

In the basic yoke dress the design line is positioned above the bust dart. In the long yoke dress in *Figure 106* the design line follows the line of the bust dart. In making the pattern for a long yoke you are actually changing the bust dart into a seam.

1. Trace around your sloper and cut out your pattern.

2. To mark the bust line, square a line from the center front to the point of the bust dart as you see in *Figure 106A*.

3. To mark your design lines, use your French curve to blend the upper line of the dart into the bust line. This forms the design line of the yoke.

4. To mark the design line of the skirt, blend a line following the bottom line of the dart into the bust line as shown in *Figure 106A*.

What you have done is made a seam across the front. The upper line of the dart forms the seam of the yoke and the lower line of the dart forms the seam of the skirt.

Next you must add seam allowance to the yoke and the skirt.

5. (See *Figure 106B*.) Place a sheet of paper larger than the yoke under your pattern. With your pencil trace around the yoke, center front, neckline, shoulder, armhole, and side seam, as shown. Trace the design line of the yoke with a tracing wheel; no carbon paper is needed.

6. Remove the dress pattern. Mark the yoke line with a pencil and curve rule, following the marks of the tracing wheel. Add 5⁄8″ seam allowance below the design line of the yoke (*Figure 106C*).

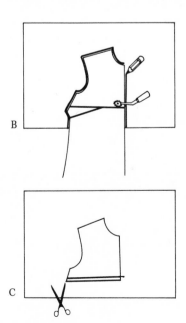

Figure 106

7. Cut out your yoke pattern, being careful to cut on the finished line, not the design line.

8. Take your dress pattern and add ⅝″ seam allowance above the design line for the skirt as shown in *Figure 106D*. Remember that the skirt design line is the lower line of the dart.

When you sew the yoke and skirt together, you may need to clip the curve to make them fit together properly. This pattern can be used with the basic back sloper or you can make a pattern with a matching yoke in the back. To make the back pattern:

9. Trace your back sloper on a new piece of paper and cut out the pattern. On your front yoke, measure the side seam from the armhole to the design line (NOT the cutting line). Mark that amount on the side seam of your back pattern.

10. (See *Figure 106E*.) Draw in your design line on the back, beginning at this mark. The design line should not be straight across but should curve down from the side seam to the center back. Use your hip curve to mark the line.

11. Place the back yoke on a new piece of paper and trace around it.

12. Following the same steps as you did for the front, add seam allowance to the back yoke and add seam allowance to the skirt above the design line. If the tip of the waist dart extends into the back yoke, tape this part of the dart closed and disregard it.

13. Cut out your back yoke and cut the skirt on the seam-allowance line.

14. Your finished pattern should look like *Figure 106F*.

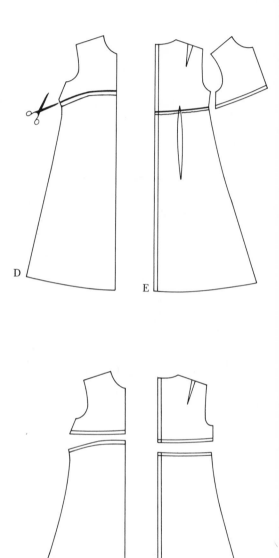

Figure 106

BIB YOKE

Figure 107. This yoke is quite similar to the long yoke above. With the bib yoke shown here, the dart is moved to the shoulder before being changed into a seam.

1. Trace your front sloper and cut out the pattern.

2. (See *Figure 107A.*) Square a line from the center front across to the point of the dart.

3. Draw a line from the dart point up to the shoulder. This line should not be parallel to the center front but should angle out slightly toward the armhole as you see here.

4. (See *Figure 107B.*) Slash the line from the shoulder to the dart point and tape the underarm dart closed. A dart will open up at the shoulder. The side of the dart toward the armhole is the seam of the dress, and the side of the dart toward the center front is the seam of the yoke.

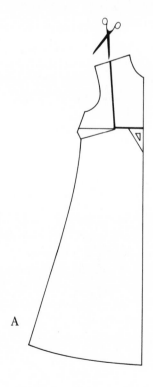

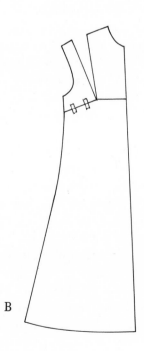

A   B

Figure 107

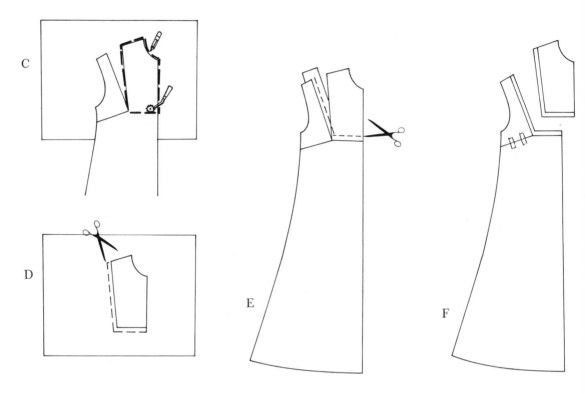

Figure 107

5. Next, you must make a separate yoke pattern and add seam allowance.

6. (See *Figure 107C.*) Place a piece of paper larger than the yoke underneath the pattern. With your pencil, trace around the yoke, center front, neckline, shoulder, and dart line as shown. Mark the yoke line with your tracing wheel; no carbon is necessary.

7. Remove the dress pattern. With a ruler and pencil, mark the yoke line you made with your tracing wheel.

8. (See *Figure 107D.*) Add ⅝″ seam allowance at the yoke-seam line at the side and bottom, as you see here.

9. Cut out your yoke pattern on the seam-allowance line.

10. To finish the dress pattern, tape a strip of paper to the dart opening on the dress so that you have a place to add seam allowance (*Figure 107E*). Add ⅝″ seam allowance to the dart line near the armhole and at the yoke line as shown.

11. Cut out on the seam-allowance line.

12. Your finished pattern should look like *Figure 107F.* This front pattern is used with the basic back sloper.

MORE BIB YOKES

Figure 108. Variations are made by shifting the dart to a different location and drawing the design line to form a new shape for the bib. Then the steps followed are the same as those just given for the square-bib yoke. You can experiment with your miniature slopers to see what new designs you can create for bib yokes.

Figure 108

PRINCESS-LINE DRESSES

Once you have learned to make the basic princess-line pattern, you can make almost innumerable variations. The steps in making a princess pattern are similar to the steps in making a long yoke pattern. Basically, you move the dart to a new position, then change the dart into a seam. The princess seam can begin at the neck, shoulder, center-front seam, armhole, or side seam, and end at the side seam, hemline, or center front. The princess style can be made with or without a center-front seam to achieve different effects. You can vary a style by inserting ties, belts, flaps, pockets, etc., into the princess seams. Princess styles generally look best in simple fabrics, which emphasize the design lines. You can add further emphasis to the design lines by topstitching or saddle stitching both sides of the seam. You can create more styles by combining the princess line with a yoke. Making a princess-line pattern with a waistline seam is covered in Chapter 14.

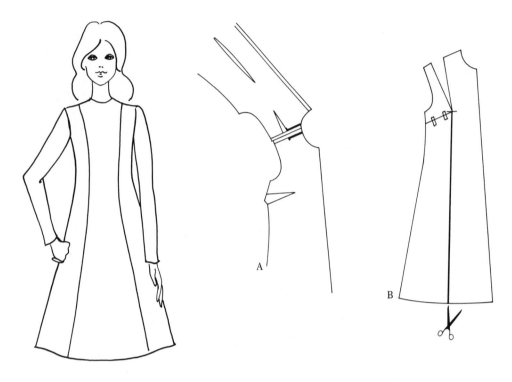

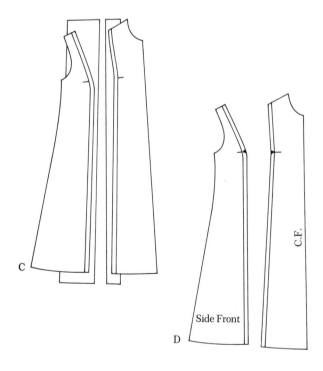

Figure 109

BASIC PRINCESS DRESS

Figure 109.

1. Trace your front sloper.

2. On your back sloper, measure along the shoulder seam the distance from the neckline to the first notch of the shoulder dart. On your front sloper, measure along the shoulder seam from the neckline, and mark the same distance as the back. See heavy line in *Figure 109A*. This is done so that the front princess seam will meet the back shoulder dart or back princess seam.

3. Draw the new dart line from this mark at the shoulder. Shift the dart to the shoulder but don't add the paper or draw in a new dart (*Figure 109B*). (See page 160 on moving the dart.)

4. To make the princess-seam line, use your yardstick to draw a line from the bust point to the hem. This line should slant toward the side seam slightly (that is, it should not be parallel to the center front). Draw a crossmark at the bust point.

5. Cut along your style line so that you have two pattern pieces.

6. To finish the pattern, you need to add seam allowance and blend the curve (*Figure 109C*). Tape a long strip of paper to the right and left side of the front along the style line. Add ⅝″ seam allowance. Using your French curve, smooth the point at the dart.

7. Extend the crossmarks and mark notches on the seam allowance at the end of the crossmarks.

8. Cut along your seam-allowance line on both pattern pieces. When you stitch the right and left sides together, the notches at the bust point should match.

9. Your finished pattern should look like *Figure 109D*.

If you add a princess seam to the front, but don't change the basic shape of the sloper, you can use the back sloper as your back pattern. I think it looks more balanced, however, to have the princess seam in the back when you have it in the front.

BASIC BACK PRINCESS

1. Trace your back sloper.

2. See *Figure 110A* and mark your design lines as shown. On the left side of your pattern, the design line follows the left side of the shoulder and waistline darts. On the right side of the pattern, the design follows the right side of the shoulder and waistline darts. The style line on the back should be the same slant as the style line of the front pattern.

3. Draw crossmarks at the top and bottom of the waist dart.

4. Cut along your design lines; be sure to cut along the correct line for each side of your pattern.

5. To finish the pattern, follow the same steps as you did on the front, taping paper and adding seam allowance. Extend the crossmarks to make notches.

6. Your finished back pattern should look like *Figure 110B*.

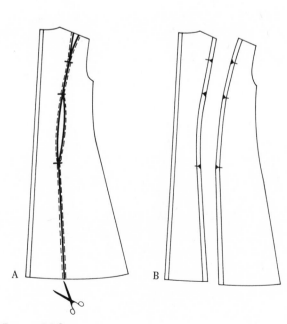

Figure 110

Figure 111

PRINCESS VARIATIONS

The variations in *Figures 111A* and *B* are made by shifting the bust dart to a new position and drawing the style line as shown. Use your French curve or curve rule to draw curved lines. Follow the same steps used to make the basic princess-style pattern. If you are making a sleeveless pattern, make the adjustments at the armhole first. Changes such as a new neckline or adding a front opening should be made after you trace your sloper and before you mark your princess line. *Figure 111C* shows the basic princess with a center-front seam.

BACK PRINCESS VARIATIONS

The back princess pattern usually follows the same design line as the front. If the design line does not end at the shoulder, retain the shoulder dart and mark your princess line on each side of the waist dart the same as the basic princess (*Figure 111D*). Cut along your design lines on the right and left side of your pattern, add seam allowance and finish the pattern the same way as the basic princess pattern.

PRINCESS DRESS WITH YOKE

Figure 112.

1. Follow the directions on page 176, to make the basic yoke pattern.

2. Shift the bust dart to the yoke seam.

3. Mark your style line and continue the same as for the basic princess pattern.

4. To make the back pattern, follow the directions for the back yoke then make the back pattern the same as for the basic princess.

Figure 112

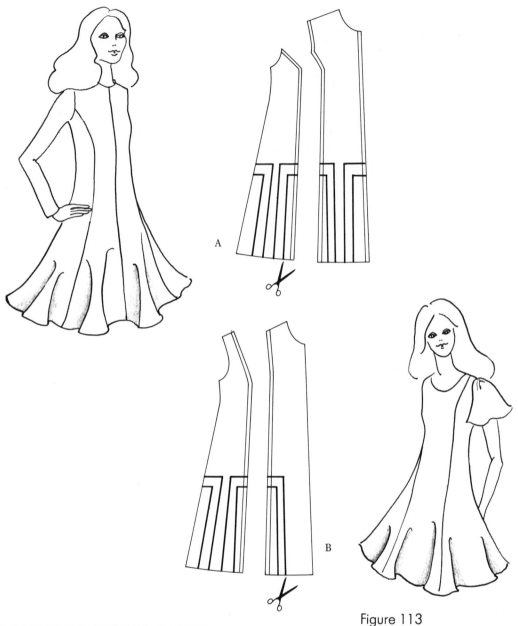

Figure 113

PRINCESS DRESS WITH FLARED SKIRT

You can make many variations in the princess style by slashing and spreading the skirt. The method is the same as that used for slashing and spreading the skirt without princess seam. The slash lines must be the same on each side of the princess seam, and you must spread the same amount on each side of your seam. *Figure 113A* shows a seam and slash lines at the center front as well as the princess seams. This gives a swingier skirt than the style shown in *Figure 113B,* where the center front is placed on the fold.

FRONT OPENINGS

SLASHED-FRONT OPENING

Figure 114. A slashed-front opening is very easy to make and can be an attractive design feature. It can be used with the basic A-line sloper or a pattern. This opening can be styled with or without a collar, and looks especially nice with a scoop neck. Slashed front can be closed with spaghetti ties, frogs, fancy hooks and eyes, or spaghetti loops with buttons. This design looks best if you cut the front and back on the fold so that there is no center-front or center-back seam. For the dress to fit easily over your head, the slash should be at least eight inches long, measured from the regular neckline. Mark the front facing line on your pattern as shown. If you're using spaghetti loops or ties, stitch them to the right side of the dress before applying the facing. Stitch the facing around the neckline and around the slit. Then slash the slit after you've done the stitching. The facing should be cut three inches longer at the bottom than the slit.

ZIPPER-FRONT OPENING

When you make a zipper-front opening, remember that you must have $5/8''$ seam allowance at the center front. The recommended minimum is a $16''$ opening from the regular neckline.

Figure 114

BUTTON-FRONT OPENINGS

EXTENSIONS

When you make a button-front opening, your pattern must have an extension beyond the center front to allow overlap for the button and buttonhole (*Figure 115A*). The amount of the extension depends on the size of your button; the larger the button the wider the extension. To figure your extension, measure the diameter of the button. There are complicated formulas for figuring the extension, but you'll do fine if you use the same measurement as the diameter of the button.

BUTTON-FRONT OPENING TO HEM

1. Trace your pattern so that the center-front line is about 7″ in from the edge of the paper.

2. Figure the amount of extension as explained above. Draw a line parallel to the center front the same distance from the center front as the extension measurement (*Figure 115B*).

3. Crease along the extension line and fold under. With the paper folded, cut out your pattern and your notches (*Figure 115C*). Unfold the paper.

4. To add the facing pattern, measure 3½″ from the extension line and draw the facing line parallel to the center front (*Figure 115D*). Shape the facing line at the neckline as shown.

5. Cut along the facing line.

BUTTON-FRONT OPENING PART WAY

When you have a front opening that buttons only part way down, you need an extension only where the buttons will be. The rest is a regular seam (*Figure 115E*).

1. Follow the instructions above for marking your extension and facing.

2. On the extension line, mark the length of the opening that you want.

3. With your triangle, square a line from the extension line to the facing line, as illustrated in *Figure 115E*. This marks the facing.

4. Below the facing, you need ⅝″ seam allowance. Measure ⅝″ from the center front. (If your extension is ⅝″, you don't need to draw the line.)

5. Cut away the lower part of the facing as shown.

BUTTON PLACEMENT

On less expensive ready to wear, manufacturers often cut cost by spacing the buttons too far apart. This results in gaps between the buttons and a look of poor quality. Lightweight fabrics need buttons placed closer together than do heavy fabrics because the weight of a heavy fabric keeps the spaces between the buttons from gaping. Button placement can also be a design feature. A row of tiny buttons placed very close together can look very pretty. A detail generally found only on more expensive ready to wear is to arrange buttons to correspond with the lines of a stripe or plaid.

Figure 115

To place buttons evenly, lay the finished garment on a flat surface and place the buttons by eye. Then use a ruler to check that you have the same space between each button. Once the buttons are spaced evenly, mark the location of each button with a pin or light-color pencil dot. Use these dots to indicate the placement of your buttonholes. Remember that button-holes should be on the right side as you wear the garment. After you make the buttonholes, cut the buttonholes open and pin the front closed, positioning very carefully. With the garment placed on a flat surface, stick the point of a pin into the center of the buttonhole. Catch the pin on the underlayer to indicate where to sew on the buttons.

JUMPERS

When making a jumper pattern, some adjustment in the shape of the armhole is necessary for good looks and good fit. Because the jumper is worn with a blouse under it, the armhole should be lowered slightly to allow for ease of movement and to keep the sleeve of the blouse from bunching up in the jumper armhole. The armhole should also be extended at the shoulder seam so that it covers the seam where the sleeve of the blouse is set in. This is the opposite of the sleeveless armhole which is made smaller.

Figure 116.

1. Trace the front sloper (*Figure 116A*).

2. Extend the shoulder seam ½".

3. At the side seam, measure from the armhole down ½" and mark.

4. From that mark, measure out from the side seam ¼".

5. With your French curve, draw a new armhole from the extended shoulder seam to the side-seam mark as shown.

6. Blend the side seam from your new armhole into the original side seam as shown. Close the dart before cutting out your pattern.

7. Trace your back sloper and make the same adjustments on the back (*Figure 116B*).

When making jumper patterns, make the armhole adjustments first, then continue with the other pattern steps. If you are using the A-line sloper as a jumper without making any other changes, you can mark your sloper and make the armhole adjustments directly on the fabric instead of making a new pattern. You can create many easy-to-make jumper styles with the A-line sloper by simple additions such as neckline variations, pockets, flaps, button fronts, or changing the position of the darts.

For other jumper ideas, see sleeveless designs in this chapter and Chapter 15. Many sleeveless styles work well as jumpers. Make the armhole adjustments for a jumper instead of the adjustments for a sleeveless dress. Then follow the same pattern instructions. Yoke-dress patterns can also work well as jumpers.

Figure 116

Figure 117

JACKETS AND COATS

Your A-line sloper can also be used to make simple jackets and coats. These are not tailoring projects; they are sewn like other styles made with the sloper. You can make a jacket, sleeveless jacket, or coat to go with a dress, skirt, pants, or as part of a sportswear group (*Figure 117*).

When you make a pattern for a jacket or coat, adjustment is necessary at the armhole and side seam to allow extra room so that the coat or jacket will fit comfortably over your garment underneath. The adjust-ments are similar to those made for a jumper pattern.

1. Trace your front sloper.

2. (See *Figure 118A.*) Extend the shoulder seam at the armhole ½″.

3. Draw a new side seam ½″ out from the original side seam as shown. On your new side seam, measure down ½″ from the armhole. Draw a new armhole using your French curve, connecting the new side seam and the extended shoulder.

4. If your coat or jacket is going to have

a zipper-front opening, add seam allowance at the center front.

5. For a button-front opening, you need to add extension and a facing to the pattern (page 193).

6. To make a jacket pattern, measure up from the hem and mark the length you want your jacket. Don't forget to add hem allowance. Blend a new hemline with your curve ruler.

7. If you're making a coat pattern to go with a dress, the coat should be one inch longer than the dress.

8. To make the back coat or jacket pattern, trace the back sloper and make the same adjustments at the armhole and side seams as you did for the front (*Figure 118B*).

Because you've made the armhole larger, the sleeve needs to be adjusted in order to fit the new armhole. The adjustment is made by simply adding ½″ to each side of the sleeve, as shown in *Figures 118C* and *D*. You can make a paper pattern or add the ½″ on the fabric after you trace the sleeve sloper.

Jacket line

A

B

C

D

Figure 118

JACKETS AND COATS WITH NO EXTENSION

The cardigan coat in *Figure 119* is cut on the center front with no extension or seam allowance because the edge is finished with foldover braid.

The jacket in *Figure 119* also has no extension because it has no buttons.

Figure 119

CHAPTER 13

DESIGNS MADE FROM THE A-LINE SKIRT

You can use the A-line-skirt sloper to make a great many different skirt styles. Very easy skirts can be made using the basic sloper and adding various pockets, different waistbands, flaps, or trimmings, or changing the waistline dart into tucks or ease (*Figure 120*). Flared skirts can be made by slashing and spreading. From this sloper you can also make patterns for wrap-around skirts, button-front skirts, and skirts with pleats. In the next chapter, which covers designs made with the bodice sloper, you will see how to make many different dress and jumper styles by combining the bodice with any of the skirts in this chapter.

Figure 120

WAISTLINES AND DARTS

WAISTBANDS

To make a waistband pattern, decide on the finished width of your waistband, then double this amount and add $1\frac{1}{4}''$. For example, if you want a $1''$ waistband, double $1''=2''+1\frac{1}{4}''=3\frac{1}{4}''$, which is the cut width of the waistband. To determine the length of the waistband, measure your waistline and, to your waistline measurement, add $3\frac{1}{4}''$ for ease, overlap, and seam allowance. The waistband can be marked directly on the fabric without making a pattern if you like. Interfacing is a good idea for most waistbands because it helps keep them from stretching out of shape and from curling.

WAISTLINE FACING

For a skirt with no waistband (*Figure 121*), you can make a bias facing to finish the waistline. From lightweight fabric, cut a strip of bias $4\frac{1}{2}''$ wide and about $2''$ longer than the measurement of the skirt waistline. Fold the strip of bias in half lengthwise and press. Use your iron to shape a curve along the fold by stretching the folded edge slightly. Pin the facing to the right side of your skirt so the fold edge is toward the hem and stitch the facing in place. Press the facing to the right side and hand tack it to the darts and seam allowance to hold it in place. Turn the raw ends of the facing under and hand stitch at the zipper opening.

BELT LOOPS

Belt loops can also be a design feature of the skirt. Consider using tabs as a different kind of belt loop. (See Chapter 9, page 104, to make tabs.) You can hold the point of the tab down with an attractive

Figure 121

button. Belt loops can also be made of braid or other trimming, scraps of leather or suede, spaghetti or thread loops.

DART VARIATIONS

Instead of stitching the dart closed, for a change you can make the dart into a little pleat like you sometimes find on men's pants. You can also eliminate the dart and just run an ease stitch around the waistline and ease the waistline into the waistband.

Figure 122

SUPER-EASY PULL-ON SKIRT

Figure 122. This style works only in stretchy knit fabrics. It is really easy to make because it has no zipper and no waistband—just elastic at the waistline. For comfort, use 1″-wide pajama elastic which is much softer than regular elastic. To make a pattern for this skirt:

1. Trace your front-skirt sloper. Do not mark the waistline dart.

2. Measure up 2½″ from the waistline and draw a new line above the original waistline. Extend the line 1½″ beyond the side seam.

3. Blend a new side seam from the new waistline into the original side seam as shown.

4. Cut out the pattern.

5. Make the pattern for the back skirt, following the same steps and measurements as the pattern for the front skirt.

To sew the skirt, stitch the side seams together, then fold the waistline down toward the wrong side to make a tunnel for the elastic. Stitch the tunnel, leaving a small opening. Then run a piece of elastic the same measurement as your waist through the tunnel.

Figure 123

A-LINE SKIRT WITH CENTER-FRONT AND CENTER-BACK SEAM

Figure 123.

1. Trace your front sloper, then add ⅝″ seam allowance at the center front.

2. Cut out your pattern.

3. To establish your grain line, fold the pattern in half lengthwise, matching the center-front line with the side seam and crease. Open up the pattern and mark the crease grain line.

4. Follow the same steps to make your back pattern.

A pattern with a center-front seam looks very nice made out of plaid or stripes, having the plaid and stripes meet at the center-front and center-back seams. If you make the skirt with a front zipper, the center front should be the grain line.

LONG SKIRT

Figure 124.

1. Trace your skirt sloper on a long piece of paper.

2. Figure the length of your skirt by measuring from your waist to your ankle.

3. Extend the center-front line of the pattern. Measure along the center front from the waist, the amount from your waistline to ankle.

4. Extend the side seam and measure the same amount from the waist along the extended side seam.

5. Add 3″ hem allowance. Draw in the new hemline, following the same curve shape as the original hemline.

6. Follow the same steps and measurements to make a back pattern.

Figure 124

Figure 125

BUTTON-FRONT SKIRT

Figure 125. You can add a button-front opening to the A-line-skirt sloper and also to a number of skirt variations which follow. The button-front skirt can have a waistband or not, whichever you like. To have a button-front opening you must add

extension and facing at the center front of the skirt pattern. To do this, see Chapter 12, page 193, for adding extensions. Use the skirt sloper instead of the A-line sloper shown in Chapter 12.

FLARED SKIRTS

There are two basic ways of making a flared skirt. For a small amount of flare, you can add to the side seam of your basic sloper. To achieve greater flare, slashing and spreading are needed. Depending on how you make your slash lines, you can make different styles of flared skirts. If you have read Chapter 12 on making the A-line dress with a flared skirt, you will see that what is done here is just about the same as in making the flared A-line-dress pattern.

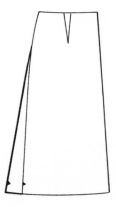

Figure 126

ADDING FLARE AT THE SIDE SEAM

1. Trace your skirt sloper.

2. (See *Figure 126.*) At the hem of the skirt, measure out from 1″ to 4″ and mark.

3. With your yardstick, blend your new side seams from the original waistline to the new point at the hem.

4. With your curve stick, extend the hemline to meet the new side seam.

4. Cut out your pattern on the new line.

5. To make your back pattern, follow the same steps. Be sure to extend out from the hemline the same amount on the back as on the front.

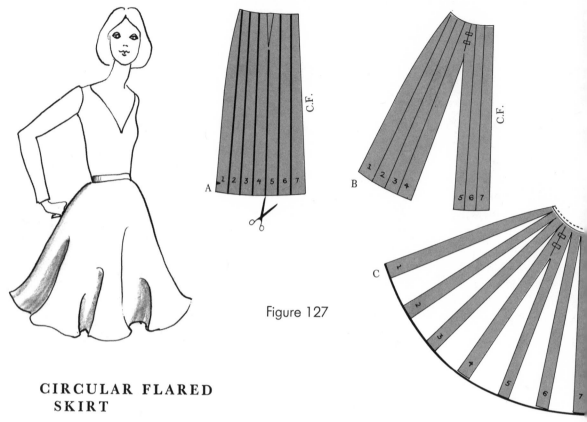

Figure 127

CIRCULAR FLARED SKIRT

Figure 127. This skirt is made by slashing and spreading. Because the slash lines are from the hem to the waist, the flare of the skirt will begin at the waistline. To make a pattern for this skirt:

1. Trace your front sloper on a piece of paper. If you want your skirt longer or shorter, make the length change next.

2. Cut out your pattern and cut away the ⅝″ seam allowance at the waistline.

3. (See *Figure 127A.*) By eye, mark five dots evenly spaced along the waistline. Also mark five dots evenly spaced along the hemline.

4. Using the dots at the waist and hem as a guide, draw five slash lines on the skirt pattern, as in *Figure 127A.* The middle slash line should come from the hem to the bottom point of the waistline dart.

5. Slash the middle line from the hem to the point of the dart and tape the waist

dart closed. A space will open at the hem (*Figure 127B*).

6. Slash the other lines to within ⅛″ of the waistline.

7. Place your working pattern on a new sheet of paper and spread each of the pieces the amount of fullness you want. You should have the same amount of space between each piece. If you spread the pieces so the side seam is at a right angle to the center front, you will have a full circle skirt.

8. When you have the pieces arranged the way you want, tape them in place.

9. Trace around the outline of your working pattern. With your curve stick, blend a new hemline, smoothing any jogs where necessary.

10. Add ⅝″ seam allowance at the waistline.

11. Untape your working pattern and

discard the pieces. Mark the center-front grain line.

If you make a very full skirt, you may not be able to cut the center front on the fold. In that case you must add ⅝″ seam allowance at the center front. You can use the same pattern for the front and back of this skirt. Because your back waist is probably a bit smaller than your front waist, you might need to run an ease thread around the waistline of the skirt and ease it into the waistband. It's a good idea to let a full skirt hang for a day before you mark the hem so that the shape can "settle." Be sure you measure up from the floor to mark the hemline, because the hem of this skirt is apt to get wavy if not marked properly.

CIRCULAR FLARED-SKIRT VARIATIONS

Figure 128. You can vary this style by spreading the pieces of the working pattern more or less than the pattern shown in *Figure 127.* Adding a center-front and center-back seam gives a different look. This is sometimes called a four-gore skirt. The skirt can be long or very short. If you are using trimming around the hem, it should be flexible because of the curve of the hem. You can use flat trim at the hem by running an ease stitch along one side of the trim and pulling the thread slightly so the trim curves. This skirt is a good style for bias.

Figure 128

SKIRT FLARED FROM HIPS

Figure 129. Because the slash lines of this skirt go to the hipline, this style skirt will fit smoothly through the hips and then flare out at the hipline.

1. Trace your front sloper.

2. Make your slash lines as shown in *Figure 129A.* The center slash line should go from the hem to the bottom point of the waistline dart.

3. Close the waistline dart (*Figure 129B*).

4. See Chapter 12, page 170, for details on spreading and finishing the pattern for this skirt. Use the skirt sloper instead of the A-line sloper shown.

5. Your spread pattern should look like *Figure 129C.*

6. Make the back pattern the same way as the front. Be sure that you spread the same amount on the front and the back.

FLARED-SKIRT VARIATIONS

The skirt in *Figure 129* can be varied by the placement of the slash lines. The lower along the seam the slash lines begin, the lower the flare of the skirt will begin. When making a long skirt, you might begin the slash lines at the thighs for a graceful silhouette. You can also vary the skirt by adding a button front, pockets, a sash, ruffles, trimming, and so on.

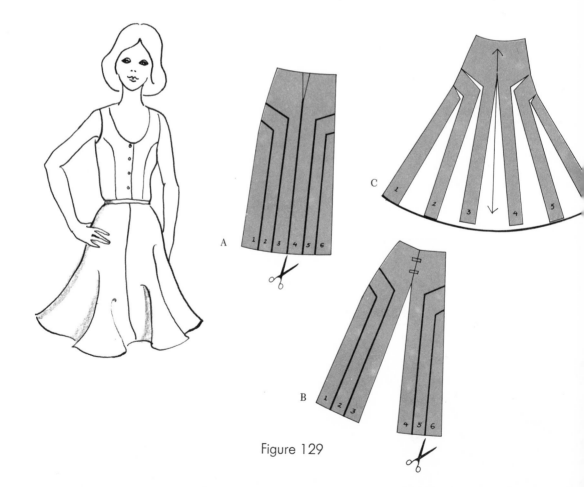

Figure 129

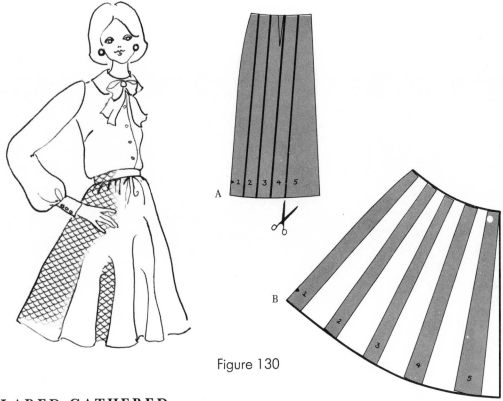

Figure 130

FLARED GATHERED SKIRTS

Figure 130. This is a lovely soft skirt shape. It is not found too often in ready to wear because it is more expensive to make than the usual gathered skirt. This style looks very nice because there aren't a lot of gathers bunched in at the waistline, yet there is a generous sweep at the hemline. It works well with fabrics that are too heavy to be gathered very much.

To make this skirt pattern:

1. Trace the A-line sloper.

2. Mark your slash lines as shown in *Figure 130A*.

3. Number the pieces of your working pattern and cut along the slash lines from hem to waist. Disregard the waist dart.

4. Take a large piece of paper and place the pieces of the working pattern as shown in *Figure 130B*. There should be more space between each piece at the hem than

at the waistline. For example, if you have ½″ between each piece at the waist, you should have 1″ or 1½″ between each piece at the hemline. Don't make the pattern a shape that won't fit on your fabric. This skirt will have to be cut with the center-front grain line on the cross grain instead of the lengthwise grain, so make sure the fabric you plan to use is suitable.

5. Once you have the pieces arranged the way you want, tape them in place.

6. Draw your new pattern. Use your curve stick to smooth out any jogs at the waistline and hemline.

7. Remove and discard the strips of your working pattern. Mark the center-front grain line.

8. Use the same pattern for the front and back skirt.

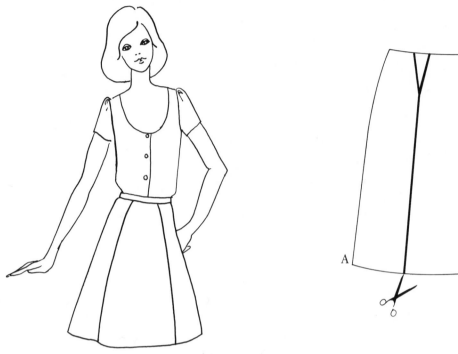

SIX-GORE SKIRTS

BASIC SIX-GORE SKIRT

Figure 131. Making a gore skirt is the same principle as making a princess-line dress. The dart is changed into a seam line. To make a six-gore skirt:

1. Trace your front-skirt sloper.

2. To mark your design line, use your yardstick to draw a line from the bottom point of the waistline dart to the hem of the skirt. This line should not be parallel to the center front, but should slant toward the side seam as in *Figure 131A.*

3. Write SIDE FRONT near the side seam.

4. Cut out your skirt pattern. Cut along the design line and along each side of the dart as you see in *Figure 131A.* On the right side of your skirt, cut along the right side of the dart; on the left side of your skirt, cut along the left side of the dart.

5. To finish the pattern, you must add seam allowance. Tape a long strip of paper along the design line of both pattern pieces (*Figure 131B*). Mark 5/8″ seam allowance on both pattern pieces.

6. Cut along your new seam line.

7. The finished pattern should look like *Figure 131C.*

8. To make your back pattern, follow the same directions given for the front pattern, using the back sloper.

FLARED SIX-GORE SKIRT

Figure 132. To make a pattern for a flared gore skirt, follow the directions above for the basic gore skirt. Next, draw slash lines as shown in *Figure 132A.* Slash and spread each pattern piece and continue the pattern following the steps for the flared skirt on page 206.

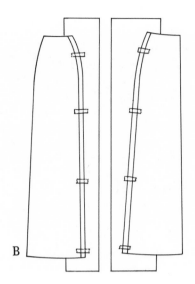
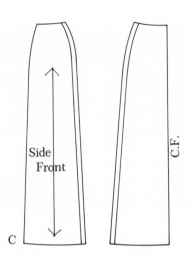

Figure 131

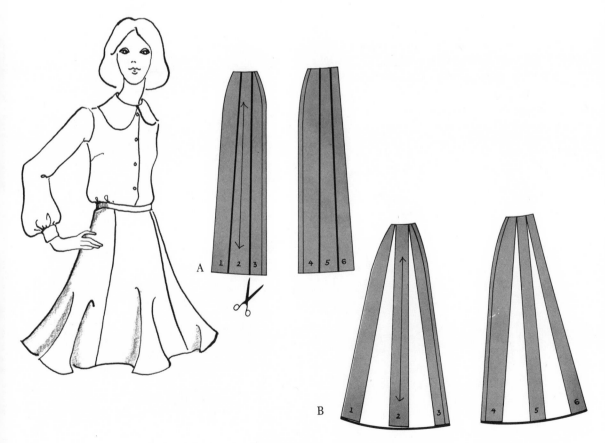

Figure 132

WRAP-AROUND SKIRTS

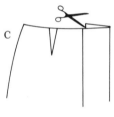

BASIC WRAP AROUND

Figure 133. To make a pattern for the basic wrap-around skirt, you need the whole front of the skirt—right and left sides—not just one side.

1. Cut a piece of paper double the size of the skirt sloper and fold the paper in half. Crease along the fold. Place the center front of your skirt sloper on the crease.

2. Trace around your skirt sloper and mark the dart as in *Figure 133A.*

3. Cut out your new pattern, with the paper folded.

4. Using the tracing wheel, mark the dart on both sides of the pattern.

5. Open up the pattern.

6. Mark the center-front crease with your yardstick; write CENTER FRONT.

7. Measure the distance from the dart point to the center-front line (*Figure 133B, Line A*).

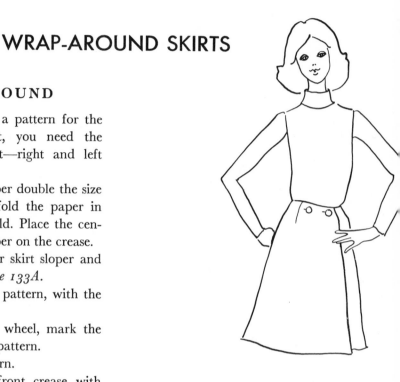

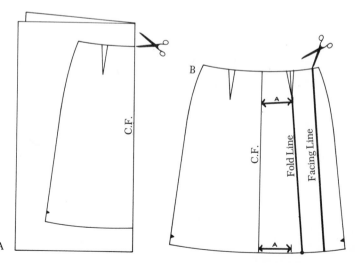

Figure 133

8. At the hemline, measure out from the center front the measurement of Line A plus 1½″ and mark.

9. With your yardstick, draw a straight line from the mark at the hem through the dart point to the waist, as in *Figure 133B*. Mark this line FOLD LINE.

10. Measure 3″ out from the fold line and draw a line parallel to the fold line. Mark this line FACING LINE.

11. Cut along the facing line.

12. Crease along the fold line and fold the facing under. Cut away the part of the facing that sticks above the waistline (*Figure 133C*).

13. Cut notches at the center front, at the waist and hem.

14. Your finished front pattern should look like *Figure 133D*.

For the back, you do not need to make any pattern. Use the basic sloper back with the wrap-front pattern.

WRAP-SKIRT VARIATIONS

Figure 134. Wrap-around skirts can wrap in the front or in the back. The wrap-around skirt looks good with patch or other pockets, flaps, or hand detailing like saddle stitching. It can have a waistband or not, and close with buttons or ties. The wrap skirt that buttons in front is a good place to use two really special buttons.

The directions given for the basic wrap are to make the skirt that wraps in the front. To make a skirt that wraps in the back, follow the same directions, using the back sloper instead of the front sloper. Use the front-skirt sloper as the front pattern if your skirt wraps in the back.

This skirt can be made reversible. You can finish the edges with foldover braid or piping, or you can stitch and turn the whole skirt. Remember to trim the hem allowance to ⅝″.

Figure 134

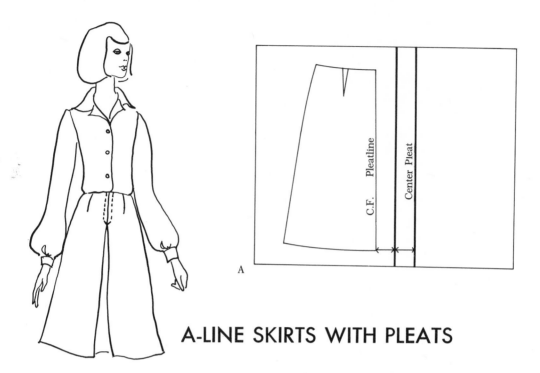

A

A-LINE SKIRTS WITH PLEATS

You can create new skirt styles by adding one or more pleats to the front only, or to both the front and back of your A-line skirt. The pleats can be topstitched from the waist to the hipline or left free.

SKIRT WITH CENTER-FRONT INVERTED PLEAT

1. *Figure 135.* Trace your skirt sloper. The center front of the skirt sloper should be about 8″ from the edge of the paper (*Figure 135A*). Mark the center front PLEAT LINE.

2. Measure 2½″ from the center front and draw a line with your yardstick parallel to the center front as you see here.

3. Measure out from that line 2½″ again and draw another line parallel to the center front, and mark this line CENTER PLEAT.

4. Crease along the pleat line. Bring the crease of your pleat line to the center pleat to make a pleat in the pattern (*Figure 135B*).

5. Using tape or paper clips to hold the pleat closed, cut out your skirt pattern.

6. Open up the pattern and cut along the center-pleat line.

7. Make notches at the waist and hem, at the center-pleat line, and at the center-front line.

8. The finished pattern should look like *Figure 135C*. When you cut out your skirt, place the center-pleat line on the fold. Cut notches at the center front and at the pleat line. Make the pleat in the fabric just as it's made in the pattern. When you hem a pleated skirt, be sure the underpart of the pleat doesn't hang below the hem of the skirt.

INVERTED-PLEAT SKIRT VARIATIONS

Figure 136. You can vary the skirt by adding trimming or pockets, or changing the length, and so on. The back skirt may have a pleat also. Follow the same directions using the back sloper. Use a side zipper.

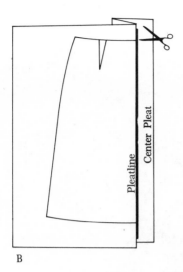

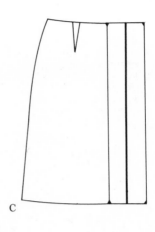

Figure 135

Figure 136

Figure 137

CHAPTER 14

DESIGNS MADE FROM THE BASIC BODICE

The basic-bodice sloper admittedly looks uninspiring, but actually it might be the most versatile of all. This sloper can be used to make many different dress styles—casual, dressy, long, or short. It can be combined with the basic A-line skirt or with any other skirt. The sloper can also be used to make many different kinds of tops, including vests, bare-midriff tops, boleros, and bib tops. The bodice sloper is also used to make sleeveless dresses and jumpers, and to make empire and high-waisted styles. Look at the chapters on necklines and collars and on sleeve variations. There are many easy dress styles you can make by combining the basic bodice and easy skirt and adding a new sleeve, interesting pocket style, collar, or new neckline. (See *Figure 137* for some ideas.)

ADDING A SKIRT TO THE BODICE

When you add a skirt to the bodice, you must have an opening in the skirt so that you can get into the dress. If you have a back opening in the bodice, you must also have a center-back seam or slash in your skirt. When the bodice has a front opening which ends at the waistline, you will need a zipper in the side seam, or hidden placket in the skirt. To figure the length of the zipper for the back-zipper opening, measure the center back from the neckline to the waist and add about 7".

Figure 138

BODICE WITH DIRNDL SKIRT

Figure 138. You can make a dirndl (gathered) skirt without a pattern by marking the measurements on the fabric. Decide the length you want your finished skirt, then add 4″ for hem and seam allowance. If you are using 36″ or 45″ fabric, cut two panels the length of your skirt and the width of the goods. For example, if you want your skirt to be 24″ finished, cut two pieces 28″ long and 36″ or 45″ across, depending on the width of your fabric. If you are using a wider fabric, cut the front and the back skirt each about 45″

and use the remaining fabric to cut other pieces of your dress. By having the gathers on the cross grain, the skirt will fall into softer folds. A lot of people cut a gathered skirt in one long length and gather it along the selvage, but unless you are using a border print or other design feature, it is better to gather the fabric on the cross grain. When you sew your dress, make the bodice and the skirt separately, then join them together around the waistline and put the zipper in last.

CHANGING THE LOCATION OF DARTS

The basic-bodice sloper has the bust dart at the side seam and a waistline dart. As you can see from *Figure 139A,* the bodice darts can radiate from the bust point in any direction. You can move one or both darts to a new position. You can also combine the darts into one large dart. Keep in mind the grain of your fabric when planning new dart locations. The center front may remain on the grain line, but the dart location will affect the direction of the fabric on other parts of the bodice. Bodice patterns with unusual dart placement may not work well with some patterned fabrics such as stripes, plaids, or complicated print designs.

The darts on the back sloper are generally left as they are.

Any change in the position of a dart begins with Step I below.

STEP I

1. (See *Figure 139B.*) Trace your sloper and cut out your pattern.

2. With your ruler, draw a line from the center of the bust dart at the side seam through the point of the dart and extended about 1½" beyond the dart point.

3. Draw another line from the center of the waist dart at the waist through the point of the dart and extended about 1½" above the dart point. The two lines should cross each other (Point A). The place where the lines cross is the apex or bust point.

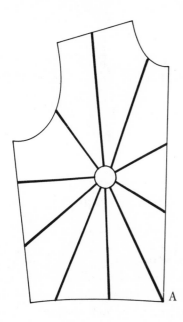

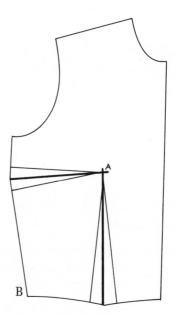

Figure 139

BODICE WITH DARTS AT WAISTLINE

Figure 140A. In this style, the amount contained in the bust dart is added to the waist dart so there is only a dart at the waist.

1. Begin with Step I on page 219 (*Figure 139B*).

2. Slash along the line which goes through the center of the waist dart from the waistline to the apex (*Figure 140B*).

3. Crease along the bust-dart line and tape the bust dart closed. The amount of the bust dart is added to the waist dart, causing the waist dart to open up (*Figure 140C*).

4. Tape a piece of paper to the back of the pattern to fill the space where the dart opened. The line indicating each side of this dart stays the same since the extra amount is added to the middle of the dart (*Figure 140D*).

5. Crease the waistline dart and close the dart with the fold toward the side seam, and tape in place.

6. With the waistline dart closed, cut along the waistline.

7. Open up the pattern.

8. Your finished pattern should look like *Figure 140E*.

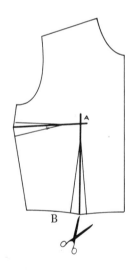

Figure 140

BODICE WITH DARTS AT SIDE SEAM

Figure 140F. In this style, the waist dart is added to the bust dart so there is only a bust dart. Reverse the same steps just given above for combining the two darts into a waist dart.

1. Begin with Step I.

2. Slash along the bust-dart line and close the waistline dart. The amount of the waistline dart will be moved into the bust dart (*Figure 140H*).

Figure 140

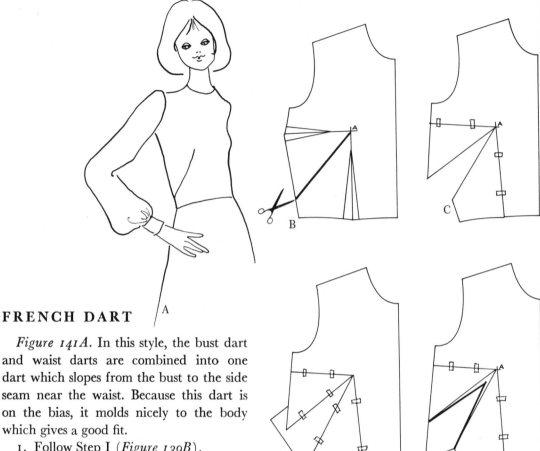

Figure 141

FRENCH DART

Figure 141A. In this style, the bust dart and waist darts are combined into one dart which slopes from the bust to the side seam near the waist. Because this dart is on the bias, it molds nicely to the body which gives a good fit.

1. Follow Step I (*Figure 139B*).

2. Draw the dart line from the apex to the side seam about 1½″ above the waist (*Figure 141B*).

3. Slash along the dart line. Crease the waist and bust darts closed so that the new dart opens up (*Figure 141C*).

4. Tape a piece of paper to the back of the pattern to fill in the space where the dart opened up (*Figure 141D*).

5. To finish the pattern, you must shorten the dart 1½″ from the apex. Mark the finished dart point 1½″ from Point A and blend a line from the dart point into the original dart (*Figure 141E*).

6. Close the dart with the fold of the dart toward the waist and tape. Cut away excess dart, if any, along the side seam and waist.

7. Open up your pattern and cut notches at the end of the dart lines. Your finished pattern should look like *Figure 141E.*

OTHER COMBINED DARTS

Figures 141F and G. Following the same directions as for the french dart above, mark your new dart line from Point A to wherever you want the new dart located. If you have a dart at the center front as in *Figure 141F*, you must add ⅝″ seam allowance at the center front.

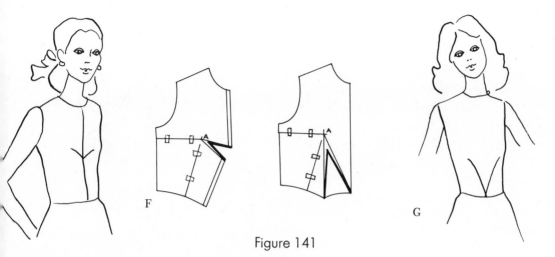

Figure 141

MOVING ONE DART

Either the bust or waist dart may be moved while keeping the other dart in the original position.

MOVING BUST DART TO ARMHOLE

1. *Figure 142.* Follow Step I (explained on page 219, *Figure 139B*).

2. Draw your dart line from the apex (Point A) to the armhole (*Figure 142A*). Do not draw your dart line into the lower part of the armhole (that is, near the side seam).

3. Slash along the dart line from the armhole to the apex.

4. Tape the bust dart closed. Your new dart will open up at the armhole.

5. Follow the same steps given above for moving other darts, taping a piece of paper in back of the dart opening and shortening the dart 1½″ from the apex (*Figure 142B*). Be sure to close your dart before you cut the armhole.

Figure 142

MOVING BUST OR WAIST DART

Following the steps above, you may move one dart to whatever position you like.

1. Begin with Step I (page 219, *Figure 139B*).

2. Draw your dart line from Point A to where you want your new dart.

3. Close whichever dart you want to eliminate.

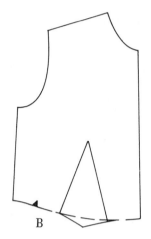

B

A

Figure 143

CHANGING THE DARTS INTO EASE OR TUCKS

In the dress in *Figure 143A,* the darts have been replaced by ease at the waistline.

1. Combine the bust dart with the waist-line dart as explained on page 220.

2. Use your curve stick at the waistline, to smooth out the jog made by the dart (*Figure 143B*).

3. Measure in at the waistline 2″ from the side seam and mark a notch. Begin your ease at this notch. If you want to change the back waistline dart to ease, follow the same directions.

In *Figure 143C* the darts have been changed to ease at the neckline.

1. Shift both darts to the neckline.

2. To finish the pattern, see page 260. Follow the directions, using the bodice sloper instead of the blouse sloper shown.

In *Figure 143D* the darts have been changed to ease at the shoulder.

1. Shift both darts to the shoulder.

2. To finish the pattern, see page 261. Follow the directions, using the bodice sloper instead of the blouse sloper shown.

The darts can also be changed into tucks at the waist, shoulder, and so on. Be sure that your tucks take in the same amount as the dart.

Figure 143

Figure 144

PRINCESS STYLES

In making a princess-line pattern, the darts are changed into seams. By moving the darts to various positions, you can create many different princess styles. If you have already made an A-line princess style, you will find making a princess-line bodice pattern quite similar.

When you design a princess-line bodice, also think about the skirt of the dress. The design lines of the bodice should relate to the design lines in the skirt if you have seams in the skirt. It is best to avoid a lot of different style lines in the bodice and in the skirt unless the lines coincide. Otherwise, the whole effect will be too chopped up. A gathered skirt or a flared skirt without darts looks nice with a princess bodice. If you want to continue the princess line into the skirt, then you can make a six-gore skirt. Do not move the bodice waistline dart, or the bodice seam line will not line up with the seam line on the skirt. You can also use the basic A-line-skirt sloper with a princess bodice. If you don't move the waistline dart of the bodice, the princess line of the bodice will continue into the dart of the skirt.

Keep to simple fabrics which will show up the princess seams. You can further emphasize the seams by topstitching, saddle stitching, or by inserting cording in the seams.

BASIC PRINCESS

On the back pattern, measure the distance along the shoulder seam from the neckline to the shoulder dart (*Figure 144A*). On the front pattern, measure

along the shoulder seam from the neckline, the same amount as on the back. Mark a point on the front shoulder.

1. *Figure 144B*. Following the directions on page 223, shift the bust dart to the shoulder, drawing the dart line to the shoulder mark. Omit the last step of taping paper to the dart opening and shortening the dart.

2. Draw your princess-seam lines as shown in *Figure 144B*. The left seam follows the left side of the bust and waist dart, and the right seam follows the right side of the bust and waist dart. Use your curve stick to blend a smooth line. Draw a crossmark at the bust point.

3. Cut along each seam line.

4. To add your seam allowance, tape a strip of paper to each pattern piece along the princess line (*Figure 144C*). Mark ⅝″ seam allowance. There should be a smooth curve, not an angle, at the bust point. Extend the crossmarks and mark notches on the seam allowance. When you sew the bodice, the notches should match. To establish the grain line of the side front, fold the pattern in half, matching the side seam and the front seam. The crease is the grain line.

5. Your finished pattern should look like *Figure 144D*.

BASIC BACK PRINCESS

The back princess pattern is made following the same steps just given for making the front pattern. Draw your seam line following the waistline and the shoulder dart as shown in *Figure 144E*.

PRINCESS VARIATIONS

Figure 145. Variations are made by shifting one or both darts to the position you want, then continuing as for the basic princess. If you are making a sleeveless princess style, first make the adjustments in the armhole, as given on page 239. When making an empire style, shorten the working pattern first, following the directions on page 251. Here are some ideas for princess-bodice variations and the new dart positions; you can make up more of your own.

BACK PRINCESS VARIATIONS

The back can follow the same design line as the front princess. If the princess line does not go to the shoulder, you should retain the shoulder dart. Draw the princess-seam line on both sides of the waist dart. To finish the design line, continue the seam line to the armhole, neckline, or wherever. Use your French curve or curve stick if necessary. If you move the waistline dart on the front, you can also move the waistline dart on the back, to give the same design. To finish the pattern, continue as for the front, cutting on each line and adding seam allowance and notches. You can also use your basic sloper for the back pattern and have the princess seams just on the front.

MORE PRINCESS STYLES

Figure 146. You can create a pinafore look by adding a ruffle to the seam of the basic princess. Some princess designs look attractive with ties in the seam. A flared skirt or six-gore skirt works well with the princess bodice. With some fabrics, you can also add interest by cutting the center panel on the bias or cross grain.

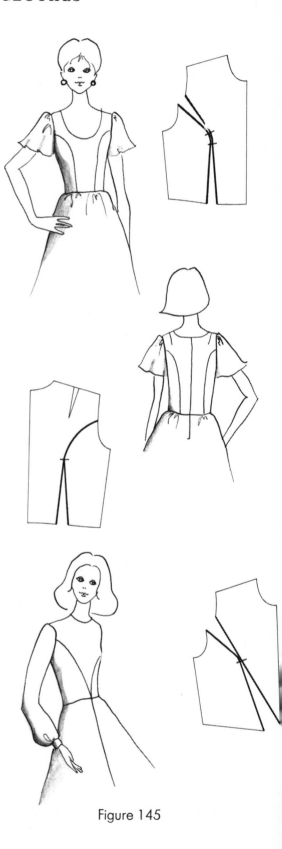

Figure 145

Figure 146

YOKES

Using yokes of various shapes is an excellent way to create new designs. Read about designing dresses with yokes, Chapter 12, page 176.

BASIC YOKES

1. *Figure 147.* Trace your bodice sloper on a new piece of paper and cut out.

2. To mark your design line, square a line from the center front across the bodice. The design line should be located at least 2″ below the neckline and 2″ above the point of the dart. (If it is higher than that, it will interfere with the neckline, and if it is too low, it will get into the bottom of the armhole, which is difficult to work with, *Figure 147A.*)

3. Take a new piece of paper larger than the yoke and place it under the bodice pattern as shown in *Figure 147B*. With a pencil trace around the yoke. Use your

tracing wheel without carbon paper, to mark the yoke line.

4. Remove the bodice pattern. Mark the yoke line with your pencil and ruler. Add seam allowance to the yoke line by drawing a line ⅝″ below the finish line (*Figure 147C*). Mark your center-front line GRAIN LINE unless you are using a different grain line.

5. Cut out your yoke pattern.

6. To finish the bodice pattern, you need to add seam allowance. Measure ⅝″ above the yoke line and draw the seam-allowance line.

7. Cut along the seam-allowance line (*Figure 147D*).

8. Your finished pattern should look like *Figure 147E.*

If you want to change the position of the dart, do that next. Follow the same directions for shifting the dart, using the bodice pattern in *Figure 147E,* instead of the sloper.

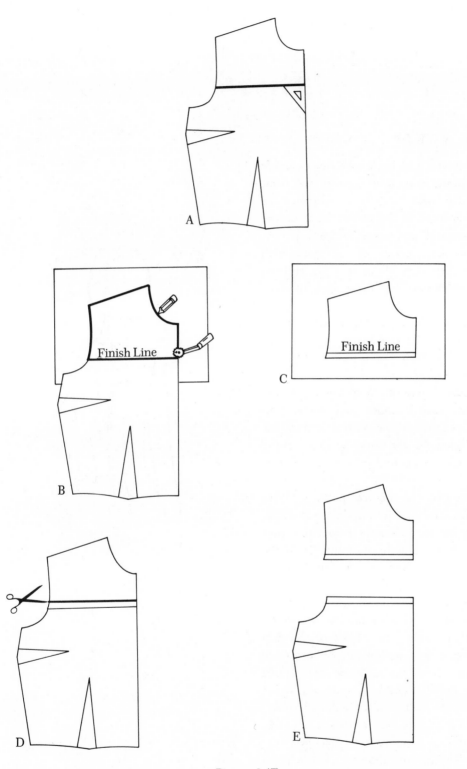

Figure 147

BACK YOKES

Figure 148. The back yoke can be made following the same directions for the front yoke. The yoke pattern should not be longer than 7" at the center back or the yoke seam will bind across the back.

The back yoke can also be made with the shoulder dart eliminated by shifting the shoulder dart into the yoke-seam line. To do this:

1. Trace your back sloper and cut out your pattern. To draw your design line, square a line from the center back across the back (*Figure 148A*).

2. Take a piece of paper larger than the yoke and place it under your bodice pattern. Trace around the yoke and mark the design line and the shoulder dart, using your tracing wheel and no carbon. (*Figure 148B*).

3. Remove the bodice pattern. With your ruler and pencil, mark the yoke line. Add ⅝" seam allowance below the yoke finish line. Extend the dart line from the shoulder to the yoke finish line (*Figure 148C*).

4. Cut out your yoke pattern.

5. To finish the pattern, close the shoulder dart, extending the crease of the dart to the yoke line, following the extended dart line. Tape the shoulder dart closed (*Figure 148D*). The yoke seam will curve up. Mark the center back GRAIN LINE.

6. To finish the bodice pattern, add ⅝" seam allowance above the yoke line, the same as adding seam allowance to the front-bodice pattern. (*Figure 147E*).

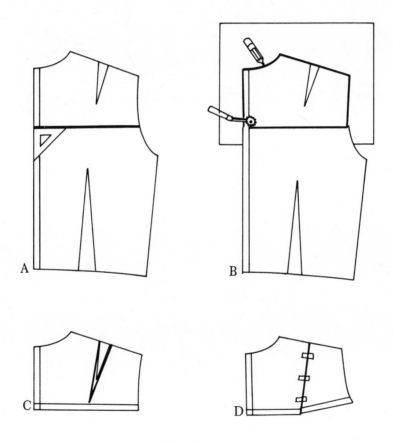

Figure 148

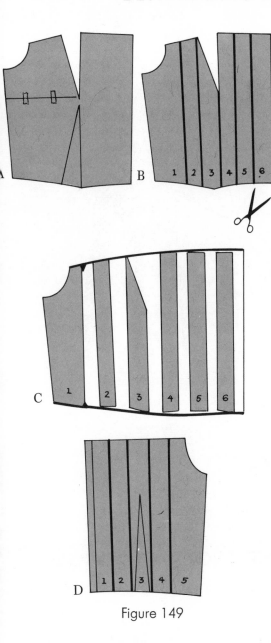

Figure 149

the bust dart to the yoke seam, but don't add the paper to the dart or make new dart lines (*Figure 149A*). The amount of the bust dart has been moved to the yoke line and will be included in the gathers at the yoke line.

3. Draw four slash lines parallel to the center front (*Figure 149B*). The first slash line should be 1½″ away from the armhole. Disregard the waistline dart. Number the pieces of the working pattern.

4. Cut along each of the slash lines.

5. Cut a piece of paper about twice the width of your bodice pattern. Draw the center-front line on the paper.

6. Spread the pieces of your working pattern parallel to the center-front line. There should be approximately ½″ to 1½″ between each piece, depending on the amount of fullness you want. You can have a little more space between pieces 2 and 3 since that is the bust area.

7. Once you have the pieces arranged, tape them in place.

8. Draw in the shape of your new pattern with your curve stick, blending a smooth line at the waist and yoke seams. At the first slash line, mark a notch at both the waistline and the yoke line. Your gathers will begin at these notches (*Figure 149C*).

9. Remove the working pattern and discard. Write GRAIN LINE on your center-front line.

10. Cut out your pattern.

BODICE WITH FRONT YOKE AND GATHERS

Figure 149. To add gathers at the yoke line and waistline, you need to slash and spread the pattern.

1. Make the basic-yoke pattern following the directions on page 230.

2. With the front-bodice pattern, shift

BODICE WITH BACK YOKE AND GATHERS

Figure 149D. Follow the same directions as in making the front pattern, but disregard the directions for shifting the bust dart. You can spread the back a little less than the front since you do not need the bust-line fullness in the back.

BIB YOKES AND OTHER YOKE VARIATIONS

Figure 150. See Chapter 12, page 176 and 183, for instructions for making other yoke variations. Follow the same directions, using the bodice sloper instead of the A-line sloper. Combine both the bust dart and waistline dart into one dart when you are making bib yokes using the bodice sloper.

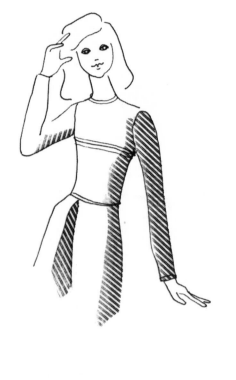

Figure 150

CENTER-FRONT SEAM AND FRONT CLOSINGS

CENTER-FRONT SEAM

Figure 151. A center-front seam can be an attractive design feature. It can be top-stitched by hand or machine for emphasis. Simply add ⅝″ seam allowance at the center front of the pattern instead of placing it on the fold.

FRONT ZIPPER

You will need to add ⅝″ seam allowance to the center front of the bodice to have a front zipper. Cut the back with the center back on the fold. Remember to have a center-front seam in the skirt.

BUTTON-FRONT CLOSING

To make a pattern for a button-front closing, you need to add extension and a facing (page 193). Use the bodice instead of the A-line sloper shown. To add extension to the skirt, see page 204.

Figure 151

Figure 152

SHIRTWAIST DRESS

Figure 152. The shirtwaist dress is a front-closing dress, usually with a collar and cuffs and often with a yoke. A shirtwaist can have ease at the waistline instead of darts, or gathers at yoke and waistline seams. This is a classic style which can be made in almost any fabric. It can be long or short, knit or woven. Some shirtwaist designs are complicated, but others are very simple. In designing shirtwaist dresses, think of contrast in color, texture, and grain of the fabric. For example, a white collar and cuffs with a dark fabric, or a smooth, shiny fabric for cuffs and yoke, with a rough-textured fabric. You can use two or three fabrics for the various parts of the dress; one print for the collar and yoke, a different print for the bodice and skirt, or a knit for the top and a woven for the skirt. Using the same fabric, you can create contrast by varying the grain. For example, stripes cut on the cross grain for the yoke and cuffs and on the straight grain for the rest of the dress, or a yoke, belt, and cuffs cut on the bias, with the rest of the dress cut on the straight grain.

SLEEVELESS STYLES

BASIC SLEEVELESS BODICE

The same principle covered in Chapter 12, page 164, for making the A-line sloper into a sleeveless-dress pattern, also applies to making the bodice sloper into a sleeveless-dress pattern. The armhole for a set-in sleeve has extra room added for ease of movement with a set-in sleeve. If you make a sleeveless dress, this armhole will be too large and won't look nice. This rule applies only to sleeveless dresses, not to jumpers which are worn over a blouse.

1. To make the adjustments in the armhole for a sleeveless bodice, trace the front sloper.

2. (See *Figure 153A*.) At the shoulder seam, measure in from the armhole ½″ and mark a point.

3. At the side seam, measure in at the armhole ½″ and mark a point. Measure up from this point ½″ and mark.

4. Using your French curve, draw in your new armhole, connecting the high point at the side seam with the point at the shoulder.

5. With your ruler, draw a new side seam from the original waistline to the new armhole.

6. Close the bust dart and cut out your pattern on the new lines.

7. To make your back pattern, trace around your back sloper and make the same adjustments at the back armhole. Use the same measurements as the front (*Figure 153B*).

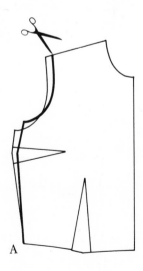

A   B

Figure 153

NOTE: If you are going to make other pattern changes, check the directions for the pattern you want to make before you cut out the pattern. (See *Figure 154* for some easy sleeveless designs.)

Figure 154

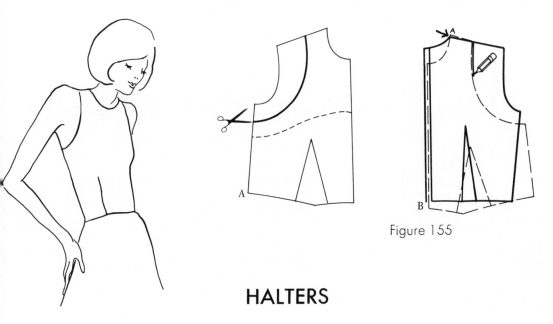

Figure 155

HALTERS

HALTER-ARMHOLE FRONT PATTERN

Figure 155. This armhole is cut high, to bare the shoulders, and low under the arm at the side seam.

1. Trace your front sloper and make the adjustment at the side seam for a sleeveless pattern (*Figure 153A*). Cut out the pattern.

2. Combine the bust dart into the waist dart (page 220). The dart is moved to the waistline so that it will not interfere with the new armhole.

3. To mark the armhole design line, measure in at the shoulder seam 2″ to 3½″ from the armhole and mark a point. At the side seam, measure down from the armhole 1″ to 3″, depending on the effect desired, and mark a point. Using your French curve, draw your new armhole connecting the point at the side seam with the point at the shoulder as you see in *Figure 155A.*

4. Mark your facing line. Keep the facing above the point of the dart.

5. Cut out your new armhole.

NOTE: If you are also making a new neckline, don't do the new neckline until after you have made the back pattern for the armhole because you need to use the original neckline as a reference point.

HALTER-ARMHOLE BACK PATTERN

Trueing the Shoulder Seam. When you change the measurement of the front-shoulder seam, you must be sure the back-shoulder seam is the same measurement. This is called trueing the shoulder seam. To do this:

1. Trace your back sloper. Make the adjustment at the side seam for a sleeveless pattern.

2. (See *Figure 155B.*) Place your new front pattern (shown in dotted line) face down on top of the back pattern so that the front- and back-shoulder seams line up together and meet at the neckline at A (see arrow). Beginning at the shoulder, trace about 3″ of the front armhole onto your back pattern. Ignore the shoulder dart since it will be omitted in this style.

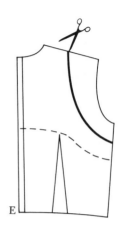

Figure 155

Trueing the Side Seam. Next you need to true the side seam. This is the same idea as trueing the shoulder seam. You must have the front- and back-side seams the same measurement so that the front and back will fit together properly.

3. (See *Figure 155C*.) Place your front pattern on your back pattern face down so that the front waistline and back waistline meet at A (see arrow) and the side seams are lined up together. Beginning at the side seam, trace about 3″ of the front armhole onto the back pattern.

4. Remove the front pattern. Your back pattern should look like *Figure 155D*.

5. Using your French curve draw in the back armhole, connecting the marks at the shoulder and side seam (*Figure 155E*).

6. Use your ruler to straighten the shoulder seam. (Remove the jog from the dart if necessary). Draw in your facing line.

7. Cut out your pattern, cutting along the new armhole.

BARE-BACK HALTER

Figure 156.

1. Make the front pattern the same as the bare-halter armhole above. For this style, the total width of the shoulder seam should be only 1½″ (*Figure 156A*).

2. To make the back pattern, trace the back sloper and make the adjustment at the side seam for sleeveless.

3. True the side seams of the front and back patterns the same as the halter-armhole pattern.

4. To mark your back design line, using your curve stick, begin at the side seam at the truing mark and blend a line across the back from the side seam to the center back. The line should dip down toward the center back as you see in *Figure 156B*.

5. Cut out your new pattern, trimming at the side seam where the side-seam adjustment was made.

6. Because of the shape of this pattern, you can eliminate the waistline dart. Simply crease along the waist dart, extending the crease to the top of the pattern and tape it closed. Blend the design line if necessary.

7. Draw your facing line.

8. Your finished pattern should look like *Figure 156C.*

9. For ties at the neck, you will need two pieces of spaghetti or ribbon about 18″ long each.

Figure 156

Figure 157 shows some other halter variations showing new design lines made on a sleeveless pattern.

Figure 157

SHORT VESTS AND BOLEROS

VESTS

Figure 158. When making vest patterns, you should omit the waistline dart (just disregard it) and use only the bust dart. The bust dart can be moved to the armhole or other location if you like. To make the vest in *Figure 158A:*

1. Trace your front sloper.

2. Add 1½″ hem allowance at the waistline.

3. Add ⅝″ seam allowance at the center front.

4. With your French curve, blend a curved neckline into the seam-allowance line at the center front.

5. Draw a facing line 3″ wide as shown.

6. Cut out your pattern.

7. To make the back pattern, trace the back sloper and add 1½″ hem allowance. Omit the waist darts.

BUTTON-FRONT VEST

Figure 158B.

1. Trace your front sloper.

2. Add 1½″ hem allowance at the waistline.

3. To add extension and a facing at the center front, see page 193.

4. The back pattern is the same as Step 7 above.

Figure 158

BOLERO

Figure 158C.

1. Trace your front sloper.

2. With your French curve and curve stick, shape the front as shown. The design line of the bolero should not come to the center front.

3. Cut out your pattern. Use the same pattern for lining.

The bolero can be made sleeveless or with a little sleeve. Use the back sloper, omitting the waist darts, for the back pattern and lining pattern.

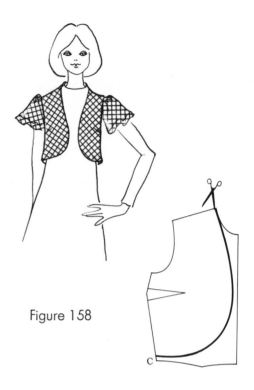

Figure 158

JUMPERS

A jumper pattern made with the bodice sloper follows the same principle as a jumper pattern made with the A-line sloper. Because the jumper is worn over a blouse or sweater, it will fit better if adjustments are made at the armhole and side seam, to allow a little extra room for ease of movement. The pattern companies will often show the same pattern as a sleeveless dress, regular dress, and jumper, but this really will not give a good fit or look well.

To make the adjustment for a jumper:

1. Trace your front sloper.

2. At the shoulder seam, extend the shoulder line ½" as in *Figure 159A.*

3. At the side seam, measure down from the armhole ½" and mark a point. Measure out from that point away from the side seam ¼" and mark a point.

4. With your French curve, draw a new armhole from this point to the extended shoulder seam as you see in *Figure 159A.*

5. Draw a new side seam from the new armhole to the original waistline.

6. Close the bust dart and cut out the pattern on the new lines.

7. To make the back-jumper pattern, make the same adjustment at the armhole and side seam as on the front (*Figure 159B*).

JUMPER VARIATIONS

Many of the styles shown as sleeveless dresses will also work as jumpers. Make the adjustments at the shoulder and armhole required for jumpers, and continue the directions given. You can also find ideas for other jumpers in Chapter 12.

Make your pattern using the bodice sloper instead of the A-line sloper shown. Look through Chapter 13 on skirt patterns. You can make many different jumper styles by combining various skirt and bodice patterns. (Also see bib and pinafore tops which follow.)

Figure 159

BIB AND PINAFORE TOPS

Bib and pinafore tops can be combined with skirts to design jumpers and with pants to design overalls. Pinafore tops can also be stitched to a waistband and worn as a vest, or made into a ruffly pinafore. When making patterns for bib and pinafore tops, the darts are omitted, but the dart shape is used as a guideline. If your bib or pinafore top will be attached to a waistband, trim away the width of your finished waistband from the waistline of your pattern after you make the pattern. For example, if you have a finished waistband 1″ wide, trim away 1″ at the waistline of your bib or pinafore-top pattern.

PINAFORE TOP

Figure 160. This top can be made with or without a ruffle.

1. Trace your front sloper.
2. Mark your design line at the shoulder seam; measure in from the armhole 2″ to 3″ and mark a point. Use your curve stick to blend a line, following the inside line of the waistline dart and up to the mark at the shoulder line as in *Figure 160A.*

3. Add ⅝″ seam allowance.
4. Cut along the seam-allowance line.
5. To make the back pattern, trace your back sloper, but omit marking the darts. Add extension for a button back if required.
6. (See *Figure 160B.*) Place your front pattern (shown in dotted line) face down on your back pattern, matching the neckline and shoulder seams of the front and back. (See arrow.) Trace the design line of the front pattern onto the back pattern. Disregard the shoulder and waistline darts.
7. Remove the front pattern. If necessary, use your ruler to straighten the shoulder seam where the shoulder dart was.
8. Cut your back pattern on the new line (*Figure 160C*).

After you make your front and back patterns, then make the neckline variations if that is part of your design. To finish your pinafore, use the same pattern to cut a lining. Use the lining as a facing for the neckline and the side of your pinafore. If you are using a ruffle on your pinafore, read about ruffles on page 106.

Figure 160

BIB TOP WITH SUSPENDERS

Figure 161. You can finish the straps of this top with buttons or metal suspender hooks or overall clips.

1. Trace your front sloper.

2. To make the design line: At the center-front line measure down from the neckline from 3″ to 5″ and mark a point. At that point, square a line from the center-front line across as shown.

3. With your ruler, draw a line from the inside line of the waist dart through the point of the waist dart up to the first design line as shown.

4. Add ⅝″ seam allowance to your design line.

5. Cut your bib pattern along your new line.

6. Use the same pattern for the lining.

SUSPENDERS

Decide how wide you want the suspenders. To figure the width to cut your suspenders, double the measurement of the finished suspenders and add 1¼″ for seam allowances. For example, if you want your suspenders 1″ finished, double 1 is 2 inches plus 1¼″=3¼″ which is the cut width of your suspenders. Cut your suspenders 30″ long. When you have finished making the garment, try it on and pin the suspenders the correct length.

Figure 161

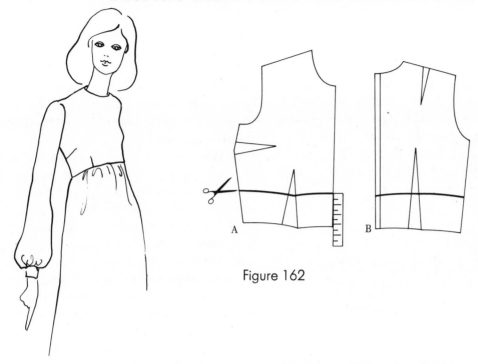

Figure 162

HIGH-WAIST AND EMPIRE-WAIST STYLES

You can make many different dress styles with a high waist or empire waist. A high waist is a few inches above the natural waistline and an empire waist is just under the bosom. The skirt can be long or short, gathered or A-line. It might also be one of the A-line-skirt variations, such as the pleated front skirt, button-front opening, flared, six-gore, or gathered flare. With the empire bodice and a simple gathered or A-line skirt, you can use any of the neckline variations in Chapter 10 and any of the sleeveless styles in Chapter 11. A sleeveless dress or jumper can also be made with an empire or high waist.

BASIC HIGH-WAIST OR EMPIRE DESIGN

1. *Figure 162.* Trace your front-bodice sloper.

2. On your body, measure up from your natural waistline to determine how far up you want to raise the waistline of your pattern. It will probably be between 2″ and 5″. Using your ruler, measure up from the normal waistline of the pattern the amount you want to raise the waistline and mark on the pattern as shown in *Figure 162A.* Draw in your new waistline with your curve stick, following the shape of the original pattern waistline.

3. Tape the waistline dart closed, with the fold toward the center front, and cut along the new waistline.

4. Release the tape and open up the dart. Cut notches at the end of the dart lines.

5. To make your back pattern, follow the same steps as the front. Be sure to measure the same amount at the back waist as at the front waist (*Figure 162B*).

After you have made your front and back patterns, work your neckline variations if that is part of your design.

MOVING THE DART

You can move the darts on an empire-waist pattern the same as on the regular waistline bodice. This style looks especially attractive with the darts at the waistline only, or with french darts. Follow the directions for shortening the bodice pattern above, then move the darts.

SKIRT PATTERNS FOR HIGH-WAIST DRESSES

If you are making a gathered skirt, no pattern is needed. Follow the same directions given for the dirndl skirt, page 218. Remember to figure the length of the skirt from the raised waistline, not the regular waistline.

A-LINE SKIRT

To make an A-line skirt for a high-waisted dress, you need to make a pattern using your A-line-skirt sloper.

1. Trace your front-skirt sloper. Lengthen the skirt if that's part of your design.

2. (See *Figure 163A*.) Measure up from the waistline of the skirt and mark in several places the same amount you measured up from the bodice waistline. For example, if your new waistline on the bodice is 3″ from the natural waistline, measure up 3″ from the skirt waistline also.

3. With your curve stick, draw in your new waistline, following the same shape curve as the original waistline.

4. The skirt waistline must be the same measurement as the waistline of the bodice (*Figure 163B*). Tape the waistline dart of

the bodice pattern closed. Measure the FINISHED waistline. This means measure on the stitching line (not on the cutting line). Beginning at the center front of your skirt pattern, measure along the new skirt waistline the same amount as the bodice waistline and mark.

5. With your curve stick, blend a new side seam from this mark to the original side seam. Disregard the waistline dart. It will not be included in this pattern.

6. Cut out the pattern following the new waistline and side seam.

7. To make your back pattern, follow the same steps as you did for the front (*Figure 168C*). Measure along the back waistline and transfer that measurement to the raised waistline of your back skirt. Add seam allowance to the center back of the skirt pattern if necessary. You can also disregard the dart in the back-skirt pattern.

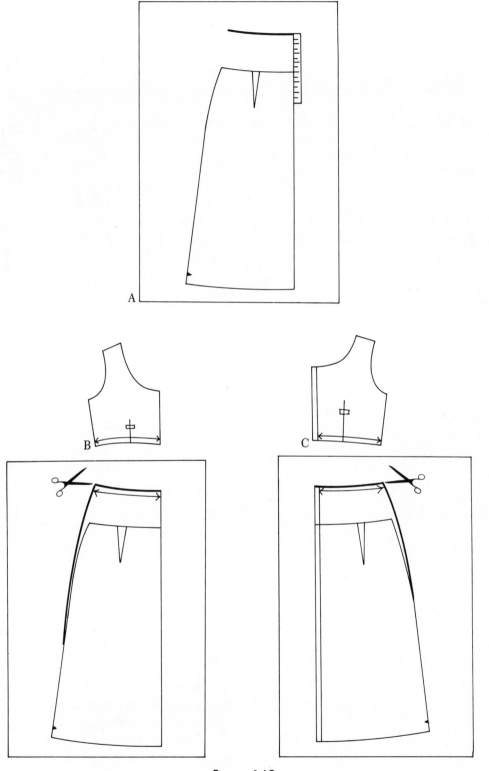

Figure 163

Figure 164

EMPIRE- AND HIGH-WAIST DESIGNS

(See *Figures 164* and *165*.) The empire style is suitable for many of the styles with a regular waistline shown in this chapter. Princess, halters, shirtwaist dresses, and jumpers all may be made with a high waist or empire waist.

Figure 165

BARE-MIDRIFF TOPS

Figure 166. You can also use a high-waist pattern to make a bare-midriff top. Use bias facing to finish the bottom.

Figure 166

CHAPTER 15

DESIGNS MADE FROM THE BLOUSE SLOPER

A great many styles can be made using the basic-blouse sloper and adding a new collar or sleeve, a different cuff, trimming, or other design touches such as tabs or pockets. Much of the information you need to make new blouse patterns has been covered in Chapter 12, "Designs Made from the A-line Sloper." Making a blouse with a yoke follows the same steps as making an A-line dress with a yoke; moving the dart of a blouse pattern follows the same steps as moving the dart of an A-line-dress pattern

and so on. Because the blouse sloper and the A-line-dress sloper are so similar, many of the directions in this chapter will refer back to Chapter 12. The blouse sloper may also be used as the bodice for dropped-waist dresses and to make patterns for jackets and vests.

Figure 167 shows some blouse designs that use the basic-blouse sloper for the front and back and various parts covered earlier in the book: collars, sleeves, pockets, necklines, ruffles, and so on.

CLOSINGS

BACK CLOSING

Instead of buttoning in the front, your blouse can close in the back either with a zipper or buttons. If you have a back opening, remember to cut your front blouse with the center-front line of the blouse sloper on the fold of your fabric. For a

blouse with a zipper in the back, mark your blouse sloper directly on the fabric and add 5⁄8″ seam allowance at the center back, instead of placing the center back on the fold.

When the blouse has a back-button

Figure 167

opening, you will need to add extension and a facing at the back. To make your back pattern, trace your back sloper on a new piece of paper. See Chapter 12, page 193, for information on figuring the amount of your extension and marking the facing on your pattern. Follow the same directions given for the A-line-dress front, using the back-blouse sloper instead. (Remember you need a two-piece collar with a back opening.)

SLASH-FRONT OPENING

Figure 168. A style with a slash-front opening pulls on over the head. Cut the blouse with the center front of your pattern or sloper on the fold and with the center back on the fold. This style looks well with or without a collar and in soft, clinging knit fabrics. See Chapter 12, page 191, for details on how to make a slash front.

Figure 168

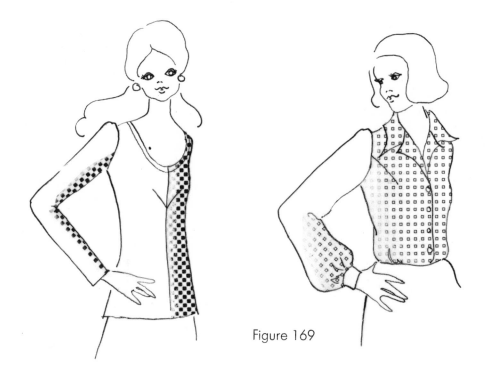

Figure 169

MOVING THE DART

As with the A-line dress, the bust dart of your blouse may be moved to a number of different positions such as the armhole, neckline, or shoulder. This is easy to do and increases the number of design possibilities. The steps in changing the dart position for a blouse pattern are the same as in changing a dart of the A-line pattern. *Figure 169* shows some blouse styles with the dart in a new position. To move the dart, see Chapter 12, page 160. Follow the same steps, using the blouse sloper instead of the A-line sloper.

CHANGING THE DART INTO EASE

You can change the bust dart into ease at the neckline or the shoulder line. The steps are similar to shifting the dart to a new position. You can use the basic sloper for the back pattern unless you are making a neckline change.

BLOUSE WITH EASE AT THE NECKLINE

1. Trace your front sloper and cut out your pattern.

2. Draw 5 slash lines from the neck to the point of the dart as you see in *Figure 170A*. Slash along each line from the neckline to the dart.

3. Tape the bust dart closed. Space will open up at the neckline.

4. Place a piece of paper underneath the space where the slashes have opened up and spread so you have the same amount of space between each piece (*Figure 170B*). Tape the pieces to the underpaper.

5. With your French curve, blend a new neckline as shown.

6. Cut along the new neckline.

7. After you gather the neckline, finish the neck with french piping or a neckband.

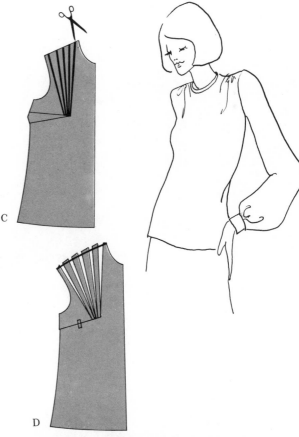

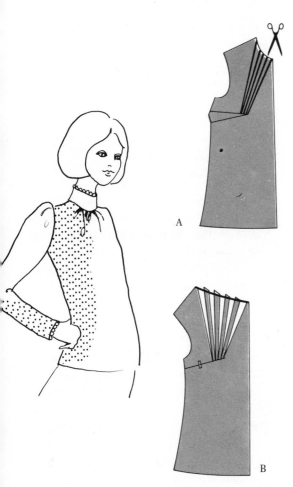

Figure 170

BLOUSE WITH EASE AT THE SHOULDER:

The steps here are almost the same as making a pattern for blouse with ease at the neckline.

1. Trace your front sloper and cut out the pattern.

2. Draw five slash lines from the point of the dart to the shoulder line as you see in *Figure 170C*.

3. Follow the same steps given above for making the blouse pattern with ease at the neckline, taping dart closed, spreading the pieces and drawing in a new shoulder line.

4. Your pattern should look like *Figure 170D*. When you sew the blouse, gather along the shoulder-seam line so the front shoulder is the same length as the back shoulder.

DARTLESS BLOUSE PATTERN

For shirt styles and blouses made out of knits, you may want to eliminate either the bust dart, the back-shoulder dart, or both darts.

6. Use your ruler to blend a new side seam from the armhole into the original side seam. Cut on the new side seam and the new hemline.

FRONT PATTERN WITH NO DART

1. Trace your front sloper and cut out your pattern.

2. (See *Figure 171A*.) With your ruler, draw a line from the notch at the bottom line of the dart to the intersection of the neckline and the center front (Point A). Draw a second line from the center of the dart at the side seam to Point A.

3. Erase your original dart.

4. At the side seam, measure up from the hemline the amount of the new dart measurement, and mark. Draw a new hemline that is shorter by the same amount as the dart measurement. For example, if your dart measures 1″, then shorten your hemline 1″.

5. Close the new dart and tape it (*Figure 171B*).

BACK PATTERN WITH NO DART

1. Trace your back sloper and cut it out.

2. (See *Figure 171C*.) Measure the width of the dart at the shoulder seam (the amount shown between the arrows).

3. Beginning at the armhole, measure along the shoulder seam and mark the same amount as the dart measurement (Point A).

4. With your French curve, blend a new armhole from Point A into the original armhole (*Figure 171D*). With your ruler, draw a new straight shoulder line from the neckline to Point A. Erase the shoulder dart.

5. Cut out your back pattern, cutting on the new armhole and new shoulder line.

Figure 171

BLOUSES WITH YOKES

A pattern for a button-front blouse with a yoke becomes quite complicated to make. If you have a front yoke, use a back opening or a front zipper. A button-front blouse, with a yoke in the back only, is the way many shirts are made.

The following blouse designs in *Figure* *172* use the basic yoke. See Chapter 12, page 175, and follow the same instructions, using your blouse sloper instead of the A-line sloper. Read through the section on yoke dresses in Chapter 12 to get some ideas for making blouses with yokes.

Figure 172

Figure 173

BLOUSES WITH BIB YOKES

Figure 173. Blouses with bib yokes can be made with the yoke of a different fabric and with some kind of trim or lace stitched to the yoke-seam line. Matching trim could also be added at the sleeves, or on the cuffs. See Chapter 12, page 181, for specific instructions for making bib yokes. Use the blouse sloper instead of the A-line-dress sloper. Many of the bib yoke-style dresses can be made as blouses.

If you are trimming a blouse with a curved yoke, remember to use a flexible trim to go around the curve.

Figure 174

SHIRTS

Figure 174. A shirt is usually made from a dartless pattern. It is a great-looking and versatile style, flattering to any figure. A shirt can be made in any fabric from lace to corduroy. There may be a yoke in the back or not. You can vary the style by using pockets, flaps, or a different collar or cuffs. The sleeve could be the basic shirt sleeve or a very full bishop. A short sleeve might be the self-cuff sleeve or a puff style. For another look, you can add ties or a drawstring at the waist.

PRINCESS-LINE BLOUSES

You can design a number of different blouse styles with princess seams. Follow the directions given in Chapter 12 for making the princess-line pattern, using the blouse sloper instead of the A-line sloper. For design ideas, some of the styles shown as princess dresses will also work as blouses, as well as princess-blouse styles shown in

Figure 175. Your blouse can have a princess seam only in the front, and use the basic-blouse sloper for the back; or it can have princess seams in both front and back. For variety, you might want to cut the side panels of the princess style on the bias, or of another fabric. A princess blouse works well as the top of a two-piece dress.

Figure 175

SLEEVELESS BLOUSES

As with the sleeveless A-line dress and sleeveless bodice, you must adjust in the size of the armhole for a sleeveless-blouse pattern to fit properly. The armhole for a set-in sleeve has been made larger for ease of movement when the sleeve is set in. With-out the sleeve, you need to make the arm-hole a little smaller so that you won't have a big, loose armhole. See Chapter 12, page 164, and follow the same directions given for adjusting the armhole of the A-line dress, using your blouse sloper instead.

Figure 176

SLEEVELESS-BLOUSE DESIGNS

(See *Figure 176.*) For other design ideas, see the halter tops in Chapter 14. Follow the same directions, using the blouse sloper instead of the bodice sloper, disregarding any information about the waistline dart. Sleeveless A-line-dress styles in Chapter 12 can also work as sleeveless blouses. Follow the directions, using your blouse sloper instead of the A-line-dress sloper.

If you have a sleeveless A-line-dress pattern and would like to make it as a blouse, you don't need to make the whole pattern again. Cut the A-line-dress pattern, shorten to blouse length, and taper the side seams so it doesn't flare out at the hip.

BLOUSONS AND TENT TOPS

A blouson pattern is made by slashing and spreading. The bottom of the blouson is gathered at the waistline or hipline. It can be gathered on a drawstring or elastic, or the gathers can be stitched to a band. A tent-top pattern is made the same as a blouson, but it is not gathered at the bottom (*Figure 179*).

BLOUSON PATTERN

Figure 177.

1. Trace your front sloper. Decide the length you want your blouson and shorten your blouse pattern if necessary. The length of your pattern should be 1″–2″ longer than the length you want your finished blouson. For example, if you want your finished blouse 18″ at the center back, your blouson pattern should be about 20″ long at the center back to give extra allowance for blousing.

2. After you have traced your sloper and shortened your pattern, cut out your pattern.

3. Make three slash lines as shown in *Figure 177A.* The first slash line begins at the point of the bust dart and extends to the hem. The second two slash lines are parallel to this line and form an L shape toward the armhole.

4. Cut along your first slash line up to the bust point. Cut your other two slash lines to within ⅛″ of the armhole.

5. (See *Figure 177B.*) Tape the bust dart closed. A space will open up at the waistline.

6. Place your working pattern on a new piece of paper. Spread the pieces of the working pattern between 1″–2″. You will probably have more space between the slash line that extends from the bust dart than between the other two slash lines.

7. Once you spread your pieces, tape

them in place. Draw a new hemline, blending a smooth line with your curve ruler. Trace around the rest of the pattern.

8. Discard your working pattern. In this pattern, the bust dart has been eliminated and the fullness from the bust dart transferred to the gathers at the waistline.

9. Cut out your pattern.

10. To make the back-blouson pattern, follow the same steps as in making your front pattern. Trace your sloper and shorten the same amount as you shortened the front. Make your three slash lines as shown in *Figure 177C*. Spread the back blouson the same as the front pattern. The finished back pattern should look like *Figure 177D*.

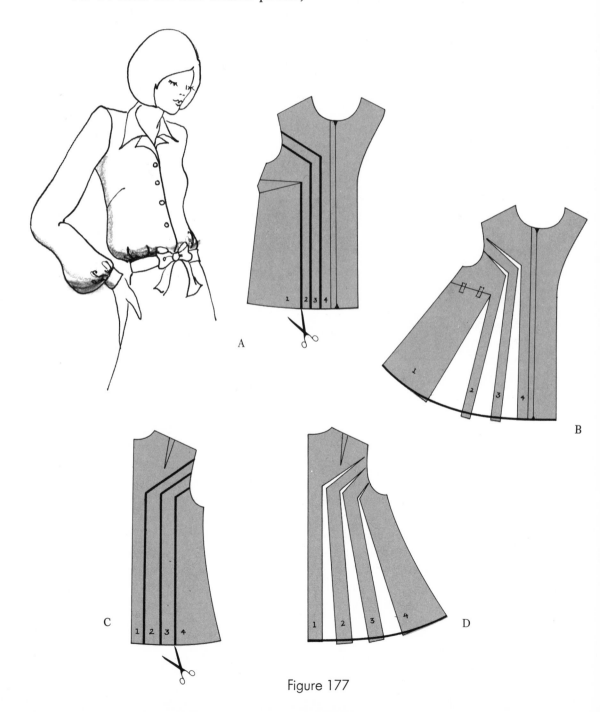

Figure 177

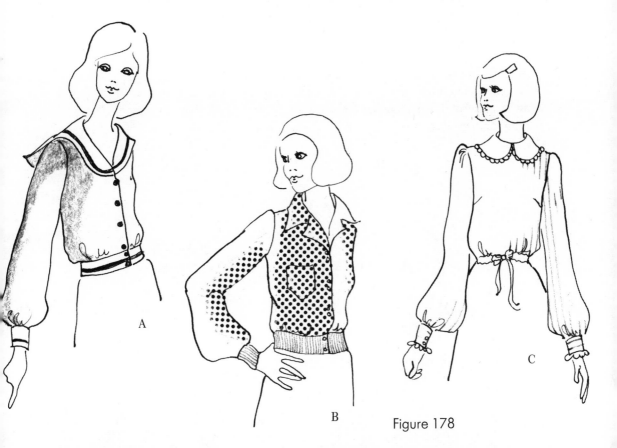

A

B

C

Figure 178

HOW TO FINISH THE BOTTOM OF A BLOUSON

1. Drawstring bottom, *Figure 178C*. Use spaghetti or a narrow stitch and turn tie. The length should be your waistline or hipline measurement plus about 36 inches to tie a bow. BEFORE you turn up the hem, make two buttonholes, one to the right and one to the left of the center front, to pull the drawstring through.

2. Waistbands or Hipbands: You can make a band at the bottom of your blouson to go around your waistline or hipline (*Figure 178A*). It is made the same as a skirt waistband. To figure the amount of your band, measure your waistline or hipline (wherever your blouson will end) and to that measurement, add $2\frac{1}{4}''$ for seam allowance and ease. Then you must also add twice the amount of your button extension. For example, if your waistline is $24''$, you would add $2\frac{1}{4}''$, making it $26\frac{1}{4}''$; then to that, add twice the amount of your extension. If your extension is $\frac{5}{8}''$, twice that is $1\frac{1}{4}''$, so your total waistband would be $27\frac{1}{2}''$ long. With this kind of band, your blouse must open from neck to bottom, or you won't be able to get into it.

You can also use a ready-made, stretchy knit ribbed waistband at the bottom of a blouson (*Figure 178B*). As you sew, stretch the knit band so it will gather up when released. The band should be applied with a zigzag stitch.

TENT TOPS

Figure 179. To make a tent-top pattern, follow the directions just given for the blouson pattern. Then hem the bottom instead of gathering it.

Figure 179

Figure 180

SHORT JACKETS AND VESTS

Figure 180. With a simple change, the blouse sloper may be used to make patterns for untailored jackets and vests. Some adjustment is necessary because a jacket must have a larger armhole to fit properly. To make short-jacket patterns, follow the directions on page 196, using the blouse sloper instead of the A-line sloper shown. Remember to add extra seam allowance at each side of your sleeve pattern, as explained on page 197, when you make a jacket. For sleeveless jackets (vests), follow the same instructions given for making a jacket pattern. Omit the sleeve and draw in an armhole-facing line.

If you are making a jacket that will be worn only over a sleeveless dress or top, it is not necessary to make the adjustments for a jacket pattern. The regular blouse sloper will have enough extra room for ease of movement because of the close fit of a sleeveless style worn underneath.

The knit cardigan jacket is made without a bust dart. Follow the directions for removing the dart on page 262.

Figure 181

TWO-PIECE DRESSES

Figure 181. A two-piece dress is made by combining a blouse with a skirt of the same or co-ordinated fabric. The skirt and top relate to each other more closely than sportswear separates. If you use a different fabric for the skirt, some skirt fabric should generally be used on the blouse to pull the look together. The top is usually worn out, rather than tucked in. It can be hip length, or waist length with a band added. Besides the styles shown in *Figure 181,* many of the blouses shown in this chapter will work as the top of a two-piece dress.

For the matching skirt, the basic A-line, flared, six-gore, or A-line with pleats would be a good choice.

LONG-WAIST DRESSES AND JUMPERS

The blouse sloper can be used as the bodice of long-waist dresses or jumpers. The skirt can be flared or gathered. Some of the A-line-skirt variations in Chapter 13 can be applied to the flared skirt shown here. A long-waist design might be a tennis dress, beach dress, short dressy dress, or jumper. This proportion looks best with a short skirt.

To make your bodice pattern for a long-waist dress, follow the same steps as making a blouse pattern. If you want a back opening, remember to add extension (page 193) or seam allowance at your center back. Remove the extension and facing and add seam allowance for a front-zipper opening.

The blouse sloper has a 1½″ hem. For a long-waist dress, you will need only ⅝″ seam allowance and will probably want to shorten your sloper so that your dress will end somewhere around your hipbone.

SKIRTS FOR LONG-WAIST DRESSES

GATHERED SKIRT

This is the simplest kind of skirt to make for a long-waist dress. Figure the length you want your skirt, then add 4″ for hem and seam allowance. For example, if your finished skirt will be 15″, your skirt should be cut 19″. Follow the directions for dirndl skirts given on page 218. A gathered skirt for a long-waist dress looks attractive cut on the bias.

FLARED SKIRT FOR
LONG-WAIST DRESS

Figure 182. You will need to make a pattern for a flared skirt.

1. Measure along the FINISH line (not cutting line) of your dropped-waist pattern from the center front to your finished side seam. Do not include the seam allowance at the side seam (*Figure 182A*). Decide the finished length of your skirt and add 2″ for the hem allowance. The seam allowance will be added later.

2. Draw a rectangle as shown in *Figure 182B.* The waist measurement is the top and bottom of the rectangle and the skirt length is the two sides of the rectangle. Draw slash lines parallel to the center front about every inch and number the pieces of your pattern.

3. Cut out the rectangle. Cut along your slash lines to within ⅛″ of the waist.

4. Take a new piece of paper and spread the pieces of your pattern to achieve the amount of flare you want. If the side seam of your pattern is at a right angle to the center front, as shown in *Figure 182C,* the skirt will be a full circle, which looks very good with a long-waist bodice. Spread your pieces so you have the same amount of space between each one and tape them in place.

5. Trace the pattern. Blend a smooth curved line at the hem and the waistline. Add ⅝″ seam allowance at the waistline and side seam.

6. Remove the strips of your working pattern and discard. Mark the center-front fold line. If your pattern piece is too big to cut on the fold, add ⅝″ seam allowance at the center front.

You can use the same pattern for the back and front skirt. After you stitch the side seams of your skirt together, run an

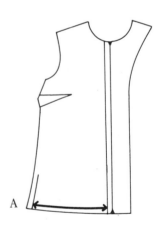

Figure 182

ease stitch around the waist. This will keep the waistline from stretching and can be used to ease the skirt into the waistline of the bodice. Since part of this skirt is on the bias, it's best to let it hang for a day or two before hemming it.

LONG-WAIST STYLES

Figure 183. You can make a long-waist style, using the basic pattern for the top and adding a new neckline or collar and sleeve. The bodice and sleeves might be of a different fabric from the skirt. Many of the blouse styles in this chapter can work as the bodice of a long-waist dress. Princess-line blouses, shirts, slashed-front opening blouses, and dartless knit tops, among others, can be used as a bodice.

Figure 182

Figure 183

CHAPTER 16

DESIGNS MADE FROM THE PANTS SLOPER

Figure 184

Besides the usual denims, corduroys, and woolens, you can also make pants out of lightweight fabrics such as sateen prints, gingham or eyelet. With lightweight fabrics you will need a backing fabric such as batiste. Cut the backing and the pants at the same time and sew the backing with the pants as one piece of fabric, not as a separate lining. Lightweight single knits are not usually a good choice for pants because they stretch out of shape too much. For design interest, you can use different color or different fabric for the waistband or pockets. Washable suede pockets are a very luxurious touch and won't cost a lot of money if you buy scraps or elbow patches. You can use flaps and tabs as belt loops at the waistband as well as for design interest on the pants themselves. Interesting pockets can be the focal point of your design. Pockets can be placed on the front or back or on the legs. See *Figure 184* for some pants styles made from the basic sloper.

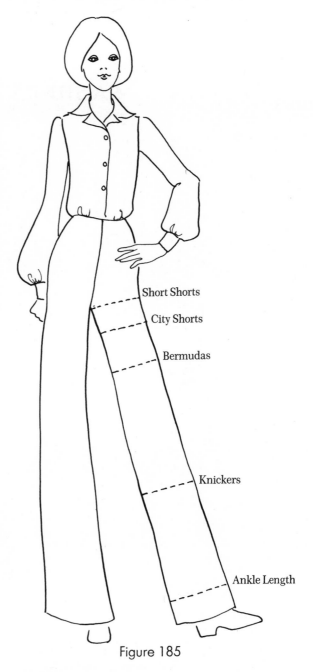

Figure 185

PANTS LENGTHS

The drawing in *Figure 185* shows some of the well-known lengths. Making a different length doesn't require a new pattern. Just trace your pattern or your sloper on the fabric and mark whatever length you want. Don't forget to include hem allowance and make the back and front the same length.

WAISTLINES AND DARTS

DART VARIATIONS

The pants dart can be made as one or two tucks like the little pleats you find in some men's pants. The darts can also be changed into ease so there is no dart (*Figure 186C*).

WAISTBANDS

Pants can be made with a waistband (*Figure 186A*), or no band and a bias facing. (See page 200 on making waistbands.) The directions are the same for pants as for a skirt.

Knit pants can be made pull-on style, with an elastic waist (*Figure 186B*). To make this kind of pants, see page 201. Follow the same instructions given for making a knit pull-on skirt, using your pants sloper instead.

Figure 186

Figure 187

PANTS WITH CUFFS

Figure 187. Cuffs may be added to pants of any length.

1. Trace your pants sloper or pattern.

2. Extend the side and inner-leg seams 6″ below the hem of the pants leg.

3. Figure the width you want your finished cuff and double it. Add that amount at the bottom of the pants leg below the hem. For example, if you want a 2″ cuff, add 4″ to the bottom of the pants leg. This can be done directly on the fab-

ric if you prefer. If you make a short-pants pattern, add hem allowance in addition to the cuff width.

The turnback cuff does not work well on pants with a very wide flared leg because there is so much curve at the bottom of the leg. To keep your cuff from flopping down, stitch by hand at the side seam and inner-leg seam, attaching the inside of the cuff to the pants leg.

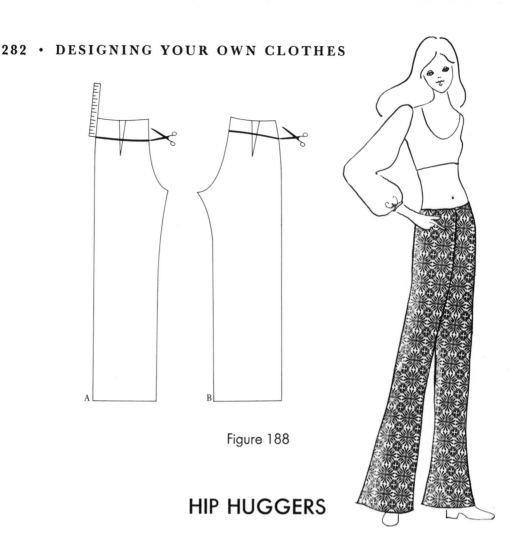

Figure 188

HIP HUGGERS

Figure 188. Hip huggers can be lowered about 2″ to 5″ below the natural waistline, depending on your figure and the effect you want. A new pattern is not necessary if you are not making any other pattern changes. You can trace your pants sloper and mark the adjustments directly on the fabric.

1. Trace your front- and back-pants sloper.

2. Mark the front waistline. With your ruler, measure down from the natural waistline at the center-front and side seams the amount you want to lower your pants and mark as you see in *Figure 188A*. With your curve stick, blend a new waistline.

3. Tape the dart closed and cut on the new waistline.

If you have only 2″ or less of the dart remaining, you may omit the dart and take in your pants a little more at the side seam near the waist. Do this when you try on your pants before you put on the waistband.

4. Mark the waistline on your back pattern. At the side seam, measure down from the waistline the same amount that you measured on the front. At the center back, measure down the amount less ¾″. (The center back of the pants will be ¾″ higher than at the side seam.) For example, if you measured down 3½″ at the side seam, you would measure down 2¾″ at the center back. Mark the back waistline, using your curve stick to draw a gently arching line from the side seam to the center back. This shape gives a better fit to the back of your pants.

5. Your back pattern should look like *Figure 188B*.

TAPERED-LEG PANTS

Figure 189. In this style the legs are tapered and end near the ankle.

1. Trace your sloper and cut it out. At the hemline, measure in from the side seam 1″ to 2″. Measure in the same amount at the inner-leg seam. Remember you need enough room to get your foot through.

2. With your curve stick, blend a new side seam from the mark at the hem into your original side seam.

3. Blend a new inner-leg seam into the original seam, as you see in *Figure 189.*

4. The back pattern is made the same as the front.

To make 1950s pedal pushers, follow the same instructions, but shorten the pants to just below knee length.

Figure 189

Flare point — — — — Flare point

Figure 190

BELL-BOTTOM PANTS

EASY BELL BOTTOM

Figure 190. This style bell-bottom pants is made by adding at the side seam. Bell bottoms can flare from above or below the knee, depending on the effect you want. To make a pattern for bell-bottom pants:

1. Trace your front sloper.

2. At the side seam, mark where you want your flare to begin (flare point in *Figure 190*). At the inner-leg seam, mark the flare point opposite the flare point at the side seam.

3. At the hem of your pants, measure out from the side seam 1″ to 4″ (A).

Measure out from the inner-leg seam the same amount and mark (B).

4. Blend a new side seam from Point A to the original side seam. Blend a new inner-leg seam from Point B the same way.

5. Extend the hemline to the new side seam and inner-leg seam.

6. To make your back pattern, trace your back sloper and follow the same directions just given for the front pattern. Be sure you use the same measurement on the back pattern as you did on the front.

BELL BOTTOMS MADE BY SLASHING AND SPREADING

The way bell bottoms look depends on how the slash lines are drawn. The flare will begin where the slash line begins. If you want bell bottoms that fit snugly through the hips and begin to flare out at the thighs, start your slash lines at the thighs (*Figure 191*). For bell bottoms that fit tightly at the thighs and flare out below the knees, begin your slash line below the knees.

1. Trace your front sloper on a new piece of paper.

2. Mark slash lines as you see in *Figure 191A*. Notice that the slash lines are opposites; the two at the side seam are the same length and shape as the two at the inner-leg seam.

3. Beginning at the hem, cut your slash lines to within ⅛″ of the side seam and the inner-leg seam.

4. Place the bottom part of your working pattern on a new piece of paper and spread the pieces for the fullness you want (*Figure 191B*). You should have the same amount of space between each piece. Tape the pattern in place.

5. Trace around the bottom of your working pattern. Blend a new hemline, smoothing out any jogs.

6. Cut on the new lines.

7. Your finished pattern should look like *Figure 191B*.

8. To make your back pattern, follow the same directions as for the front pattern. The length of your slash lines and the amount you spread the pieces must be the same as for the front pattern.

Figure 191

FLARED PANTS AND EVENING PANTS

Figure 192. As you can see in *Figure 192A,* the slash lines in this style are made from the hem to the waistline. This gives the pants a very different shape from bell bottoms, which have slash lines to the side seam. Evening pants have more fullness than daytime pants and are generally made of soft, drapy fabrics. If the evening-pants pattern has enough width, it will look more like a skirt than pants. The measurement of the circumference of the pants leg can be about 28″ for moderately flared pants, to 50″ or more for full evening pants.

1. Trace your front-pants sloper on a new piece of paper and cut out your pattern.

2. Trim off ⅝″ seam allowance at the waistline.

3. Mark five parallel slash lines from hem to waist and number the pieces (*Figure 192A*). Cut along each line from the hem to within ⅛″ of the waistline.

4. Tape the waistline dart closed.

5. Place your working pattern on a new sheet of paper, and spread the pieces to achieve the amount of fullness you want. The amount of space should be equal between each piece. The more you spread the pieces, the wider your pants. Once you have arranged your pieces, tape them in place.

6. Trace around your new pattern. With your curve stick, blend a smooth line at the waist and hem. Add ⅝″ seam allowance at the waistline (*Figure 192B*).

7. Clip the tape of your working pattern and discard it.

8. Cut out your new pattern.

9. To establish the grain line, fold your pattern in half longways, matching the side seam with the inner-leg seam. Crease along the fold. Mark the crease GRAIN LINE.

10. Make your pattern for the back, following the same steps as the front. Be sure you spread the same amount between the pieces on the back pattern as on the front pattern.

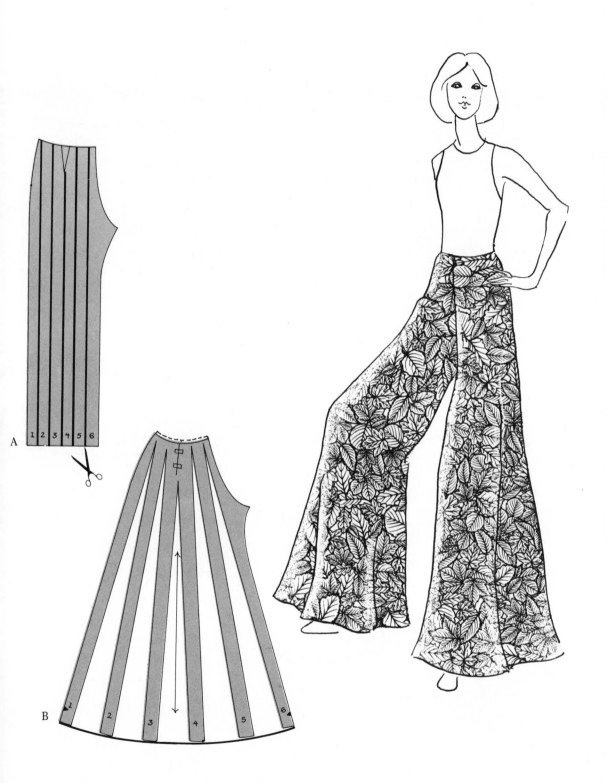

Figure 192

Figure 193

FULL EVENING PANTS WITH GATHERS AT WAISTLINE

Figure 193. This style looks more like a skirt and is best made in very soft fabrics like single knit.

1. Trace your front sloper.

2. Mark five parallel slash lines and number the pieces of your working pattern (*Figure 192A,* page 287).

3. Cut out your pattern and cut along each slash line all the way through. Disregard the dart.

4. On a new piece of paper, spread the pieces of your working pattern approximately as in *Figure 193.* There should be more space at the hem than at the waistline and an equal amount of space between each piece. The more the pattern is spread, the fuller your pants will be. Once you have your pieces arranged the way you want, tape them in place.

5. Trace around the pattern. With your curve stick, blend a smooth line at the waist and hemline.

6. Discard the pieces of your working pattern and cut out your new pattern.

7. To establish the grain line, fold your pattern in half lengthwise, matching the side seam and inner-leg seam. Crease along the fold. Open up your pattern and mark the fold GRAIN LINE.

8. To make your back pattern, follow the same steps as in making the front pattern. Be sure you spread the pieces of your back working pattern the same amount as the front.

Figure 194

KNICKERS

Figure 194B. Knickers can be made using pants sloper or a pants pattern such as the knit pull-on or flared leg. If you prefer, you don't need to make a new pattern for this but can mark directly onto your fabric.

1. Trace your front sloper.

2. Beginning at the waistline, measure along the side seam to 2″ below the knee.

3. Draw a straight line across the leg and cut off the pants leg at this point (*Figure 194D*).

4. To make a cuff pattern, measure the circumference of your leg just below the knee. To this measurement add 2¼″ for ease and seam allowance. To finish, see "All-Around Cuff" on page 154.

The cuff of a knicker is made the same as the cuff for the shirt sleeve that has no button opening. For a really quick finish, you can omit the cuff and use elastic instead. When you do this, measure at the side seam to 3½″ below the knee. Turn up the hem to make a tunnel for the elastic and run a piece of 1″-wide elastic through the tunnel.

BLOOMERS

Figure 194C. Bloomers are made the same as knickers except they end above the knee. They can be whatever length you like.

HAREM PANTS

Figure 194A. This style can be made from the pattern for flared pants with no gathers at the waist, (*Figure 192*) or pants with gathers at the waist (*Figure 193*). The waist can also be lowered as for hip huggers. To make the cuff pattern for harem pants, follow directions given on page 154 for making cuffs on shirt sleeves. The circumference of the cuff should be just big enough for you to put your foot through. Gather up the bottom of the pants and attach the cuffs just as you would a cuff on a shirt sleeve.

SHORTS

Figure 195. Any of the styles in this chapter can be made as shorts. They can be styled with pockets, flaps, or topstitching and with or without cuffs. For city or office wear, shorts can be made longer and with more flare, to look like a skirt. To make this style short, shorten the working pattern to the length you want, then follow the directions for the flare-leg pants on page 286.

Figure 195

Figure 196

OVERALLS

Overalls are made by attaching a bib and suspenders or a pinafore top to pants. You can use the pants sloper or other pants pattern such as bell bottoms. The pants can be made with or without a waistband, but should come to the natural waistline. (See page 248 for directions on making the bib top and pinafore top shown in *Figure 196*.)

Figure 197

JUMPSUITS

Jumpsuits are made by combining a bodice with pants. Both the bodice or pants can be either the basic sloper or a new pattern. Jumpsuits can be any length from short little tennis suits to full length for evening. They can also be made sleeveless or as jumpers. With a basic jumpsuit you can use most any neckline or sleeve style. The jumpsuit can be made in one piece from shoulders to hem, or with a waistline seam.

BASIC JUMPSUIT WITH SEAM AT WAISTLINE

Figure 197. For the top of the jumpsuit, you can use the bodice sloper or another bodice pattern. Just remember to add seam allowance to the center front of the bodice if the jumpsuit has a front opening. An adjustment is needed at the waistline of the pants pattern for ease.

If your jumpsuit bodice and pants pattern both have darts at the waistline, you should be sure the darts of the pants pattern line up with the darts of the bodice. To check this:

1. Measure along the finished waistline of your bodice pattern the distance from the center front to the first line of the dart (*Figure 197*).

2. At the pants waistline, measure from the center front (NOT the cutting line) the same distance as on the bodice and mark. If the mark indicating the position of the dart on the bodice does not match the dart at the waist of your pants, you will need to move the dart over to this mark.

3. Trace your pants sloper or pattern. Draw the new dart mark at the waist. Redraw the new dart at the new mark. If your pants pattern has two darts, the dart closest to the center front should line up with the dart on the bodice.

4. Raise the waistline 1″ (*Figure 197*). Extend the lines of the dart up to the raised waistline and mark notches.

5. To make the back pattern for your jumpsuit, follow the same steps as you did for the front, adding 1″ ease at the waistline and moving the pants dart to line up with the waist dart if necessary.

BASIC JUMPSUIT WITH NO SEAM AT WAIST

Figure 198. For this you will need a large piece of paper from 5 to 6 feet long.

1. Draw the center-front line on one side of the paper.

2. Place the bodice sloper so the center-front line of the bodice is against the center-front line on your paper.

3. Trace around your bodice sloper. Mark the bust dart and the waistline dart.

4. Remove the bodice sloper.

5. Add ⅝″ seam allowance parallel to the center-front line. On your seam-allowance line, measure down ½″ from the waist of the bodice sloper and mark (Point A).

6. Take your pants sloper or pattern and place it so that the waistline of the pants sloper is at Point A and the grain line of the pants is parallel to the center front of the bodice (*Figure 198A*). You can extend the grain line of the pants with a yardstick to see if you have it in the right position.

7. Trace around the pants pattern, marking the notches and point of the waist dart.

8. Remove your pants pattern.

9. Blend a smooth line from the bodice, connecting the side seam of the bodice with the side seam of the pants as you see in *Figure 198A.*

10. To mark the waistline dart, use your curve stick to blend a smooth line from the point of the bust dart to the dart point on the pants. The left and right sides of the dart should be the same.

11. To avoid confusion, erase the waistline and the old dart marks.

12. Cut out your pattern.

13. To make your back pattern, follow

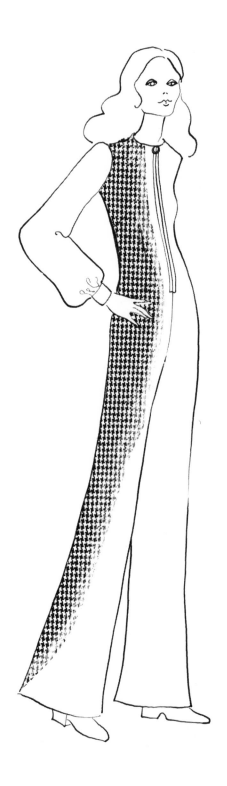

the same steps as for the front pattern but do not add seam allowance at the center-back bodice. The side seam of the back pattern should have the same shape and be the same length as the side seam of the front pattern. The back pattern should look like *Figure 198B*.

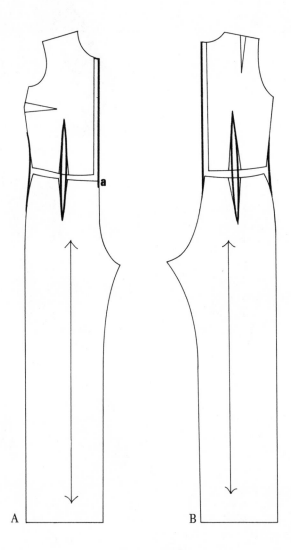

Figure 198

JUMPSUIT STYLES

Figure 199 shows jumpsuits made by combining a bodice pattern from Chapter 14 with a pants pattern from this chapter.

Figure 199

Figure 201

Figure 200

SLEEVELESS JUMPSUIT

Figure 200. You can make the pattern for a sleeveless jumpsuit using a sleeveless-bodice pattern or by tracing the bodice sloper and marking the adjustments for a sleeveless armhole as explained on page 239.

JUMPER JUMPSUIT

Figure 201. You can make a jumper-jumpsuit pattern using a jumpsuit-bodice pattern you've already made or by tracing the bodice sloper and making the adjustments, explained on page 246, to make a jumper.

INDEX